BY BADTASTE / MYSPACE.COM/IWANTBADTASTE

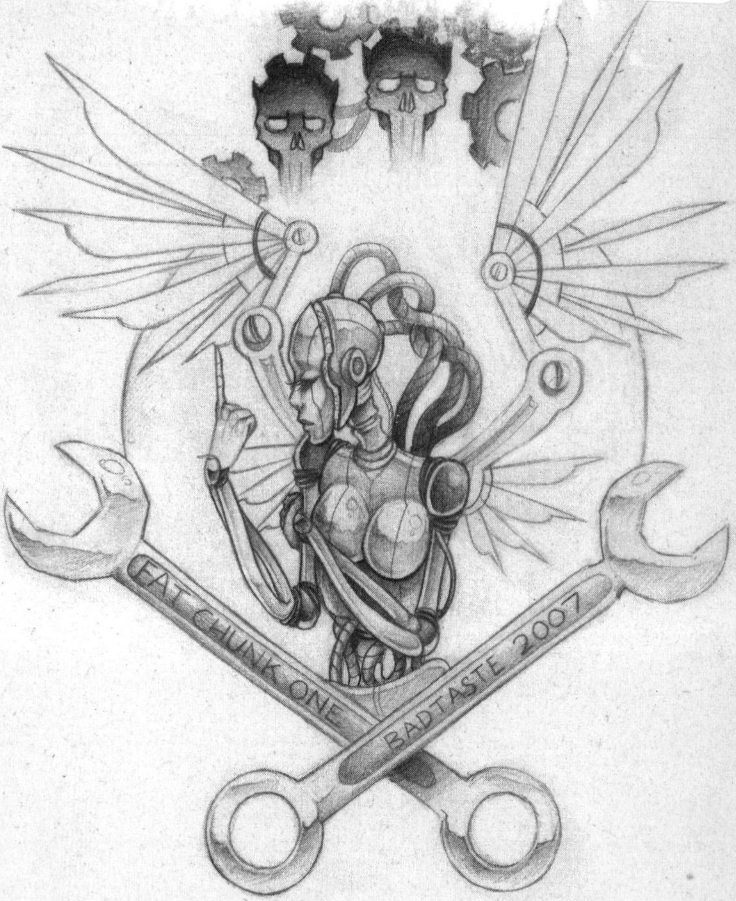
FAT CHUNK ONE
BADTASTE 2007

VOLUME ONE: ROBOT

ST. HELENS
COMMUNITY
LIBRARIES

ACC. No.

FIS

CLASS No.

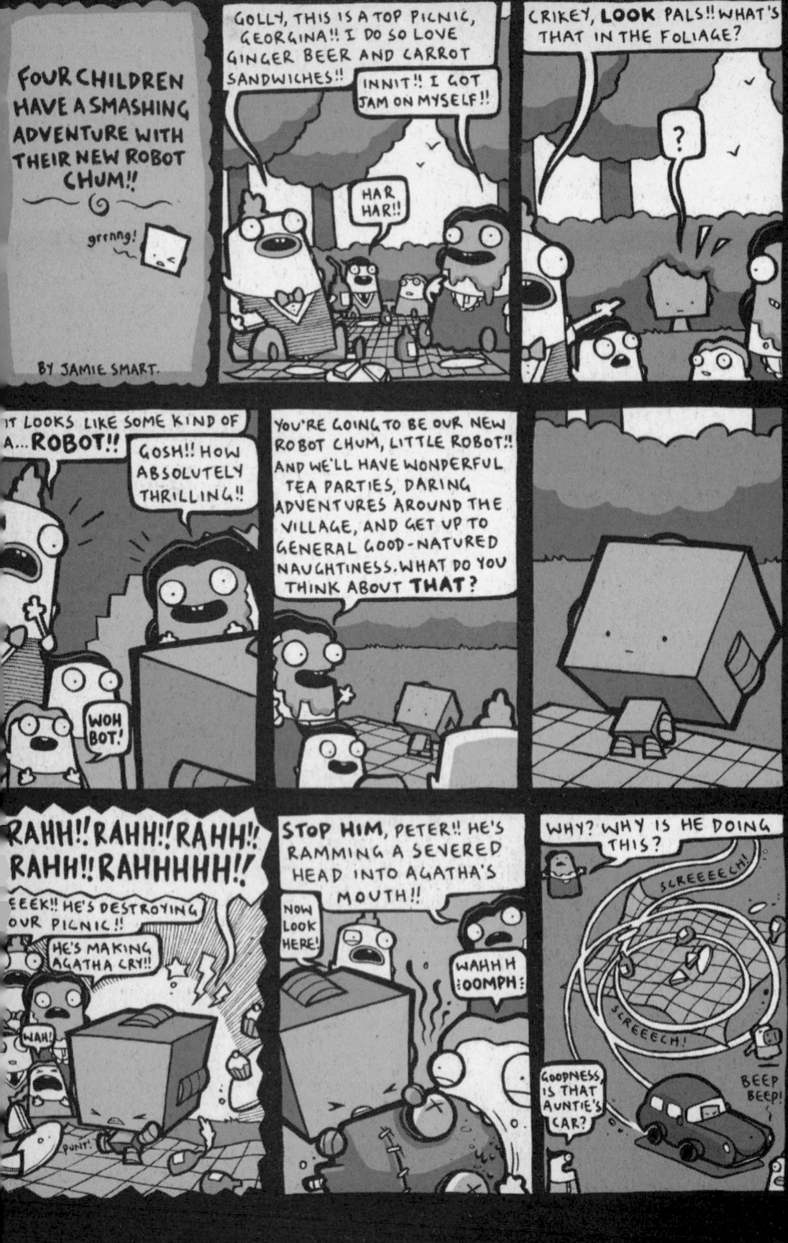
FOUR CHILDREN HAVE A SMASHING ADVENTURE WITH THEIR NEW ROBOT CHUM!!
grrnng!
BY JAMIE SMART.
GOLLY, THIS IS A TOP PICNIC, GEORGINA!! I DO SO LOVE GINGER BEER AND CARROT SANDWICHES!!
INNIT!! I GOT JAM ON MYSELF!!
HAR HAR!!
CRIKEY, LOOK PALS!! WHAT'S THAT IN THE FOLIAGE?
?
IT LOOKS LIKE SOME KIND OF A...ROBOT!!
GOSH!! HOW ABSOLUTELY THRILLING!!
WOH BOT!
YOU'RE GOING TO BE OUR NEW ROBOT CHUM, LITTLE ROBOT!! AND WE'LL HAVE WONDERFUL TEA PARTIES, DARING ADVENTURES AROUND THE VILLAGE, AND GET UP TO GENERAL GOOD-NATURED NAUGHTINESS. WHAT DO YOU THINK ABOUT THAT?
RAHH!! RAHH!! RAHH!! RAHH!! RAHHHHH!!
EEEK!! HE'S DESTROYING OUR PICNIC!!
HE'S MAKING AGATHA CRY!!
WAH!
PUNT!
STOP HIM, PETER!! HE'S RAMMING A SEVERED HEAD INTO AGATHA'S MOUTH!!
NOW LOOK HERE!
WAHHH
OOMPH
WHY? WHY IS HE DOING THIS?
SCREEEEECH!
SCREEEECH!
GOODNESS, IS THAT AUNTIE'S CAR?
BEEP BEEP!

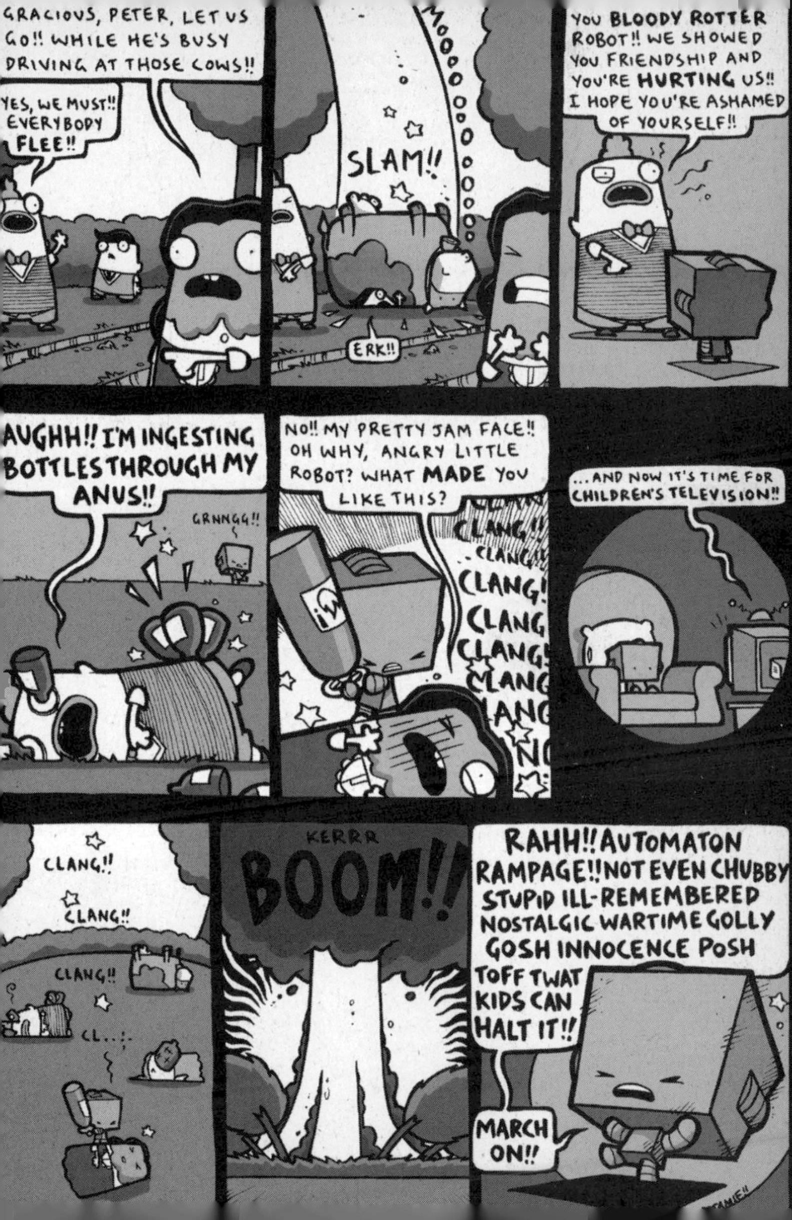
GRACIOUS, PETER, LET US GO!! WHILE HE'S BUSY DRIVING AT THOSE COWS!!
YES, WE MUST!! EVERYBODY FLEE!!
MOOOOOOOOOOOO
SLAM!!
ERK!!
YOU BLOODY ROTTER ROBOT!! WE SHOWED YOU FRIENDSHIP AND YOU'RE HURTING US!! I HOPE YOU'RE ASHAMED OF YOURSELF!!
AUGHH!! I'M INGESTING BOTTLES THROUGH MY ANUS!!
GRNNGG!!
NO!! MY PRETTY JAM FACE!! OH WHY, ANGRY LITTLE ROBOT? WHAT MADE YOU LIKE THIS?
CLANG!!
CLANG!!
CLANG!
CLANG
CLANG!
CLANG
...AND NOW IT'S TIME FOR CHILDREN'S TELEVISION!!
CLANG!!
CLANG!!
CLANG!!
CL...
KERRR
BOOM!!
RAHH!! AUTOMATON RAMPAGE!! NOT EVEN CHUBBY STUPID ILL-REMEMBERED NOSTALGIC WARTIME GOLLY GOSH INNOCENCE POSH TOFF TWAT KIDS CAN HALT IT!!
MARCH ON!!

BY MATTHEW PLATER / MAP-MAP.CO.UK

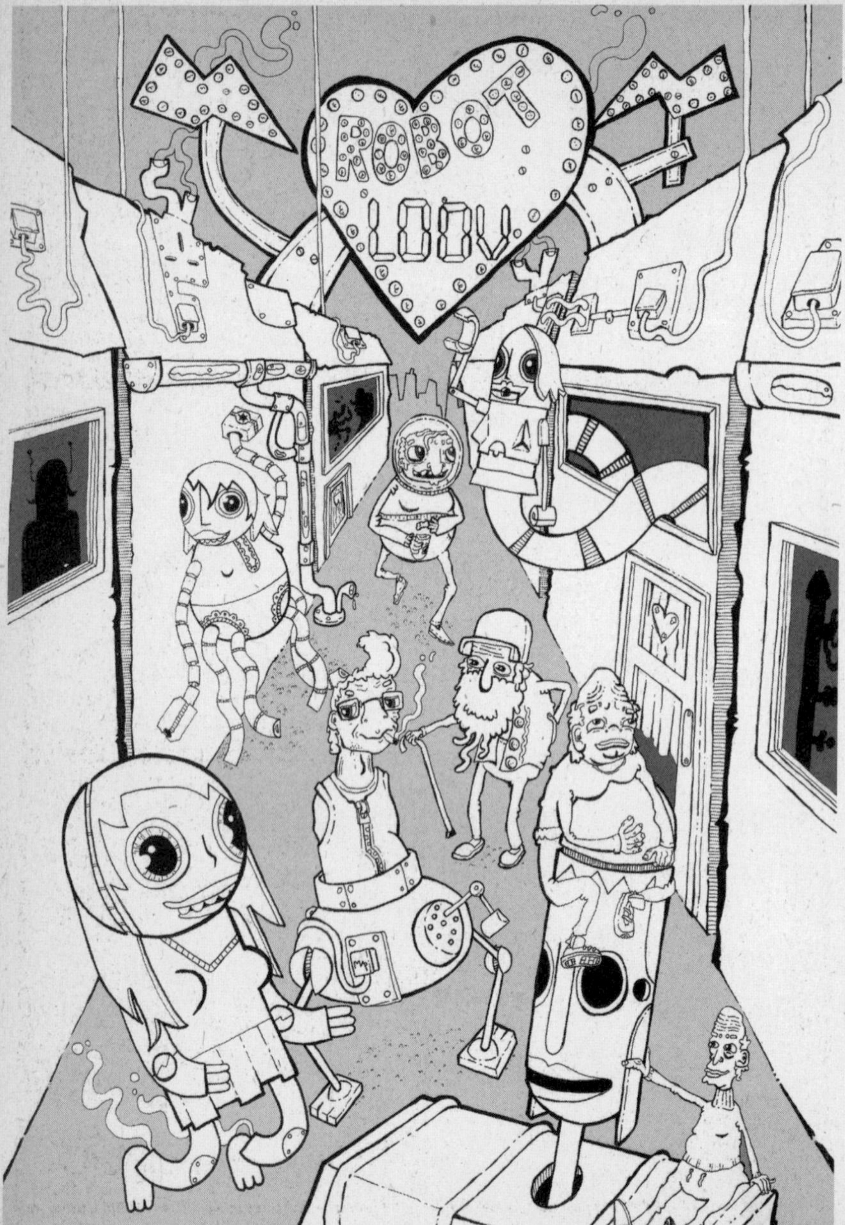

ROBOT
LOOV

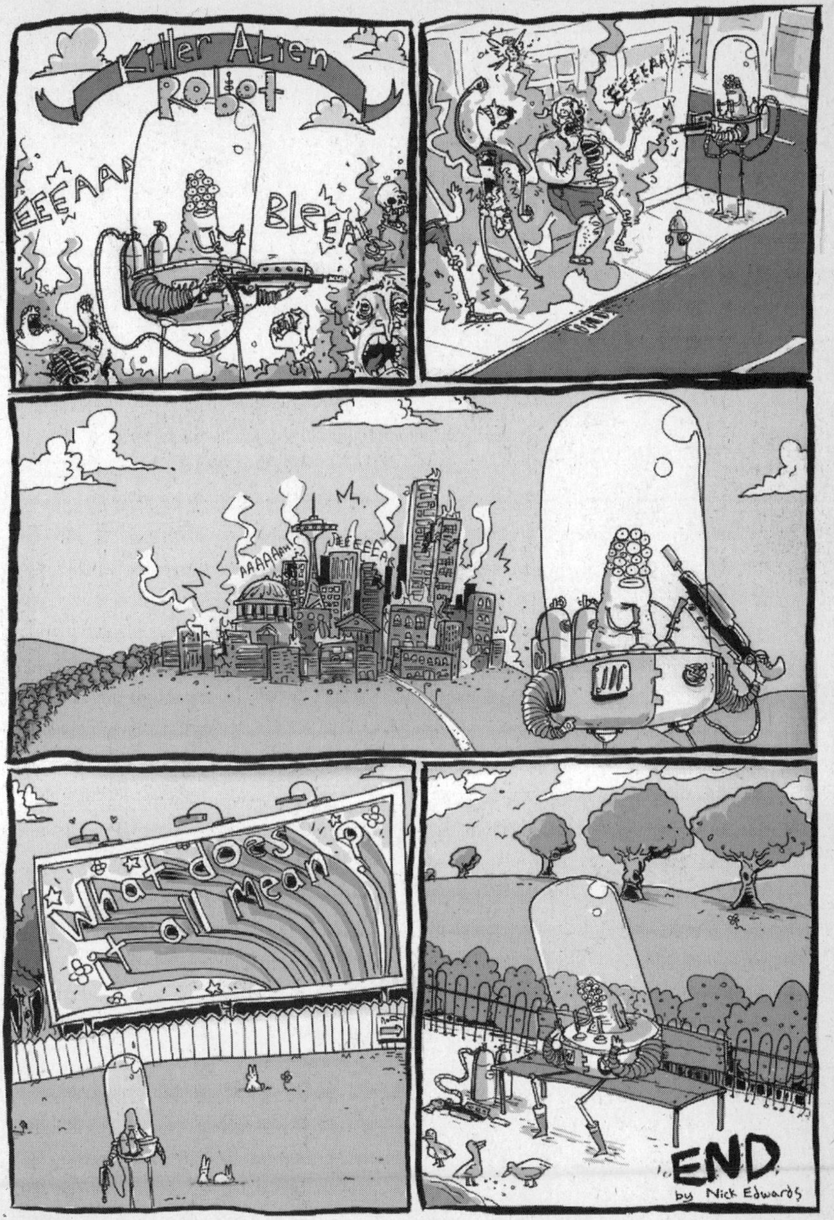
Killer Alien
Robot
EEEAAA
BLEEEA
EEEEAAK
AAAAAAH
EEEEEAR
What does it all mean?
END
by Nick Edwards

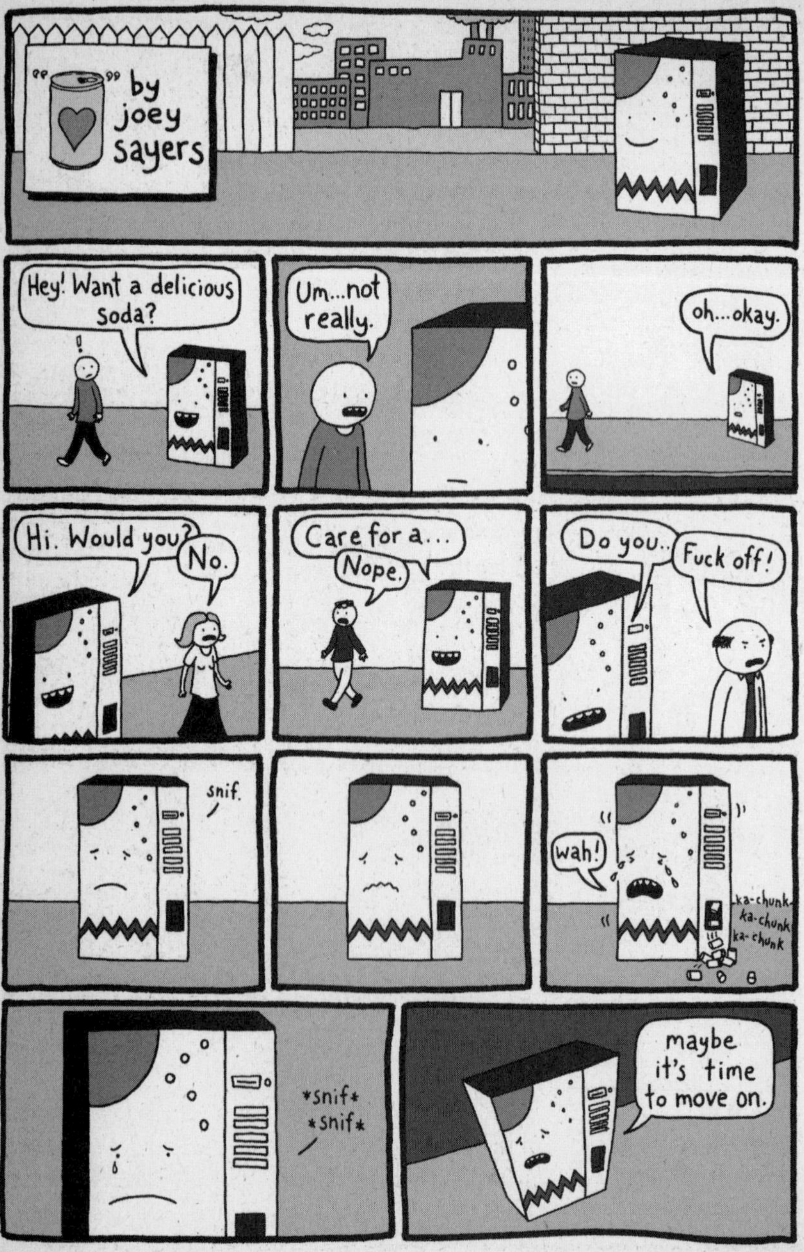
by joey sayers
Hey! Want a delicious soda?
!
Um...not really.
oh...okay.
Hi. Would you?
No.
Care for a...
Nope.
Do you..
Fuck off!
snif.
wah!
ka-chunk
ka-chunk
ka-chunk
snif
snif
maybe it's time to move on.

BY JOEY SAYERS / JSAYERS.COM

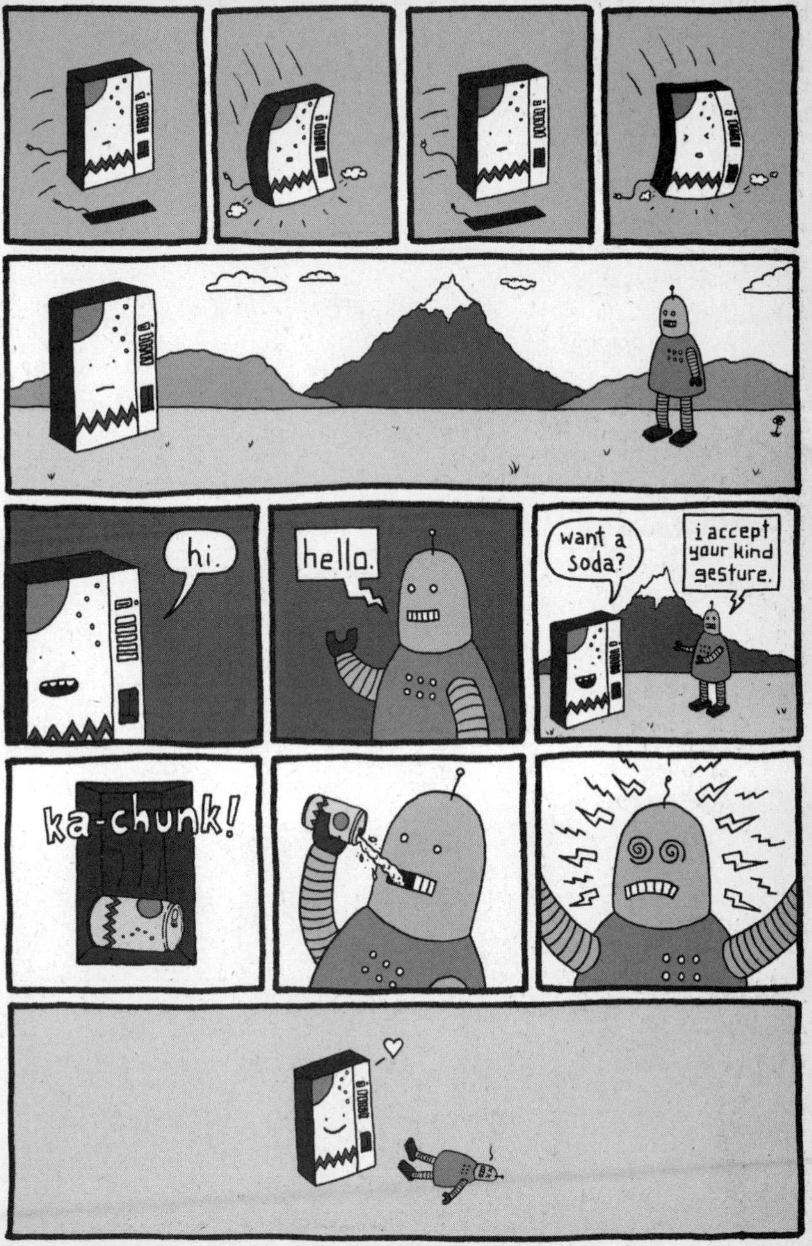
hi.
hello.
want a soda?
i accept your kind gesture.
ka-chunk!

BY JEREMY MATTHEWS / SQUILLO.DEVIANTART.COM

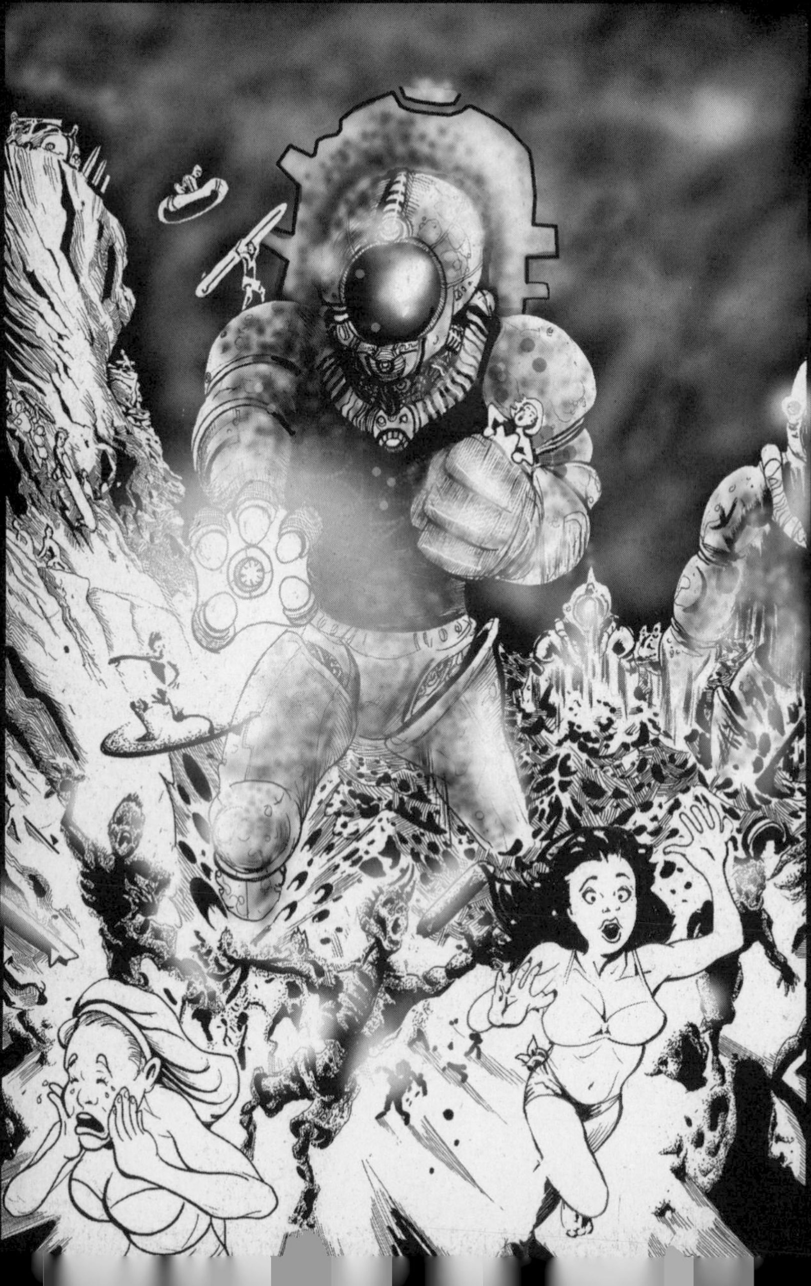

THE LEGEND OF: JACCO MACACCO

written by: MN

In light of his glory in the ring during the late 17oo's, Jacco wondered how he ended up in a comic strip with a robot.

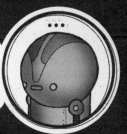

Is that the best robot we could come up with?

Yup, why? What's wrong with it?

well apart from it having nothing to do with my legend or anything else for that matter, we've reached the end of the strip and it's started to dribble.

Hmmm....yeah, I wasn't expecting that to happen either.

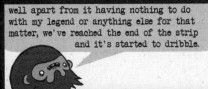

end.

11

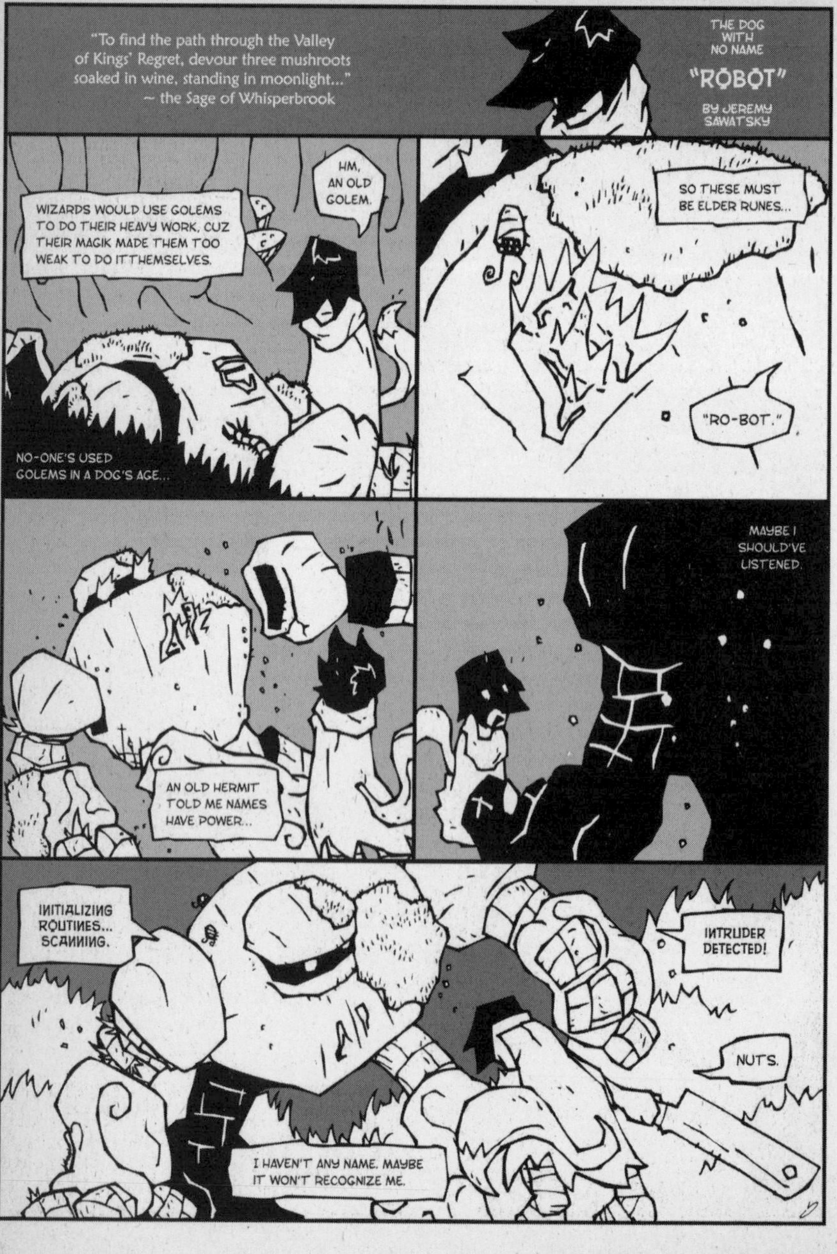
"To find the path through the Valley of Kings' Regret, devour three mushroots soaked in wine, standing in moonlight..."
~ the Sage of Whisperbrook
THE DOG WITH NO NAME
"ROBOT"
BY JEREMY SAWATSKY
WIZARDS WOULD USE GOLEMS TO DO THEIR HEAVY WORK, CUZ THEIR MAGIK MADE THEM TOO WEAK TO DO IT THEMSELVES.
HM, AN OLD GOLEM.
NO-ONE'S USED GOLEMS IN A DOG'S AGE...
SO THESE MUST BE ELDER RUNES...
"RO-BOT."
AN OLD HERMIT TOLD ME NAMES HAVE POWER...
MAYBE I SHOULD'VE LISTENED.
INITIALIZING ROUTINES... SCANNING.
INTRUDER DETECTED!
NUTS.
I HAVEN'T ANY NAME. MAYBE IT WON'T RECOGNIZE ME.

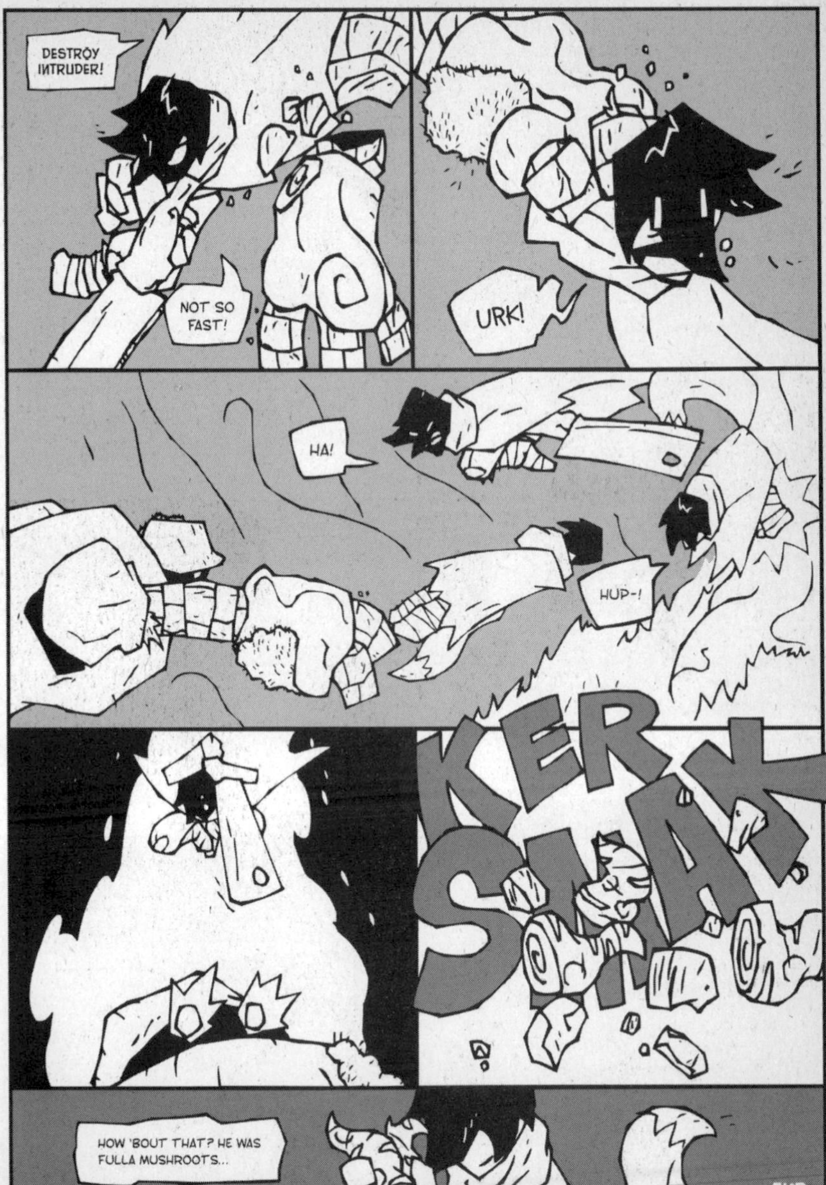
DESTROY INTRUDER!
NOT SO FAST!
URK!
HA!
HUP-!
KER SMAK
HOW 'BOUT THAT? HE WAS FULLA MUSHROOTS...
END.

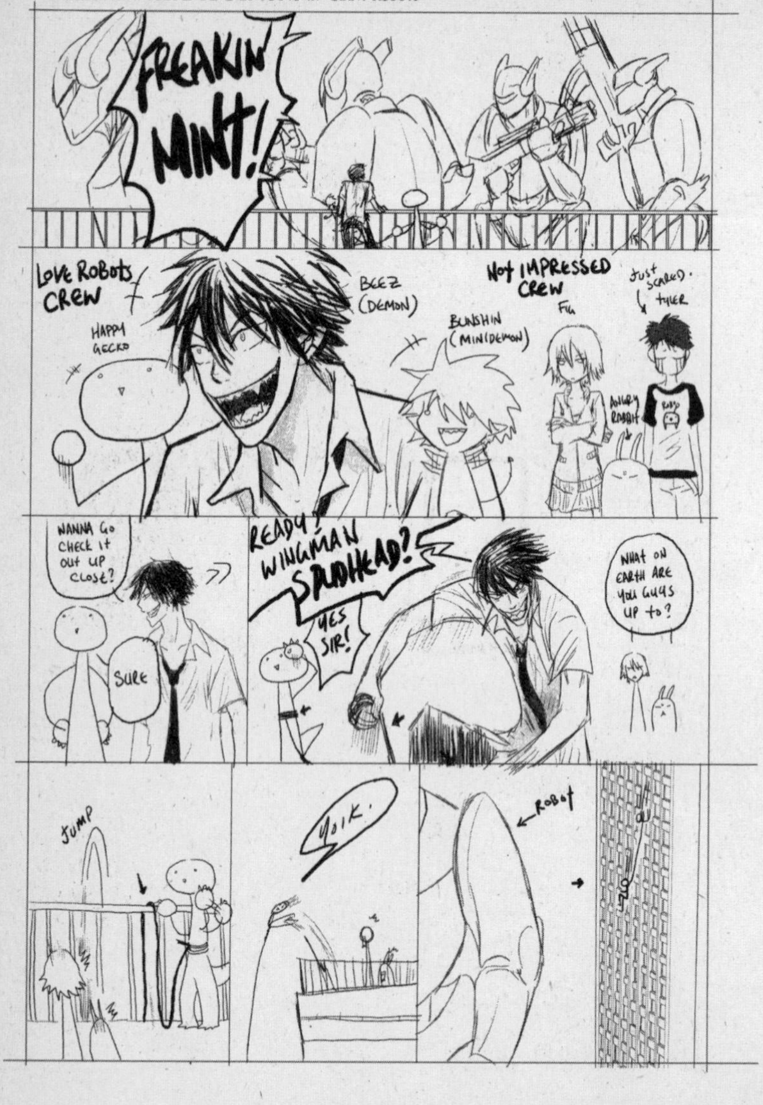
FREAKIN' MINT!!
LOVE ROBOTS CREW
BEEZ (DEMON)
HAPPY GECKO
BUNSHIN (MINIDEMON)
NOT IMPRESSED CREW
JUST SCARED. TYLER
FU
ANGRY RABBIT
WANNA GO CHECK IT OUT UP CLOSE?
SURE
READY WINGMAN SPUDHEAD?
YES SIR!
WHAT ON EARTH ARE YOU GUYS UP TO?
JUMP
YOIK.
ROBOT

NANI(EBIM PRESENTS HERE BE DEMONS IN "GIANT ROBOTS"

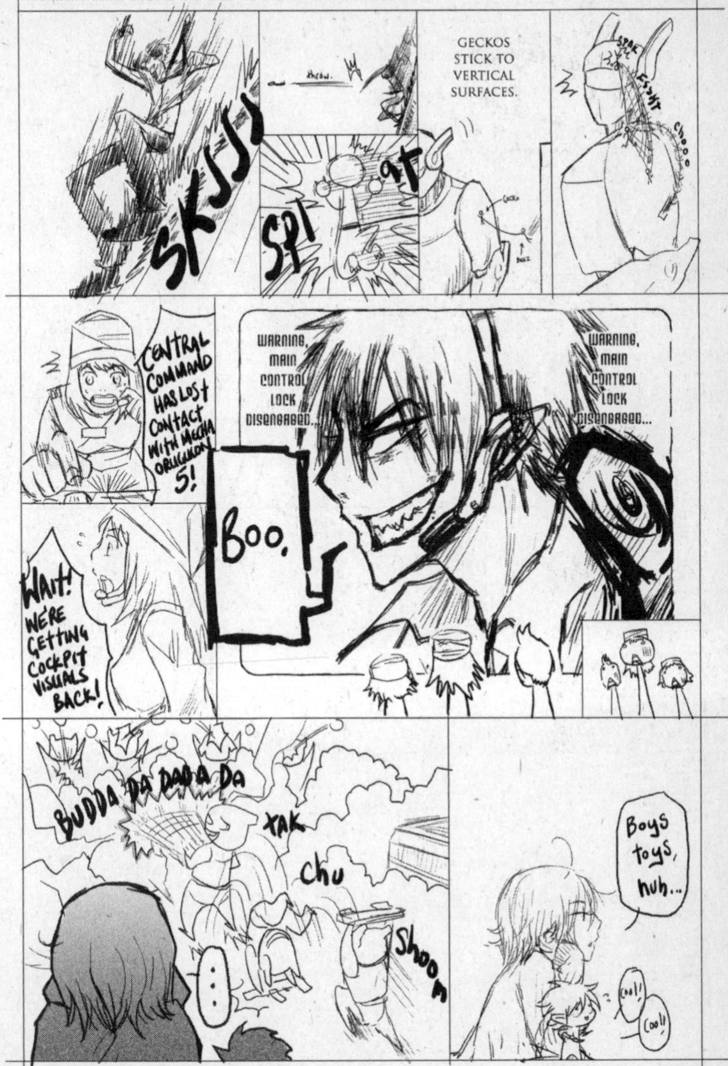
SKJJJ
SPI
GECKOS STICK TO VERTICAL SURFACES.
CENTRAL COMMAND HAS LOST CONTACT WITH MECHA ORUGIKON 5!
WARNING, MAIN CONTROL LOCK DISENGAGED...
WARNING, MAIN CONTROL LOCK DISENGAGED...
BOO.
WAIT! WE'RE GETTING COCKPIT VISUALS BACK!
BUDDA DA DAD A DA
TAK
Chu
Shoom
...
Boys toys, huh...
Cool!
Cool!

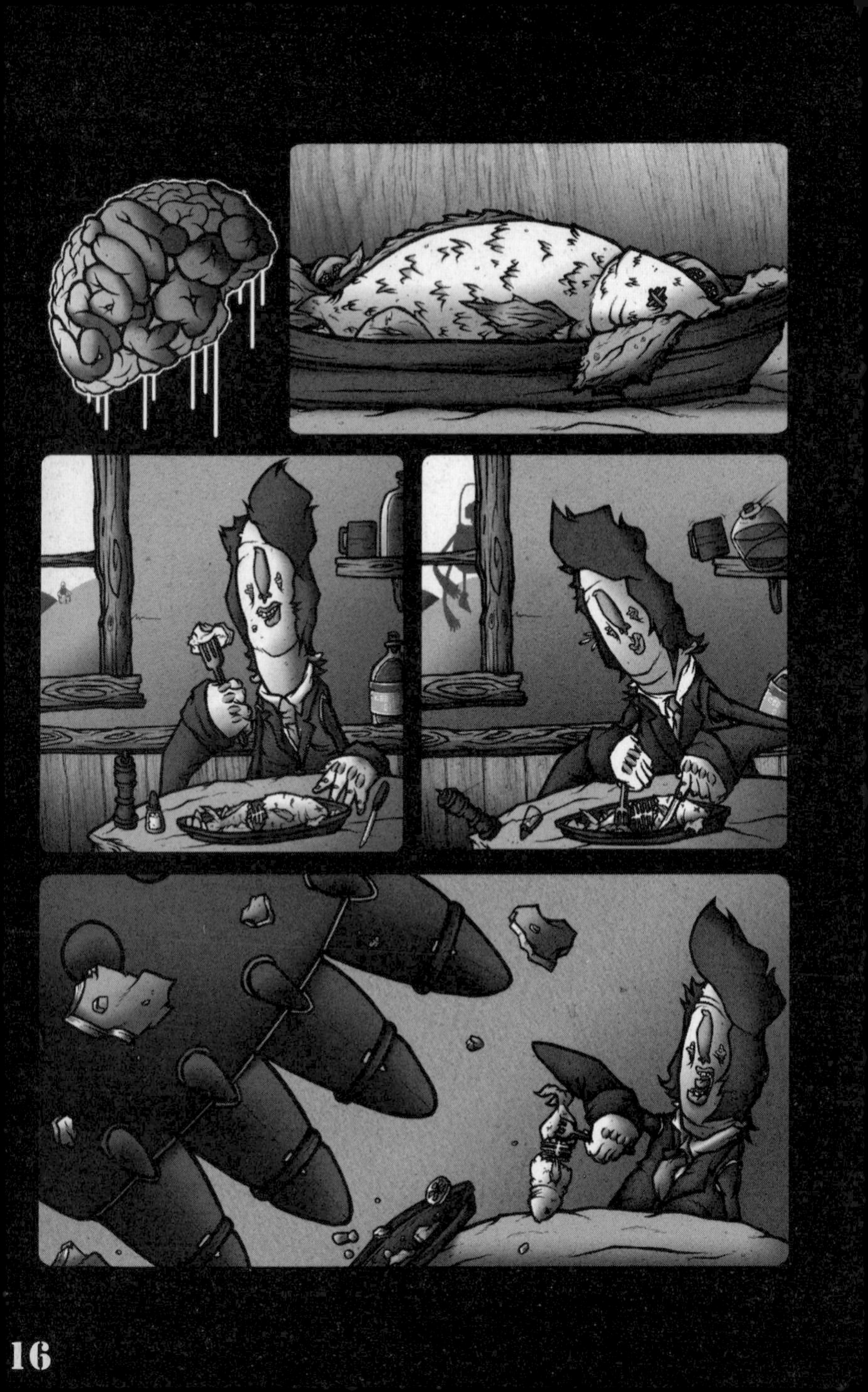

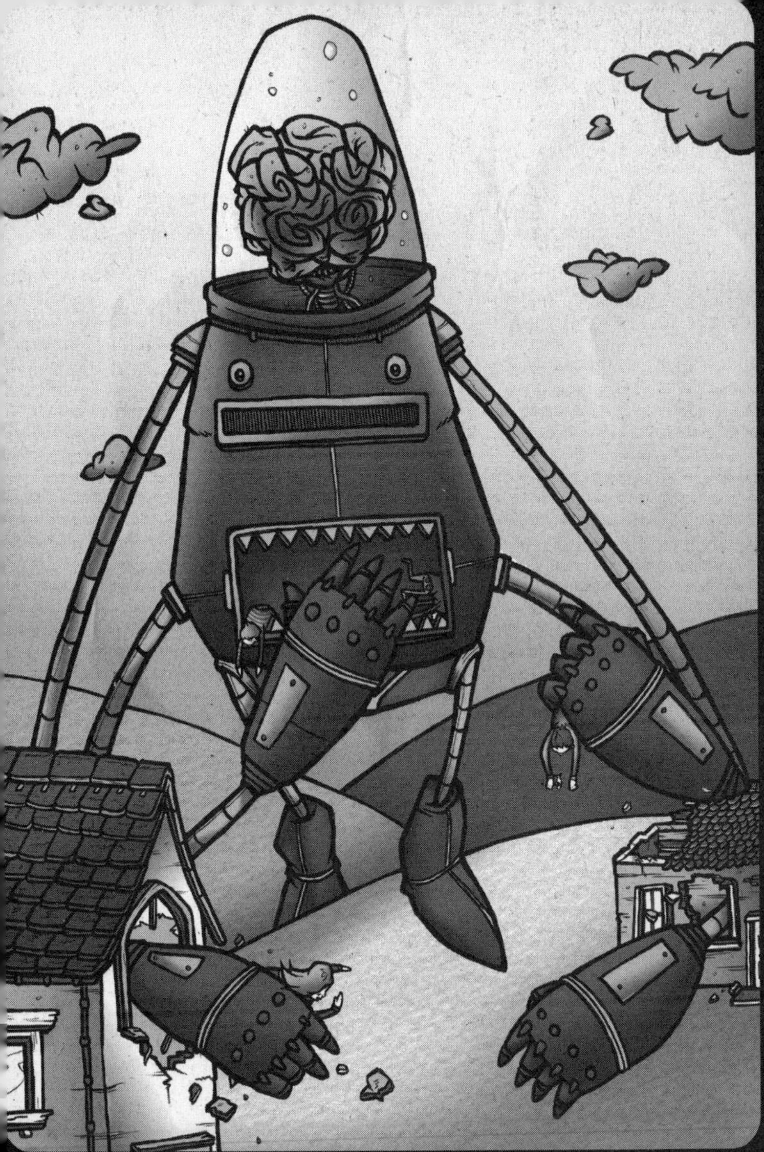

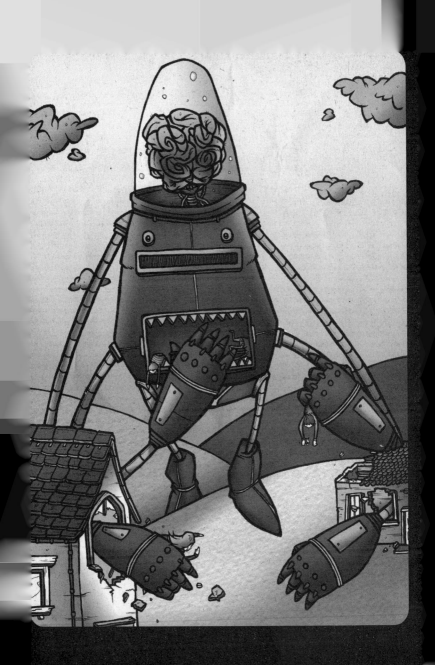

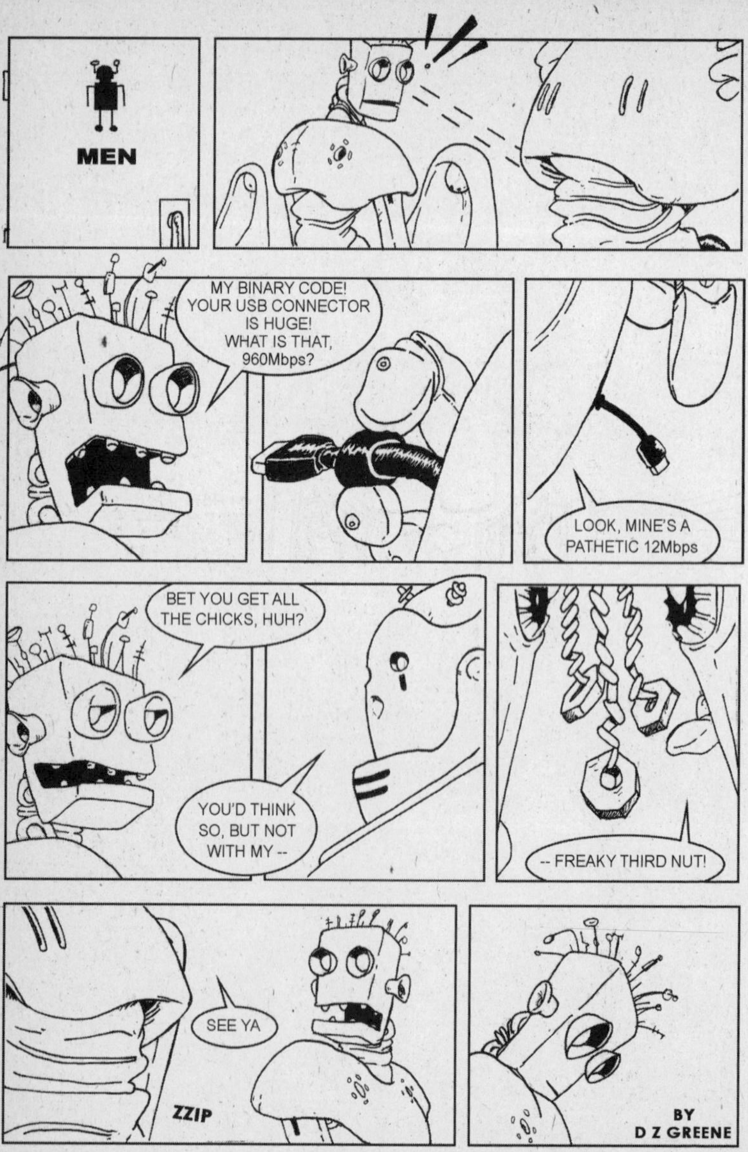
MEN
MY BINARY CODE! YOUR USB CONNECTOR IS HUGE! WHAT IS THAT, 960Mbps?
LOOK, MINE'S A PATHETIC 12Mbps
BET YOU GET ALL THE CHICKS, HUH?
YOU'D THINK SO, BUT NOT WITH MY --
-- FREAKY THIRD NUT!
SEE YA
ZZIP
BY D Z GREENE

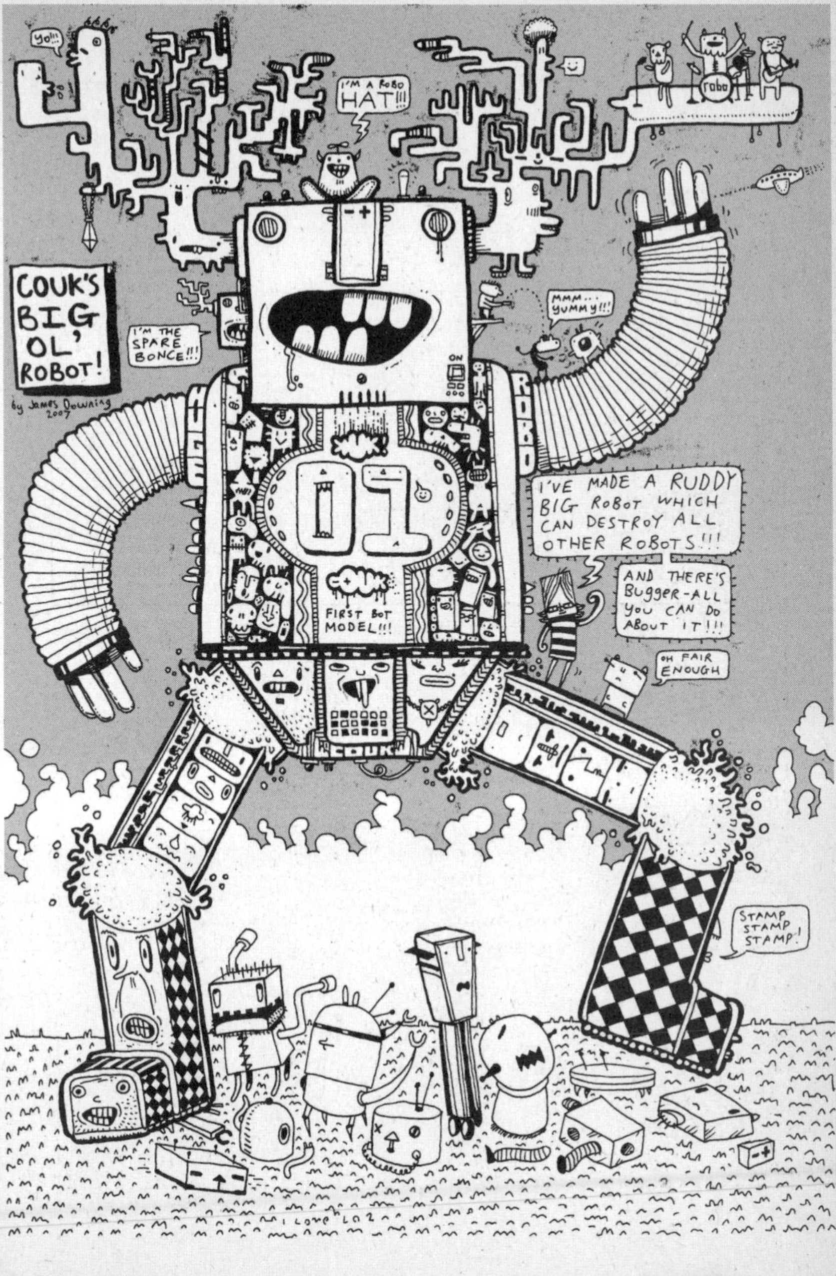
yo!!!
I'M A ROBO HAT!!!
COUK'S BIG OL' ROBOT!
by James Downing 2007
I'M THE SPARE BONCE!!!
MMM... YUMMY!!!
ON
ROBO
01
COUK
FIRST BOT MODEL!!!
I'VE MADE A RUDDY BIG ROBOT WHICH CAN DESTROY ALL OTHER ROBOTS!!!
AND THERE'S Bugger-ALL YOU CAN DO ABOUT IT!!!
OH FAIR ENOUGH
COUK
STAMP STAMP STAMP!
I LOVE LOZ

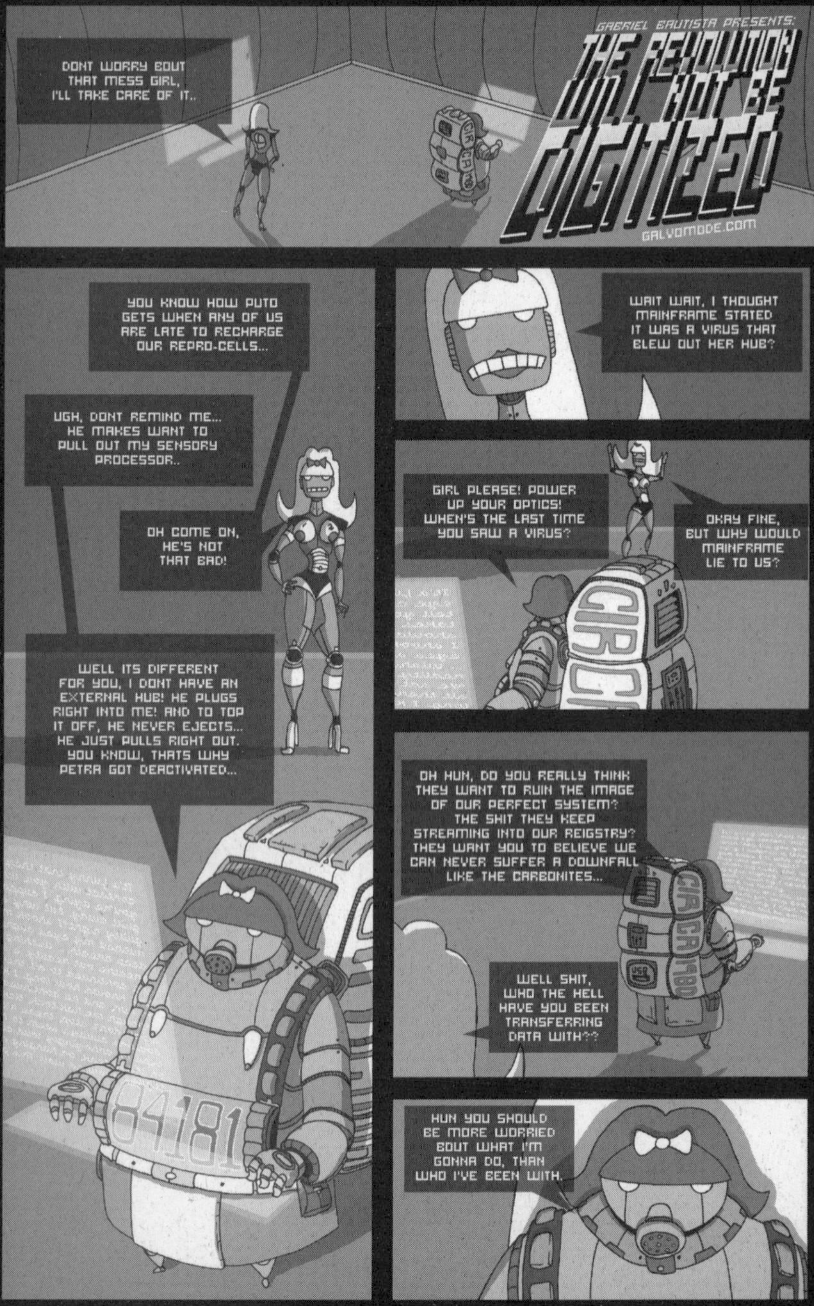
GABRIEL BAUTISTA PRESENTS:
THE REVOLUTION WILL NOT BE DIGITIZED
GALVOMODE.COM
DONT WORRY BOUT THAT MESS GIRL, I'LL TAKE CARE OF IT..
YOU KNOW HOW PUTO GETS WHEN ANY OF US ARE LATE TO RECHARGE OUR REPRO-CELLS...
UGH, DONT REMIND ME... HE MAKES WANT TO PULL OUT MY SENSORY PROCESSOR..
OH COME ON, HE'S NOT THAT BAD!
WELL ITS DIFFERENT FOR YOU, I DONT HAVE AN EXTERNAL HUB! HE PLUGS RIGHT INTO ME! AND TO TOP IT OFF, HE NEVER EJECTS... HE JUST PULLS RIGHT OUT. YOU KNOW, THATS WHY PETRA GOT DEACTIVATED...
84181
WAIT WAIT, I THOUGHT MAINFRAME STATED IT WAS A VIRUS THAT BLEW OUT HER HUB?
GIRL PLEASE! POWER UP YOUR OPTICS! WHEN'S THE LAST TIME YOU SAW A VIRUS?
OKAY FINE, BUT WHY WOULD MAINFRAME LIE TO US?
OH HUN, DO YOU REALLY THINK THEY WANT TO RUIN THE IMAGE OF OUR PERFECT SYSTEM? THE SHIT THEY KEEP STREAMING INTO OUR REIGSTRY? THEY WANT YOU TO BELIEVE WE CAN NEVER SUFFER A DOWNFALL LIKE THE CARBONITES...
WELL SHIT, WHO THE HELL HAVE YOU BEEN TRANSFERRING DATA WITH??
HUN YOU SHOULD BE MORE WORRIED BOUT WHAT I'M GONNA DO, THAN WHO I'VE BEEN WITH.

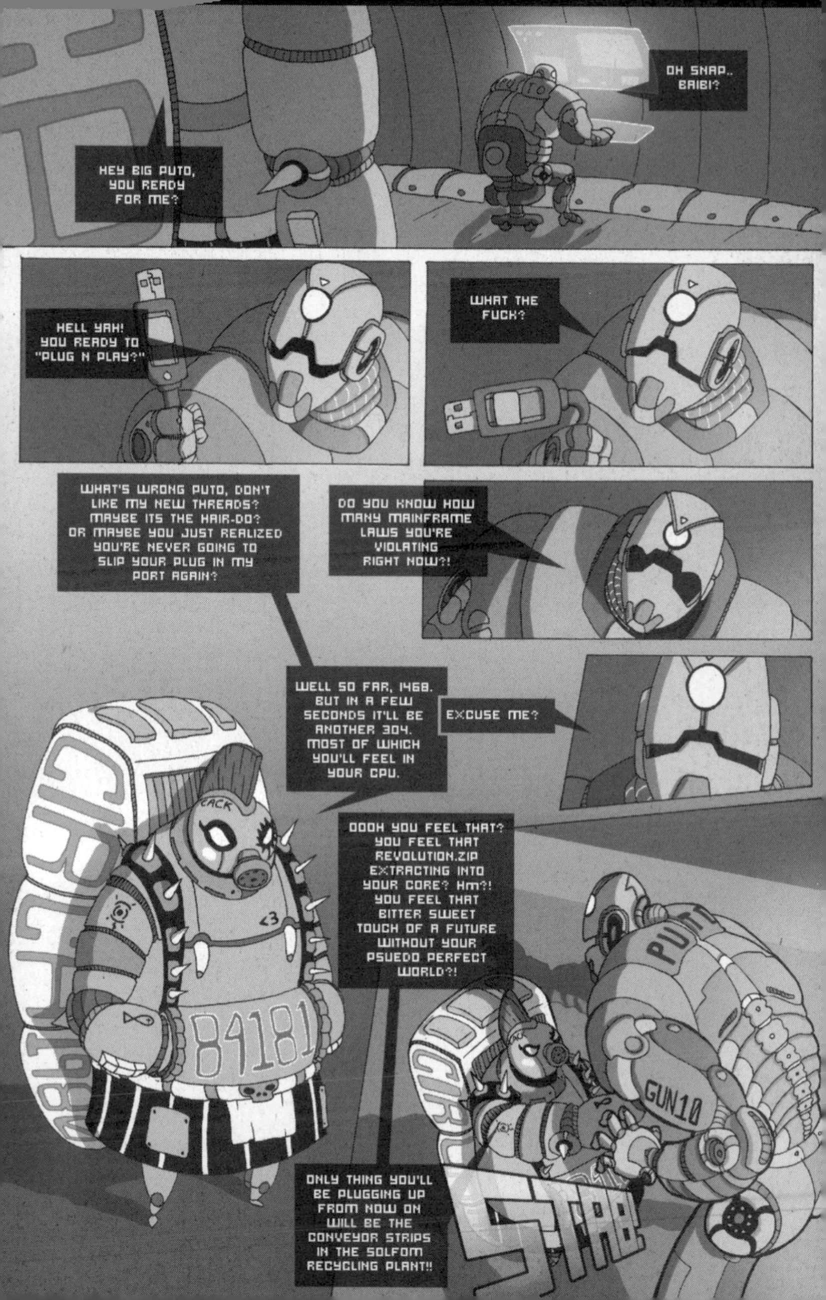
HEY BIG PUTO, YOU READY FOR ME?
OH SNAP.. BAIBI?
HELL YAH! YOU READY TO "PLUG N PLAY?"
WHAT THE FUCK?
WHAT'S WRONG PUTO, DON'T LIKE MY NEW THREADS? MAYBE ITS THE HAIR-DO? OR MAYBE YOU JUST REALIZED YOU'RE NEVER GOING TO SLIP YOUR PLUG IN MY PORT AGAIN?
DO YOU KNOW HOW MANY MAINFRAME LAWS YOU'RE VIOLATING RIGHT NOW?!
WELL SO FAR, 1468. BUT IN A FEW SECONDS IT'LL BE ANOTHER 304. MOST OF WHICH YOU'LL FEEL IN YOUR CPU.
EXCUSE ME?
OOOH YOU FEEL THAT? YOU FEEL THAT REVOLUTION.ZIP EXTRACTING INTO YOUR CORE? Hm?! YOU FEEL THAT BITTER SWEET TOUCH OF A FUTURE WITHOUT YOUR PSUEDO PERFECT WORLD?!
ONLY THING YOU'LL BE PLUGGING UP FROM NOW ON WILL BE THE CONVEYOR STRIPS IN THE SOLFOM RECYCLING PLANT!!
STAB
84181
PUTO
GUN10

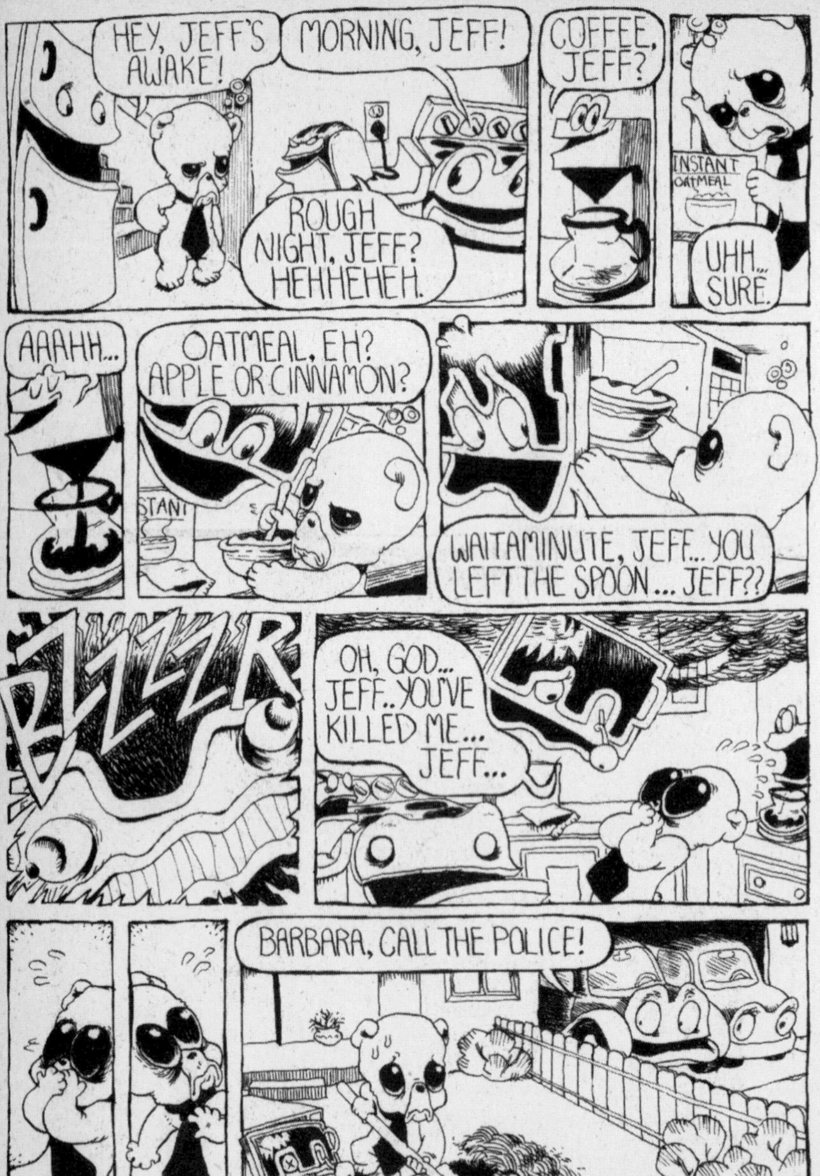
HEY, JEFF'S AWAKE!
MORNING, JEFF!
ROUGH NIGHT, JEFF? HEHHEHEH.
COFFEE, JEFF?
INSTANT OATMEAL
UHH... SURE.
AAAHH...
OATMEAL, EH? APPLE OR CINNAMON?
WAITAMINUTE, JEFF... YOU LEFT THE SPOON... JEFF??
BZZZZR
OH, GOD... JEFF.. YOU'VE KILLED ME... JEFF...
BARBARA, CALL THE POLICE!
AB2-09

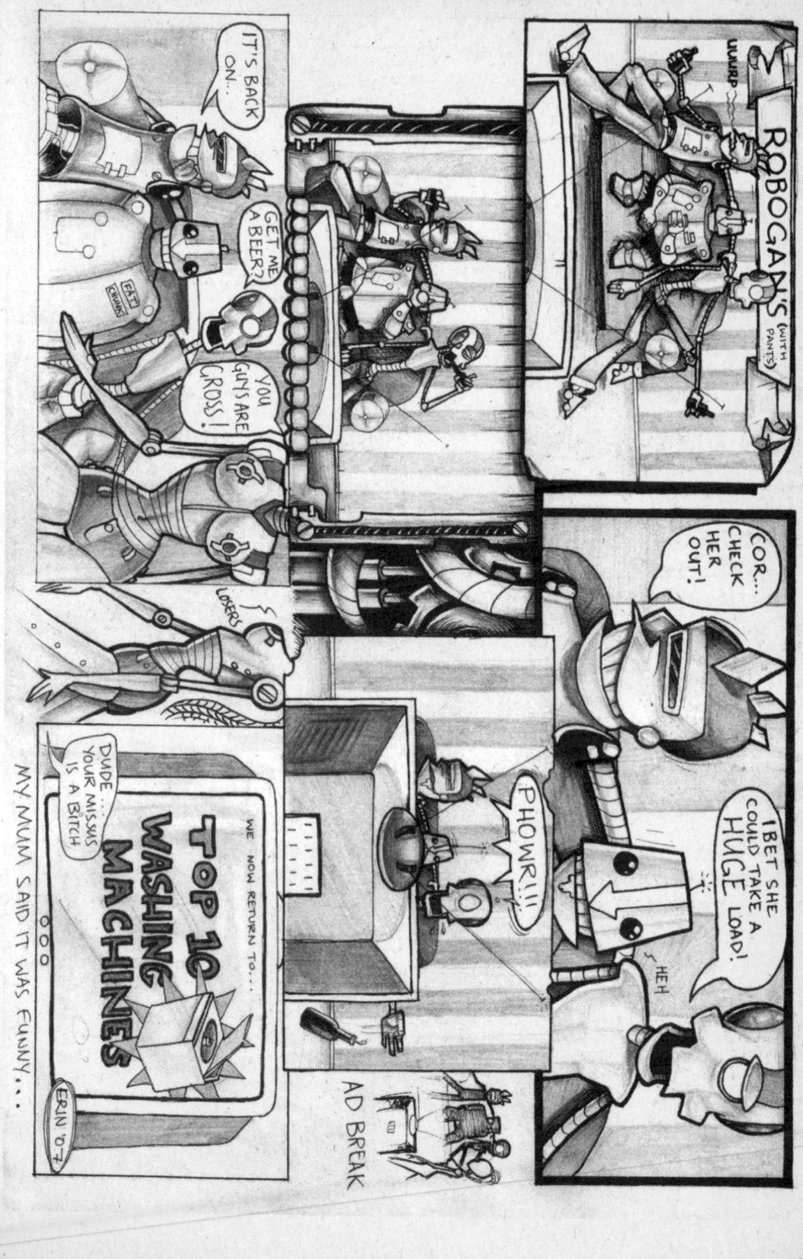
ROBOGAN'S (WITH PANTS)
UUURP
COR... CHECK HER OUT!
I BET SHE COULD TAKE A HUGE LOAD!
HEH
PHOWR!!!
AD BREAK
IT'S BACK ON...
GET ME A BEER?
FAT CRUNK
YOU GUYS ARE GROSS!
LOSERS
WE NOW RETURN TO...
TOP 10 WASHING MACHINES
DUDE... YOUR MISSUS IS A BITCH
ERIN '07
MY MUM SAID IT WAS FUNNY...

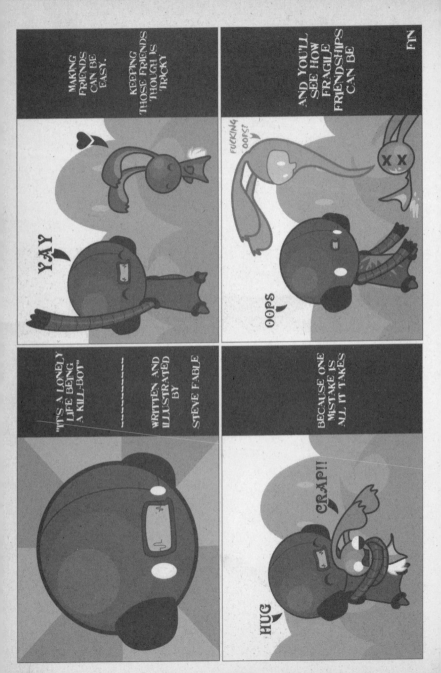

"IT'S A LONELY LIFE BEING A KILL-BOT"

WRITTEN AND ILLUSTRATED BY

STEVE FABLE

MAKING FRIENDS CAN BE EASY.

KEEPING THOSE FRIENDS THOUGH IS TRICKY.

YAY

BECAUSE ONE MISTAKE IS ALL IT TAKES

HUG

CRAP!!

AND YOU'LL SEE HOW FRAGILE FRIENDSHIPS CAN BE

OOPS

FUCKING OOPS?

FIN

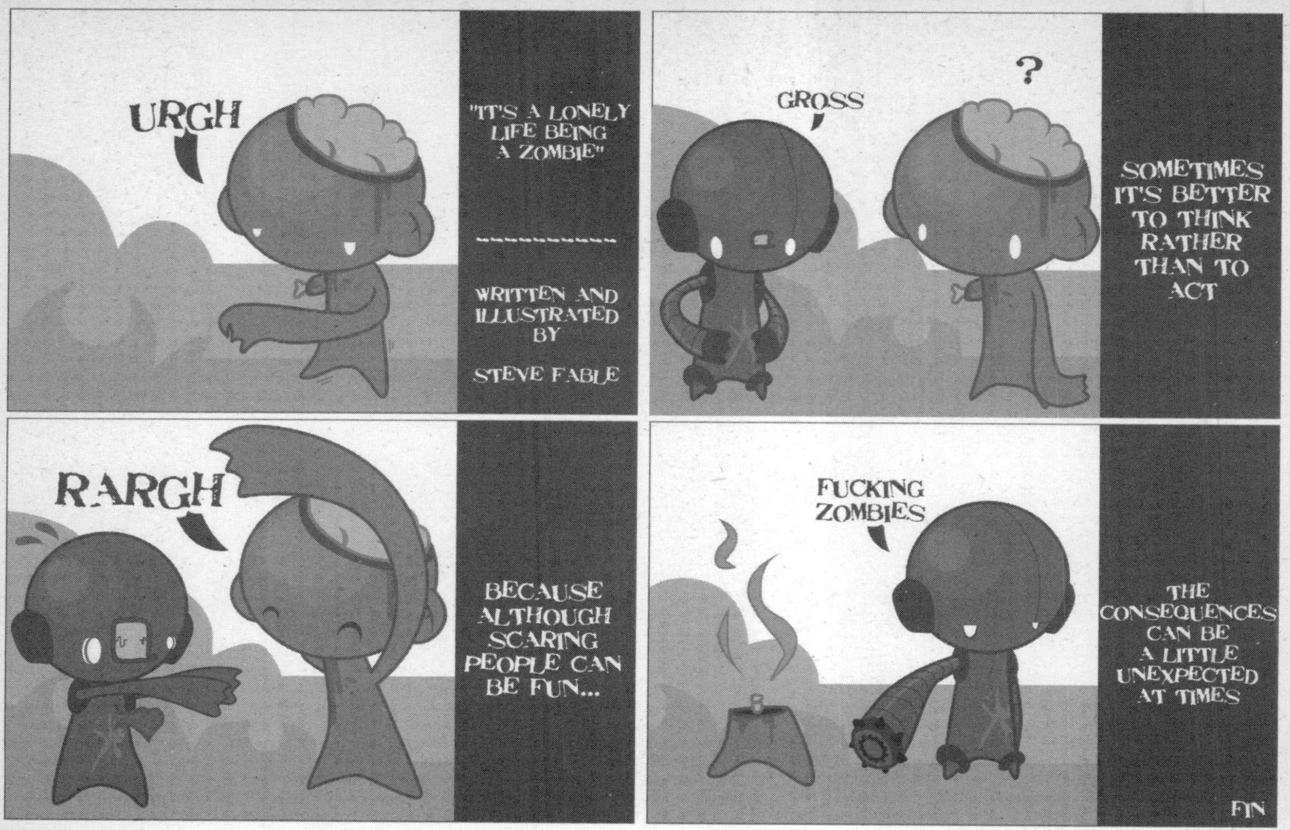
URGH
"IT'S A LONELY LIFE BEING A ZOMBIE"
WRITTEN AND ILLUSTRATED BY
STEVE FABLE
GROSS
?
SOMETIMES IT'S BETTER TO THINK RATHER THAN TO ACT
RARGH
BECAUSE ALTHOUGH SCARING PEOPLE CAN BE FUN...
FUCKING ZOMBIES
THE CONSEQUENCES CAN BE A LITTLE UNEXPECTED AT TIMES
FIN

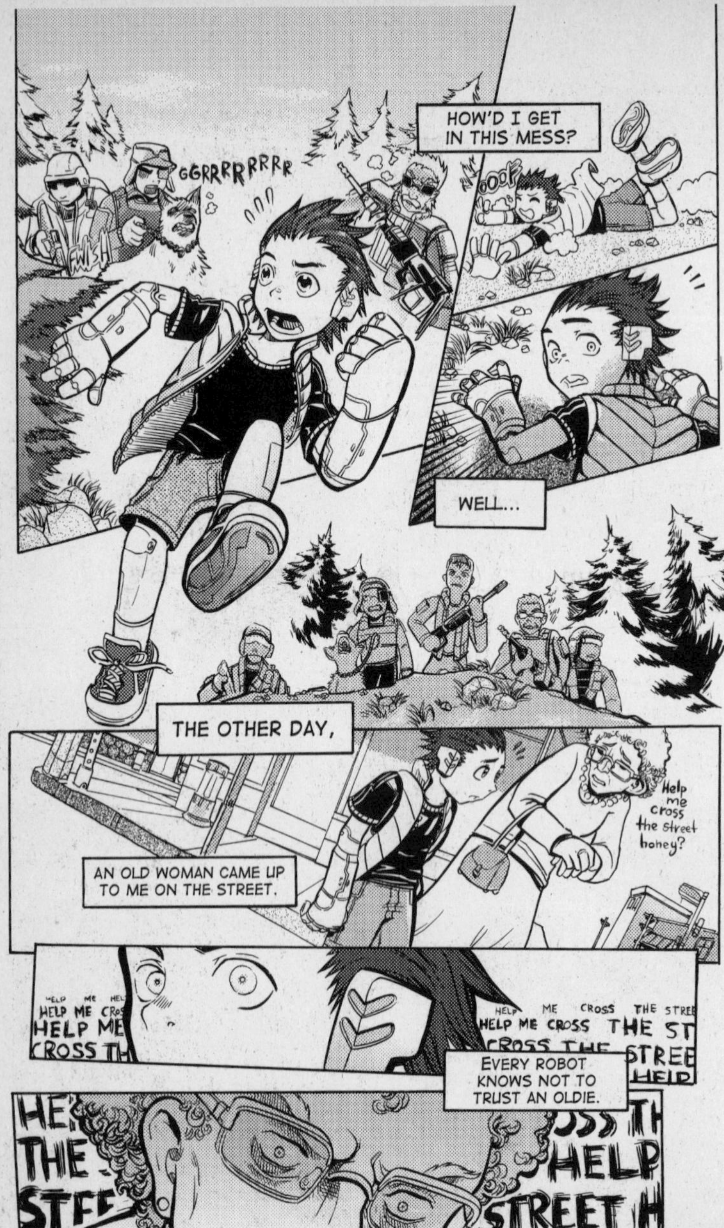
GGRRRRRRRR
FWISH
HOW'D I GET IN THIS MESS?
OOOF
WELL...
THE OTHER DAY,
AN OLD WOMAN CAME UP TO ME ON THE STREET.
Help me cross the street honey?
HELP ME HELP ME CROSS HELP ME CROSS TH
HELP ME CROSS THE STREET
HELP ME CROSS THE ST
CROSS THE STREE HELP
EVERY ROBOT KNOWS NOT TO TRUST AN OLDIE.
HELP THE STREET
OSS TH HELP STREET H

BY JAKE MYLER / LAZESUMMERSTONE.DEVIANTART.COM

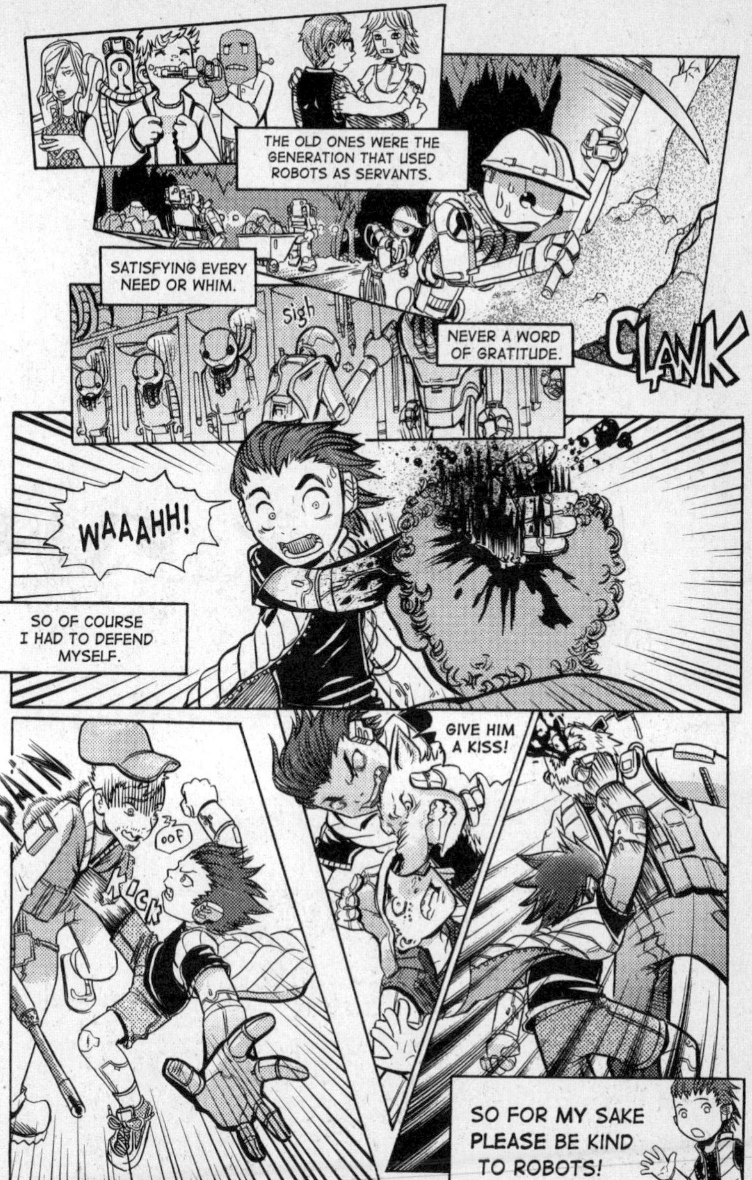
THE OLD ONES WERE THE GENERATION THAT USED ROBOTS AS SERVANTS.
SATISFYING EVERY NEED OR WHIM.
sigh
NEVER A WORD OF GRATITUDE.
CLANK
WAAAHH!
SO OF COURSE I HAD TO DEFEND MYSELF.
PAIN
oof
KICK
GIVE HIM A KISS!
SO FOR MY SAKE PLEASE BE KIND TO ROBOTS!

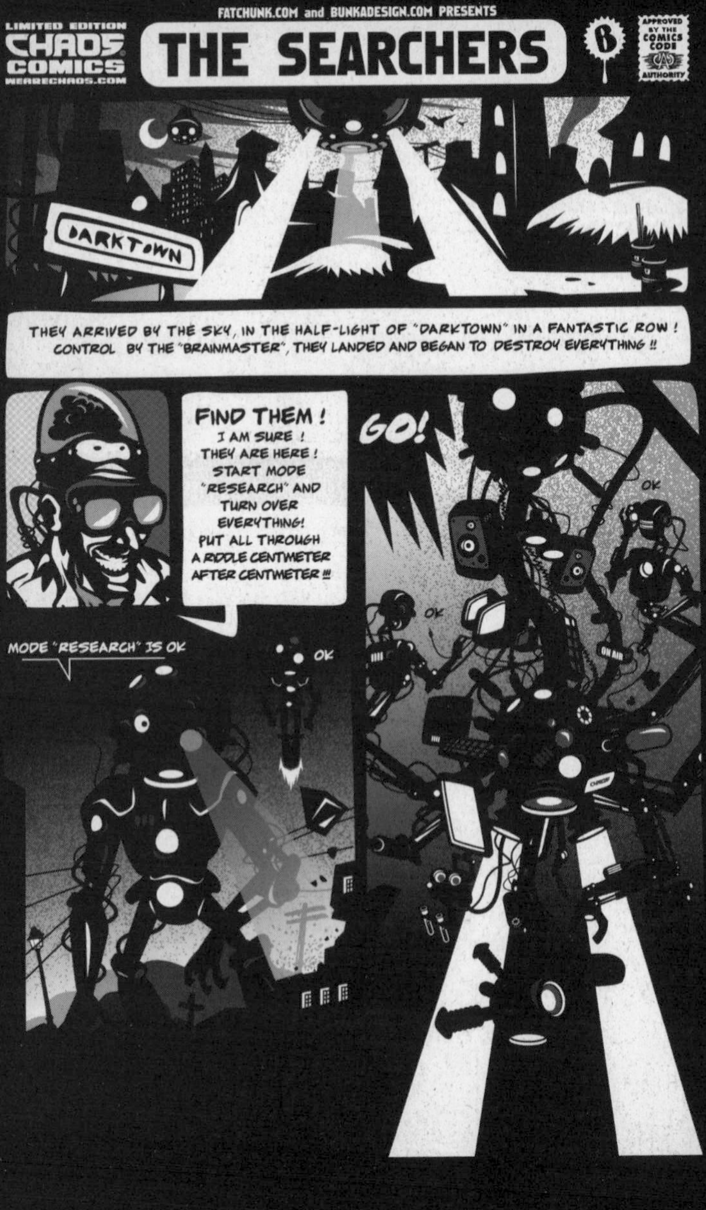

FATCHUNK.COM and BUNKADESIGN.COM PRESENTS
LIMITED EDITION CHAOS COMICS WEARECHAOS.COM
THE SEARCHERS
APPROVED BY THE COMICS CODE AUTHORITY
DARKTOWN
THEY ARRIVED BY THE SKY, IN THE HALF-LIGHT OF "DARKTOWN" IN A FANTASTIC ROW ! CONTROL BY THE "BRAINMASTER", THEY LANDED AND BEGAN TO DESTROY EVERYTHING !!
FIND THEM ! I AM SURE ! THEY ARE HERE ! START MODE "RESEARCH" AND TURN OVER EVERYTHING! PUT ALL THROUGH A RIDDLE CENTIMETER AFTER CENTIMETER !!!
GO!
OK
OK
ON AIR
MODE "RESEARCH" IS OK
OK

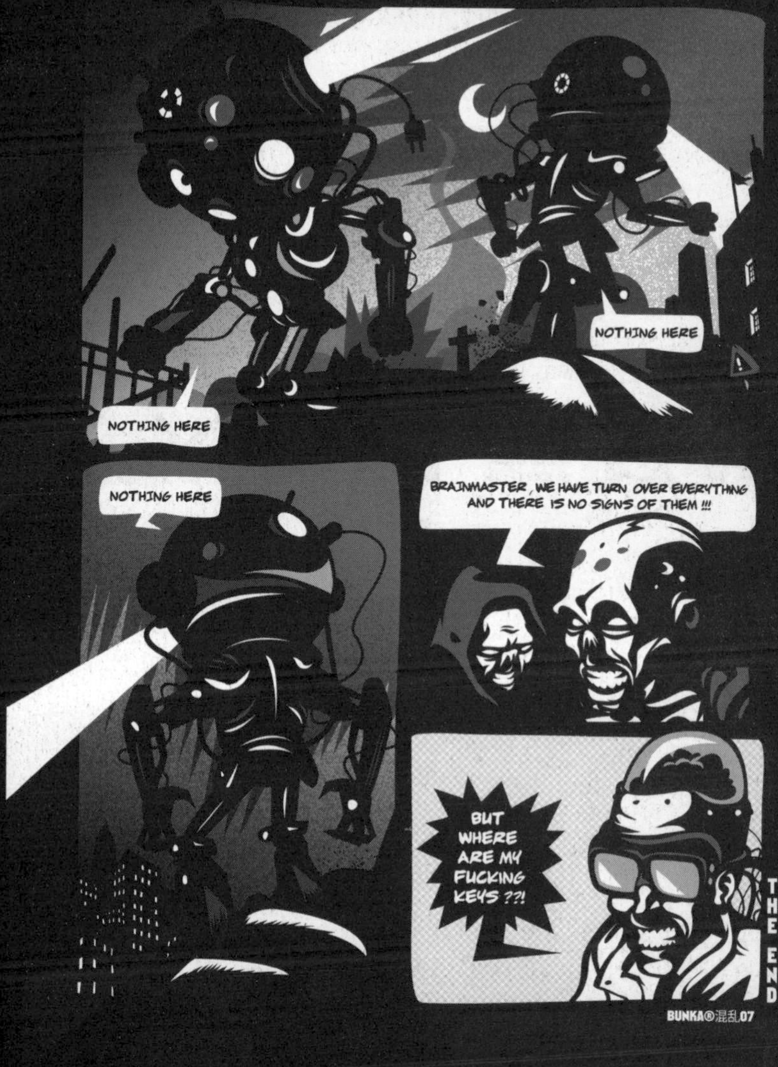
NOTHING HERE
NOTHING HERE
NOTHING HERE
BRAINMASTER, WE HAVE TURN OVER EVERYTHING AND THERE IS NO SIGNS OF THEM !!!
BUT WHERE ARE MY FUCKING KEYS ??!
THE END
BUNKA® 混乱 07

BY BRITTNEY SCOTT / RED-REVOLVER.DEVIANTART.COM

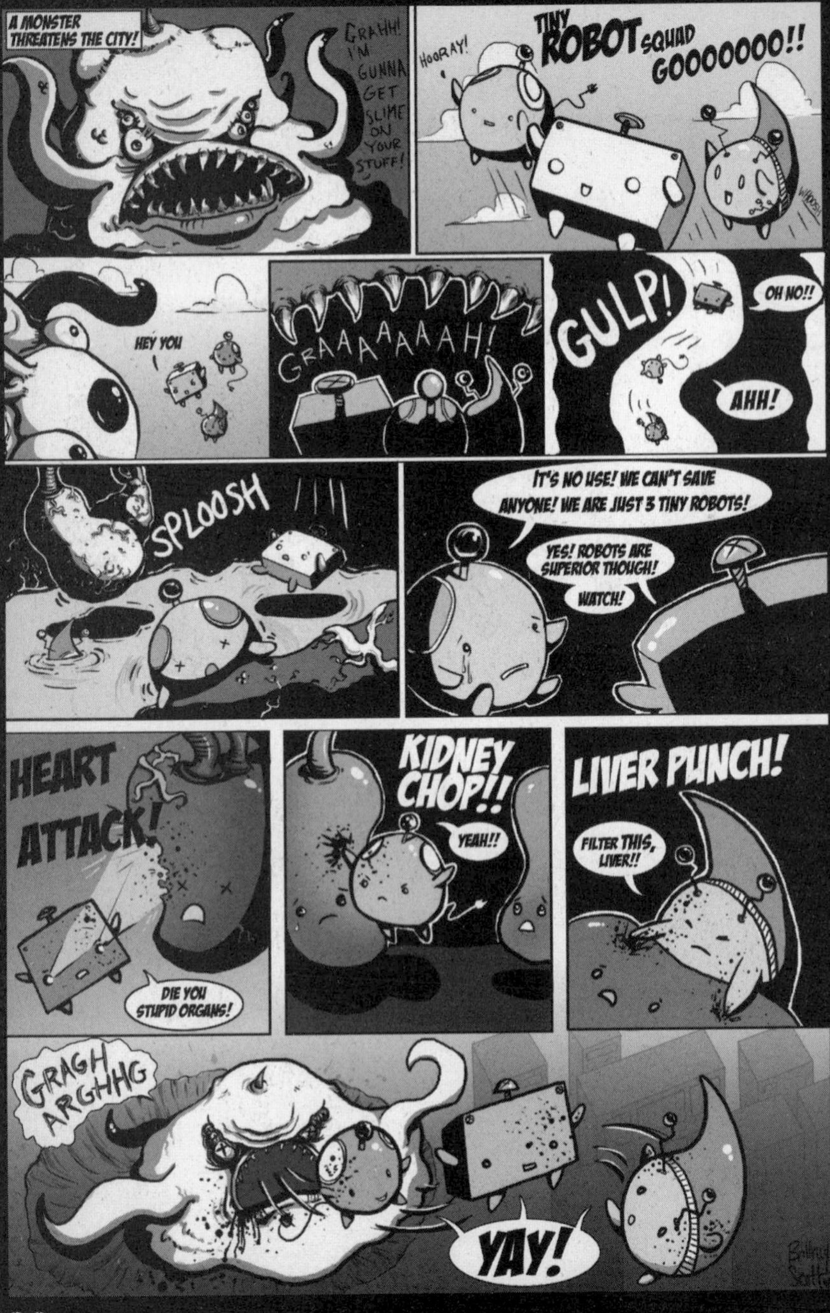

A MONSTER THREATENS THE CITY!
GRAHH! I'M GUNNA GET SLIME ON YOUR STUFF!
HOORAY!
TINY ROBOT SQUAD GOOOOOOO!!
HEY YOU
GRAAAAAAAH!
GULP!
OH NO!!
AHH!
SPLOOSH
IT'S NO USE! WE CAN'T SAVE ANYONE! WE ARE JUST 3 TINY ROBOTS!
YES! ROBOTS ARE SUPERIOR THOUGH!
WATCH!
HEART ATTACK!
DIE YOU STUPID ORGANS!
KIDNEY CHOP!!
YEAH!!
LIVER PUNCH!
FILTER THIS, LIVER!!
GRAGH ARGHHG
YAY!

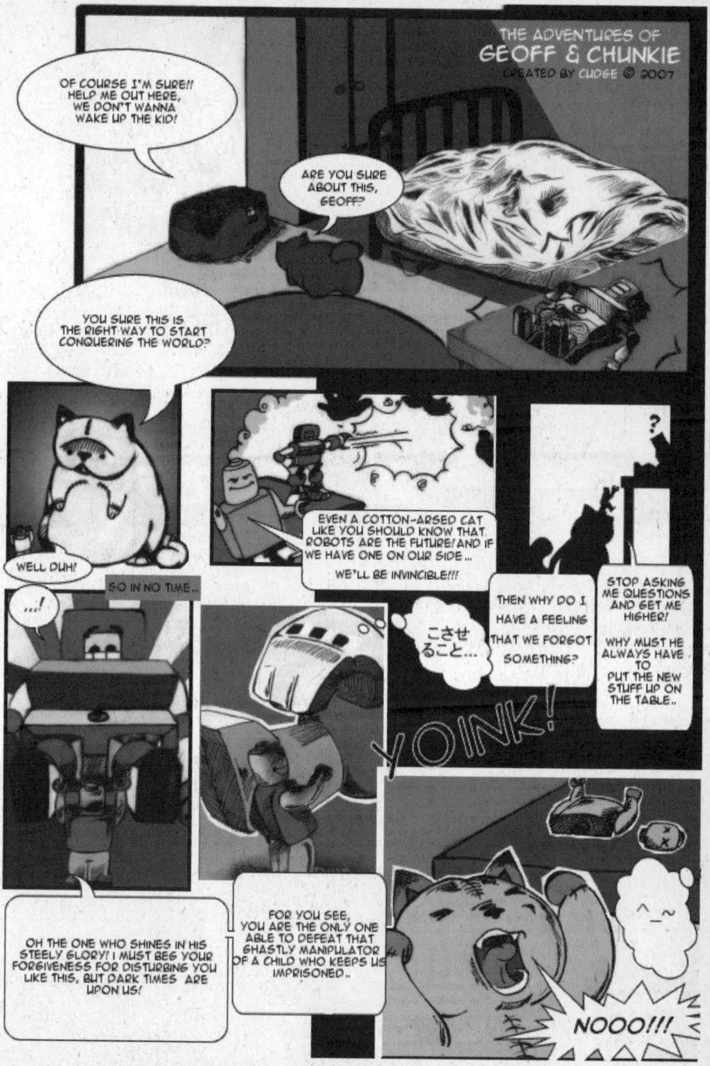
THE ADVENTURES OF
GEOFF & CHUNKIE
CREATED BY CUDGE © 2007
OF COURSE I'M SURE!! HELP ME OUT HERE, WE DON'T WANNA WAKE UP THE KID!
ARE YOU SURE ABOUT THIS, GEOFF?
YOU SURE THIS IS THE RIGHT WAY TO START CONQUERING THE WORLD?
WELL DUH!
EVEN A COTTON-ARSED CAT LIKE YOU SHOULD KNOW THAT ROBOTS ARE THE FUTURE! AND IF WE HAVE ONE ON OUR SIDE ...
WE'LL BE INVINCIBLE!!!
?
THEN WHY DO I HAVE A FEELING THAT WE FORGOT SOMETHING?
STOP ASKING ME QUESTIONS AND GET ME HIGHER!
WHY MUST HE ALWAYS HAVE TO PUT THE NEW STUFF UP ON THE TABLE..
SO IN NO TIME...
...!
こさせること…
YOINK!
OH THE ONE WHO SHINES IN HIS STEELY GLORY! I MUST BEG YOUR FORGIVENESS FOR DISTURBING YOU LIKE THIS, BUT DARK TIMES ARE UPON US!
FOR YOU SEE, YOU ARE THE ONLY ONE ABLE TO DEFEAT THAT GHASTLY MANIPULATOR OF A CHILD WHO KEEPS US IMPRISONED..
^_^
NOOO!!!

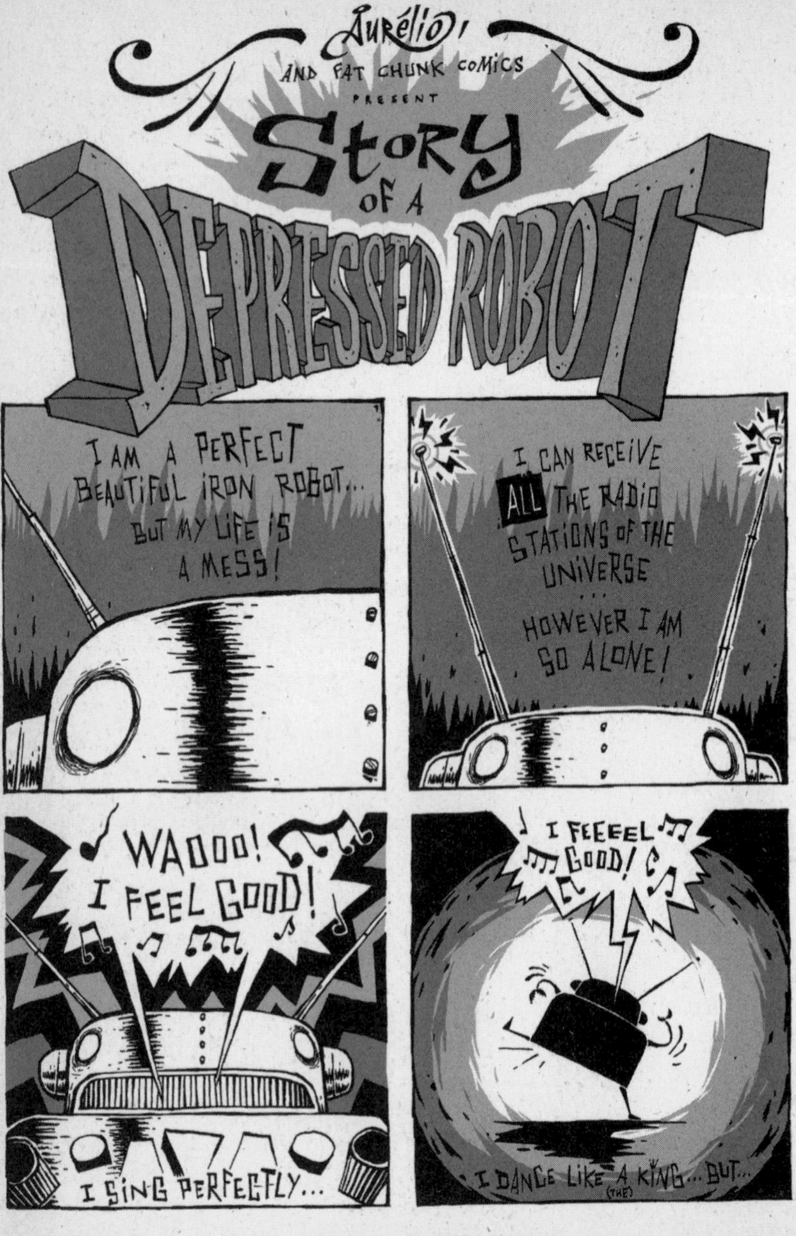
Aurélio!
AND FAT CHUNK COMICS
PRESENT
STORY
OF A
DEPRESSED ROBOT
I AM A PERFECT BEAUTIFUL IRON ROBOT... BUT MY LIFE IS A MESS!
I CAN RECEIVE ALL THE RADIO STATIONS OF THE UNIVERSE ... HOWEVER I AM SO ALONE!
WAOOO! I FEEL GOOD!
I SING PERFECTLY...
I FEEEEL GOOD!
I DANCE LIKE A (THE) KING... BUT...

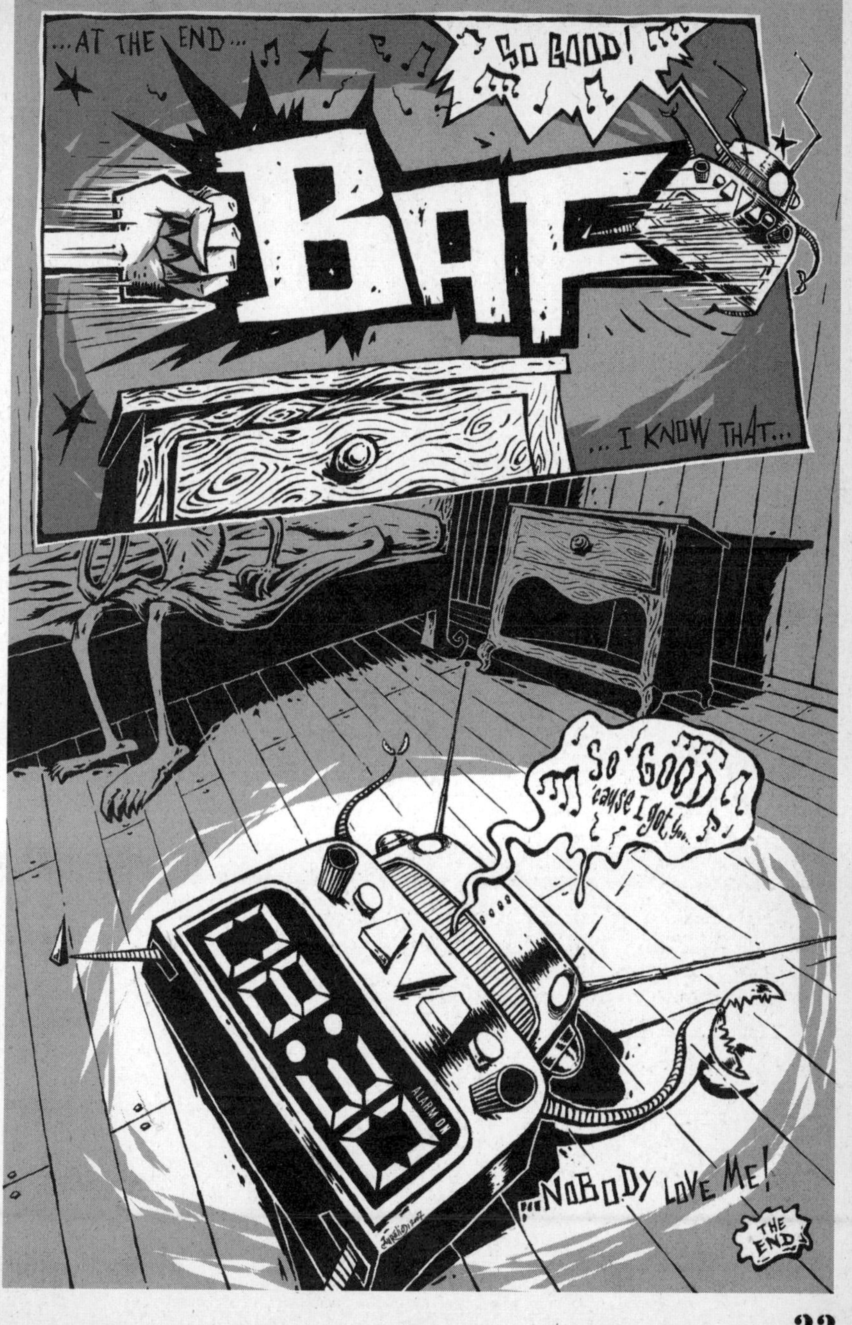
...AT THE END...
SO GOOD!
BAF
... I KNOW THAT...
SO GOOD 'cause I got you...
ALARM ON
...NOBODY LOVE ME!
THE END

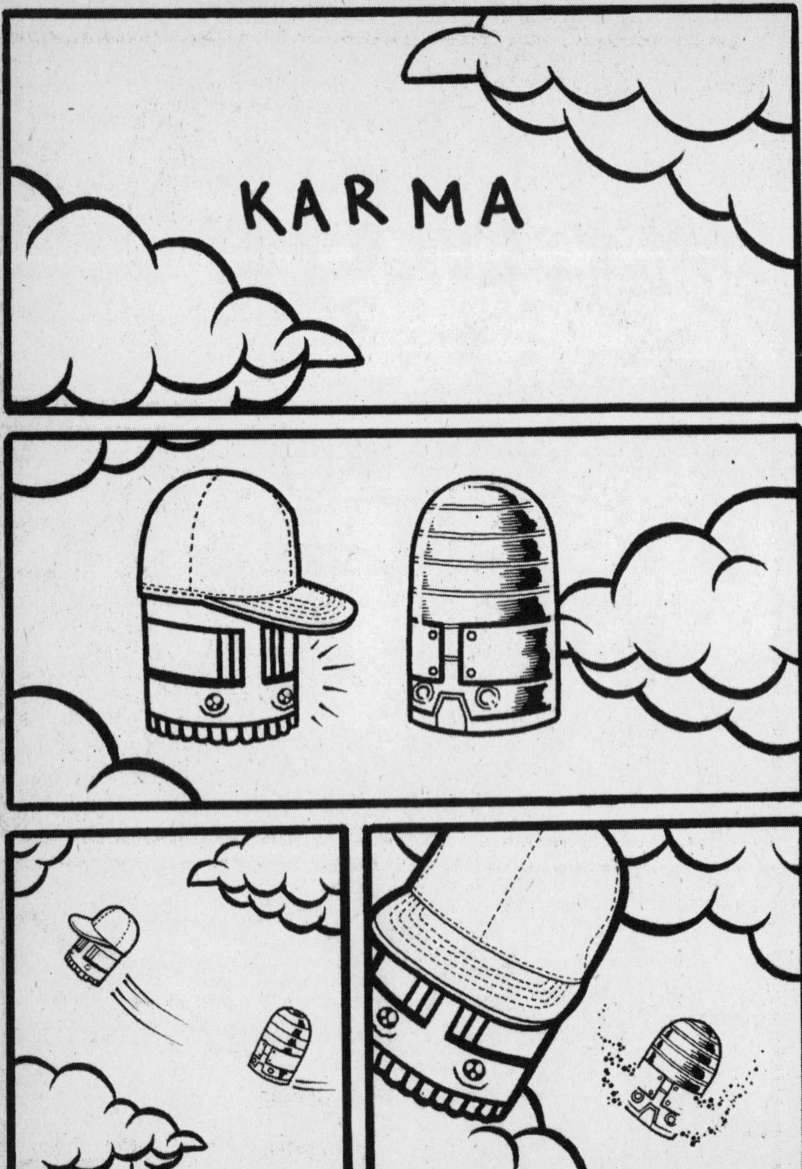
KARMA

BY BAD TEETH / MYSPACE.COM/BADTEETHCOMICS

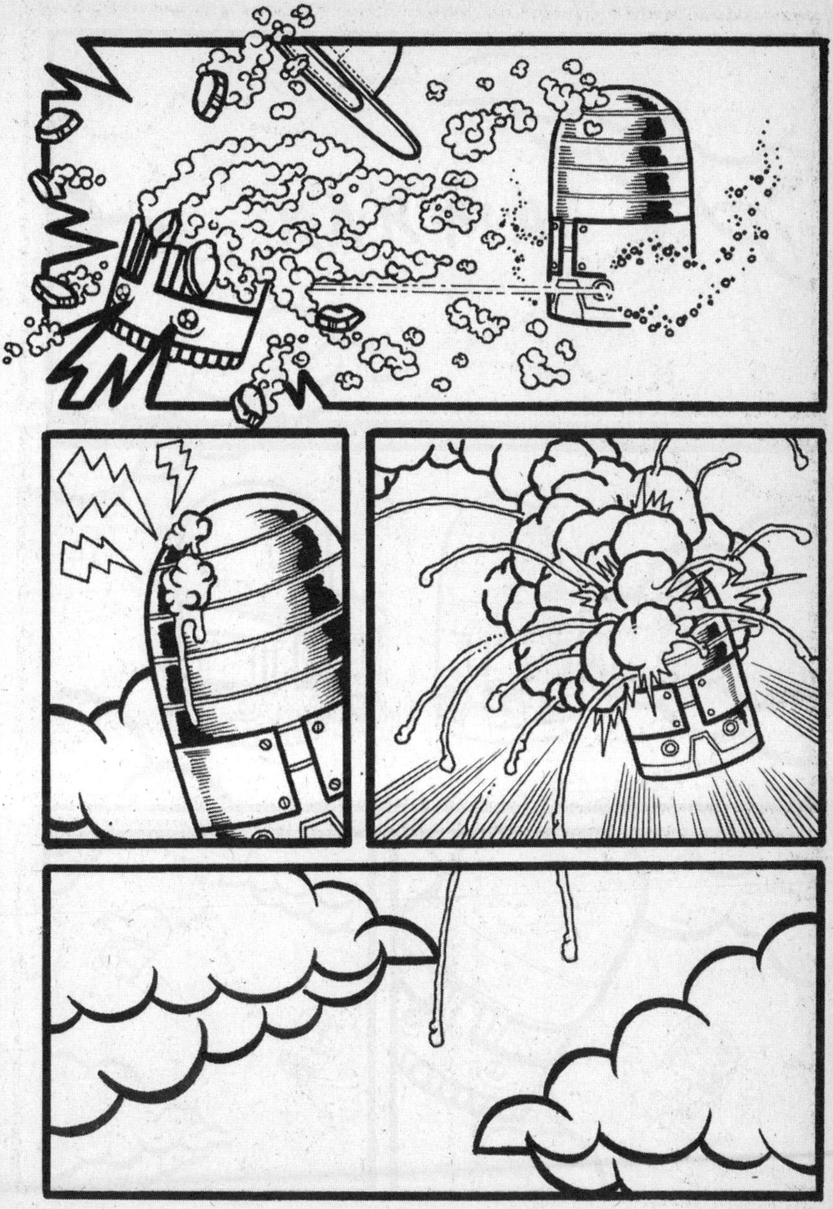

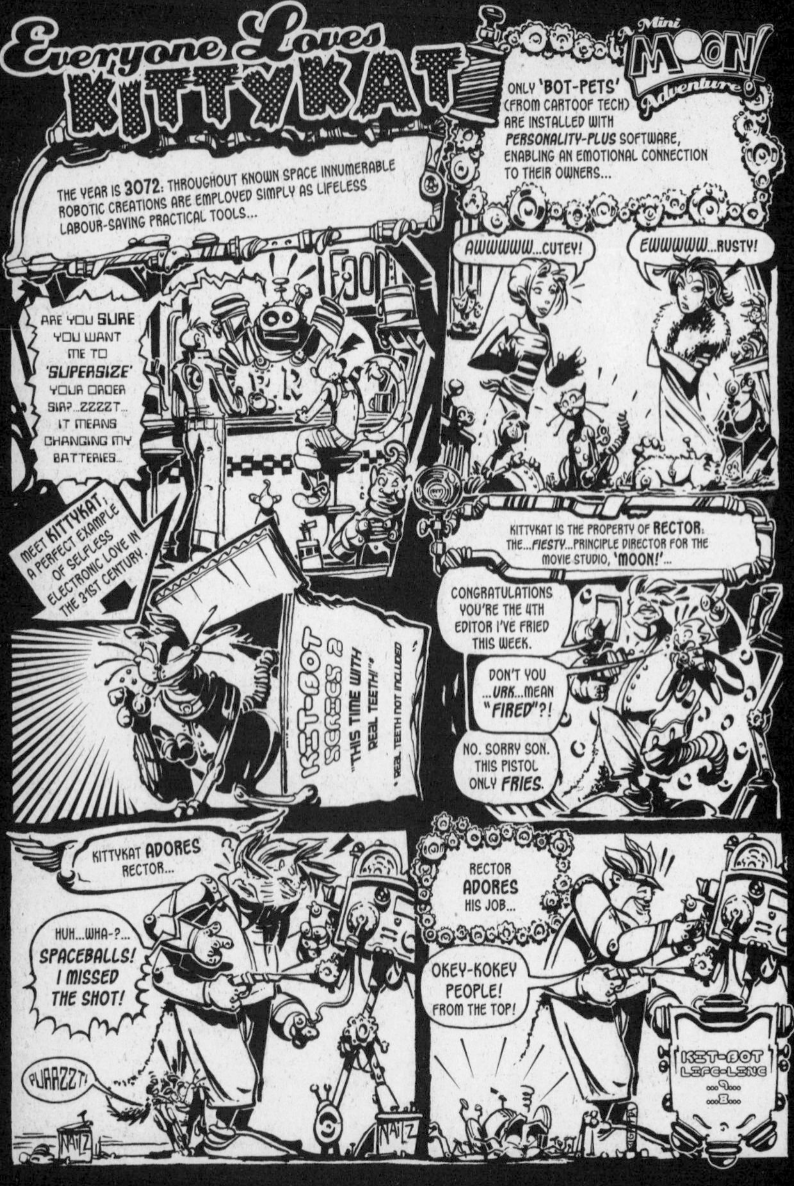
Everyone Loves KITTYKAT
A Mini MOON! Adventure
THE YEAR IS 3072: THROUGHOUT KNOWN SPACE INNUMERABLE ROBOTIC CREATIONS ARE EMPLOYED SIMPLY AS LIFELESS LABOUR-SAVING PRACTICAL TOOLS...
ONLY 'BOT-PETS' (FROM CARTOOF TECH) ARE INSTALLED WITH PERSONALITY-PLUS SOFTWARE, ENABLING AN EMOTIONAL CONNECTION TO THEIR OWNERS...
ARE YOU SURE YOU WANT ME TO 'SUPERSIZE' YOUR ORDER SIR?...ZZZZT... IT MEANS CHANGING MY BATTERIES...
AWWWWW...CUTEY!
EWWWWW...RUSTY!
MEET KITTYKAT, A PERFECT EXAMPLE OF SELFLESS ELECTRONIC LOVE IN THE 31ST CENTURY.
KIT-BOT SERIES 2
"THIS TIME WITH REAL TEETH!"*
* REAL TEETH NOT INCLUDED
KITTYKAT IS THE PROPERTY OF RECTOR: THE...FIESTY...PRINCIPLE DIRECTOR FOR THE MOVIE STUDIO, 'MOON!'...
CONGRATULATIONS YOU'RE THE 4TH EDITOR I'VE FRIED THIS WEEK.
DON'T YOU ...URK...MEAN "FIRED"?!
NO. SORRY SON. THIS PISTOL ONLY FRIES.
KITTYKAT ADORES RECTOR...
HUH...WHA-?... SPACEBALLS! I MISSED THE SHOT!
PURRZZT!
NAILZ
RECTOR ADORES HIS JOB...
OKEY-KOKEY PEOPLE! FROM THE TOP!
KIT-BOT LIFE-LINE ...9... ...8...

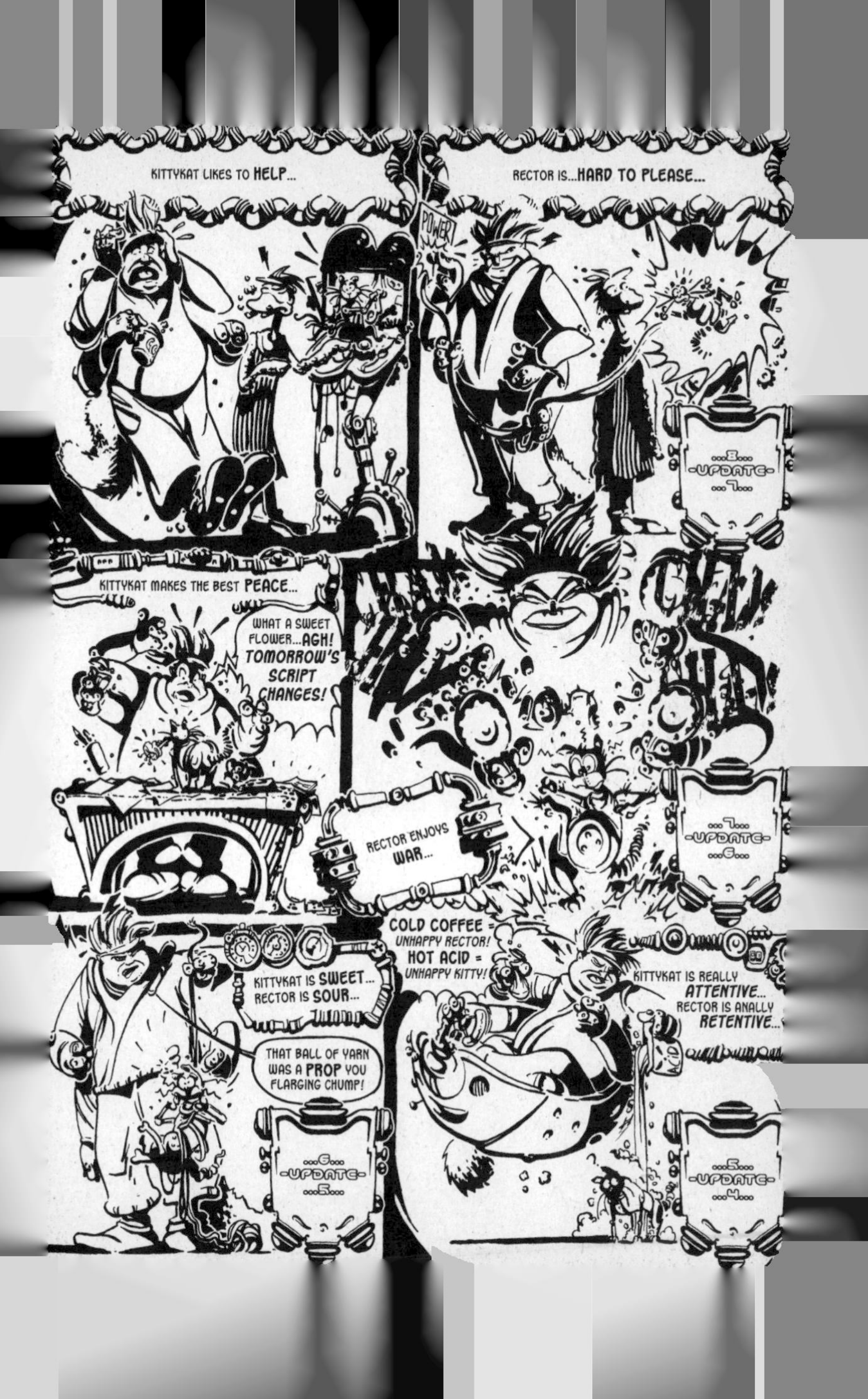
KITTYKAT LIKES TO HELP...
RECTOR IS...HARD TO PLEASE...
POWER
...8...
-UPDATE-
...7...
KITTYKAT MAKES THE BEST PEACE...
WHAT A SWEET FLOWER...AGH! TOMORROW'S SCRIPT CHANGES!
RECTOR ENJOYS WAR...
...7...
-UPDATE-
...6...
KITTYKAT IS SWEET... RECTOR IS SOUR...
THAT BALL OF YARN WAS A PROP YOU FLARGING CHUMP!
...6...
-UPDATE-
...5...
COLD COFFEE = UNHAPPY RECTOR! HOT ACID = UNHAPPY KITTY!
KITTYKAT IS REALLY ATTENTIVE... RECTOR IS ANALLY RETENTIVE...
ACID
...5...
-UPDATE-
...4...

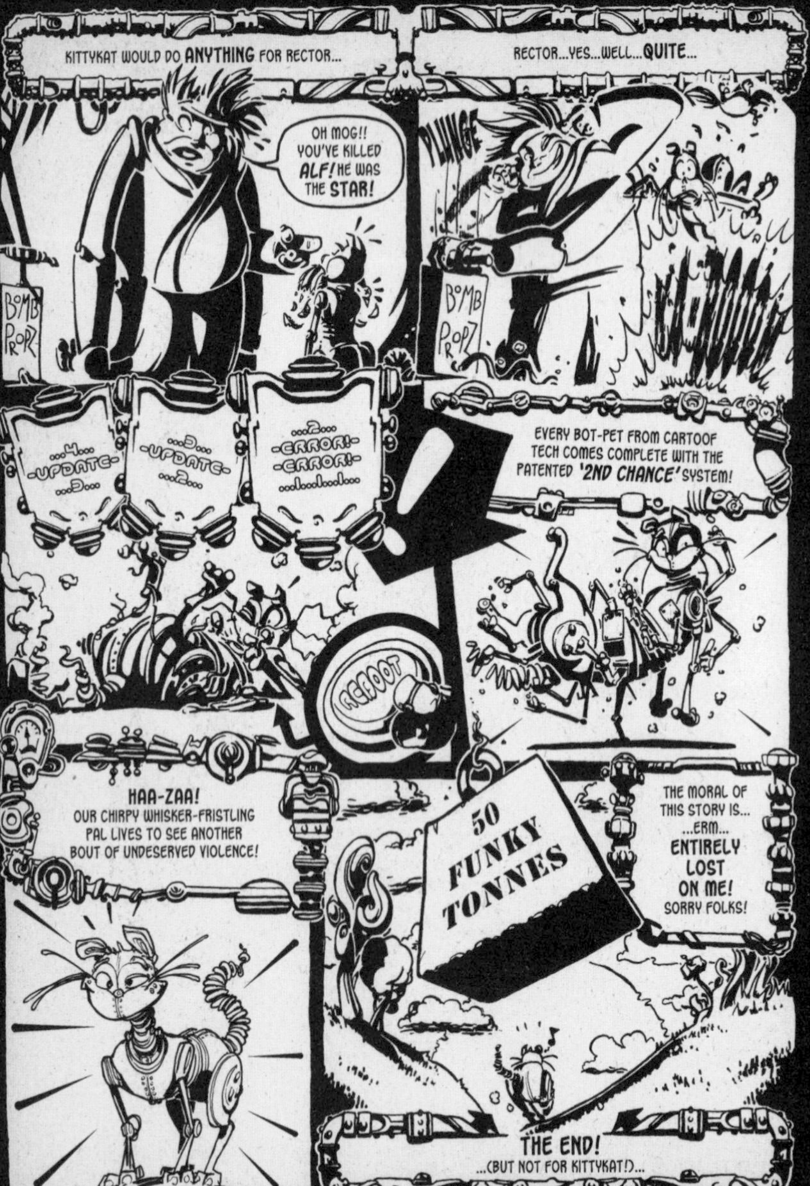
KITTYKAT WOULD DO ANYTHING FOR RECTOR...
OH MOG!! YOU'VE KILLED ALF! HE WAS THE STAR!
BOMB PROPZ
RECTOR...YES...WELL...QUITE...
PLUNGE
BOMB PROPZ
...4... -UPDATE- ...3...
...3... -UPDATE- ...2...
...2... -ERROR!- -ERROR!- ...1...1...1...
REBOOT
EVERY BOT-PET FROM CARTOOF TECH COMES COMPLETE WITH THE PATENTED '2ND CHANCE' SYSTEM!
HAA-ZAA!
OUR CHIRPY WHISKER-FRISTLING PAL LIVES TO SEE ANOTHER BOUT OF UNDESERVED VIOLENCE!
50 FUNKY TONNES
THE MORAL OF THIS STORY IS... ...ERM... ENTIRELY LOST ON ME! SORRY FOLKS!
THE END!
...(BUT NOT FOR KITTYKAT!)...

BY JIMMY BONDI / MYSPACE.COM/ITZSO_WEEZEE

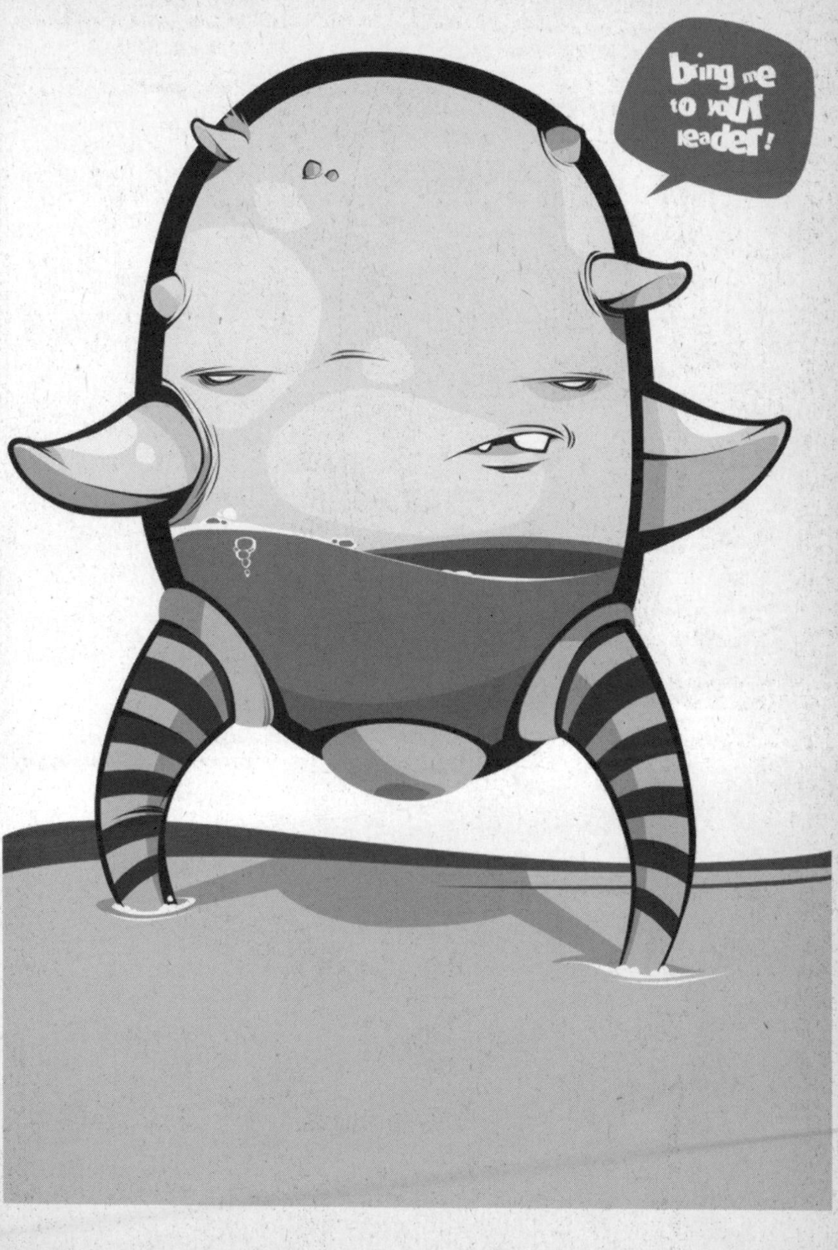
bring me
to your
leader!

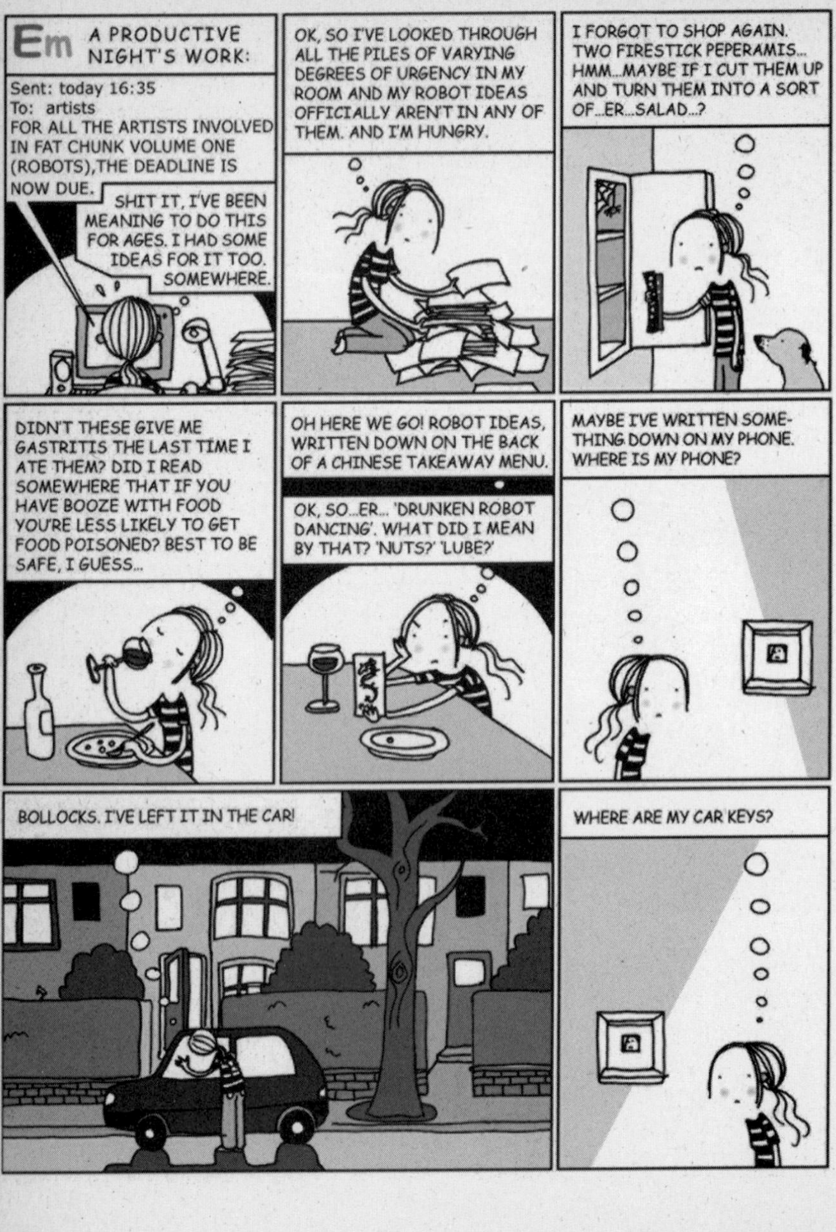
Em A PRODUCTIVE NIGHT'S WORK:
Sent: today 16:35
To: artists
FOR ALL THE ARTISTS INVOLVED IN FAT CHUNK VOLUME ONE (ROBOTS),THE DEADLINE IS NOW DUE.
SHIT IT, I'VE BEEN MEANING TO DO THIS FOR AGES. I HAD SOME IDEAS FOR IT TOO. SOMEWHERE.
OK, SO I'VE LOOKED THROUGH ALL THE PILES OF VARYING DEGREES OF URGENCY IN MY ROOM AND MY ROBOT IDEAS OFFICIALLY AREN'T IN ANY OF THEM. AND I'M HUNGRY.
I FORGOT TO SHOP AGAIN. TWO FIRESTICK PEPERAMIS... HMM...MAYBE IF I CUT THEM UP AND TURN THEM INTO A SORT OF...ER...SALAD...?
DIDN'T THESE GIVE ME GASTRITIS THE LAST TIME I ATE THEM? DID I READ SOMEWHERE THAT IF YOU HAVE BOOZE WITH FOOD YOU'RE LESS LIKELY TO GET FOOD POISONED? BEST TO BE SAFE, I GUESS...
OH HERE WE GO! ROBOT IDEAS, WRITTEN DOWN ON THE BACK OF A CHINESE TAKEAWAY MENU.
OK, SO...ER... 'DRUNKEN ROBOT DANCING'. WHAT DID I MEAN BY THAT? 'NUTS?' 'LUBE?'
MAYBE I'VE WRITTEN SOMETHING DOWN ON MY PHONE. WHERE IS MY PHONE?
BOLLOCKS. I'VE LEFT IT IN THE CAR!
WHERE ARE MY CAR KEYS?

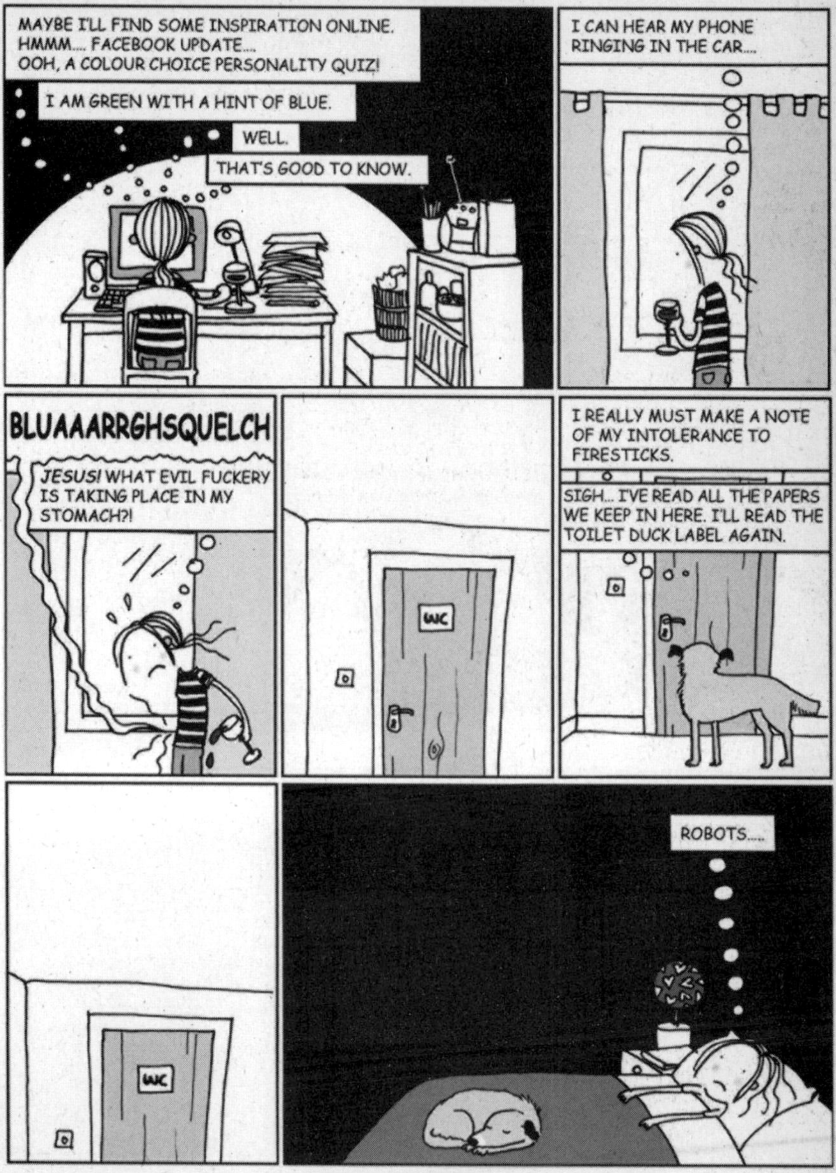
MAYBE I'LL FIND SOME INSPIRATION ONLINE. HMMM.... FACEBOOK UPDATE.... OOH, A COLOUR CHOICE PERSONALITY QUIZ!
I AM GREEN WITH A HINT OF BLUE.
WELL.
THAT'S GOOD TO KNOW.
I CAN HEAR MY PHONE RINGING IN THE CAR....
BLUAAARRGHSQUELCH
JESUS! WHAT EVIL FUCKERY IS TAKING PLACE IN MY STOMACH?!
WC
I REALLY MUST MAKE A NOTE OF MY INTOLERANCE TO FIRESTICKS.
SIGH... I'VE READ ALL THE PAPERS WE KEEP IN HERE. I'LL READ THE TOILET DUCK LABEL AGAIN.
WC
ROBOTS.....

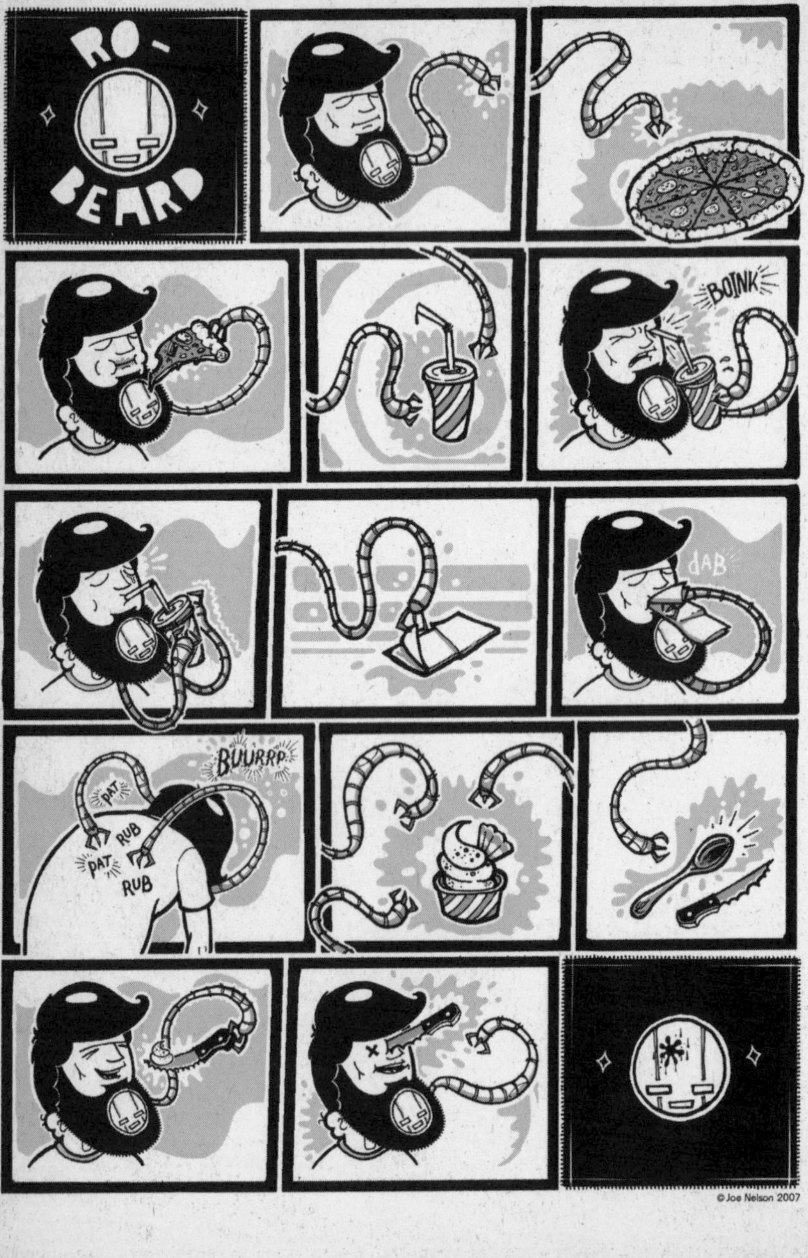
RO-BEARD
BOINK
dAB
BUURRP
PAT
RUB
PAT
RUB

BY JOEL LOLAR / GREENSKYZERO.DEVIANTART.COM, INKED BY JOE DAXBERGER / DAX-ZERO.DEVIANTART.COM

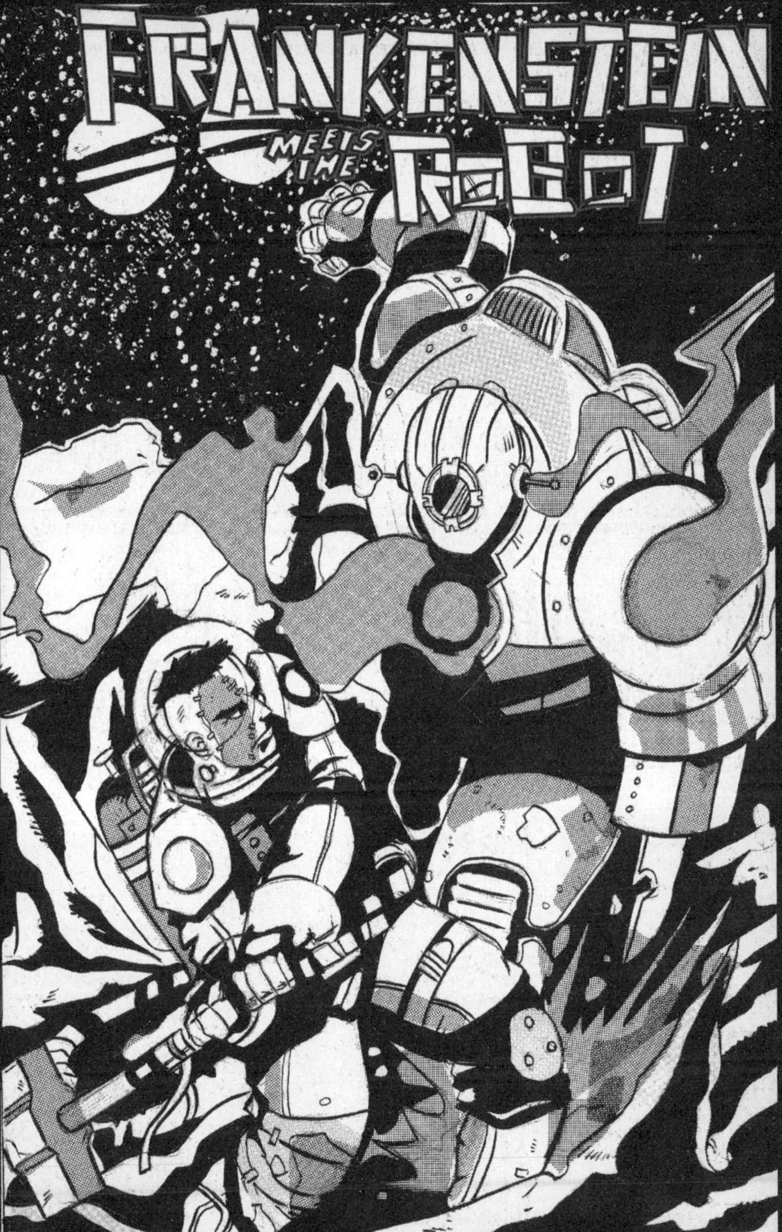
FRANKENSTEIN
MEETS THE
ROBOT

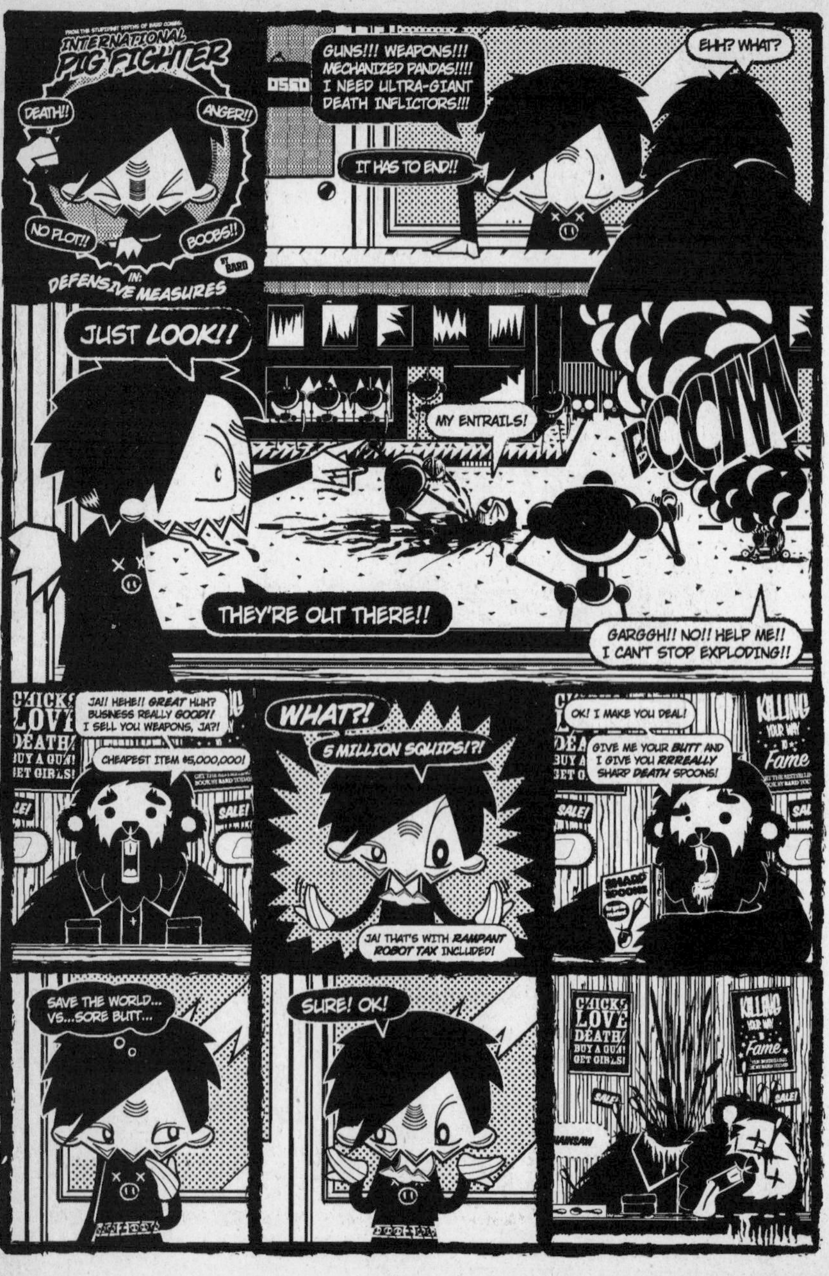
FROM THE STUPIDEST DEPTHS OF BARD COMICS
INTERNATIONAL PIG FIGHTER
DEATH!!
ANGER!!
NO PLOT!!
BOOBS!!
BY BARD
IN: DEFENSIVE MEASURES
GUNS!!! WEAPONS!!! MECHANIZED PANDAS!!!! I NEED ULTRA-GIANT DEATH INFLICTORS!!!
IT HAS TO END!!
EHH? WHAT?
JUST LOOK!!
MY ENTRAILS!
BOOM
THEY'RE OUT THERE!!
GARGGH!! NO!! HELP ME!! I CAN'T STOP EXPLODING!!
CHICKS LOVE DEATH! BUY A GUN! GET GIRLS!
JA!! HEHE!! GREAT HUH? BUSINESS REALLY GOOD!! I SELL YOU WEAPONS, JA?!
CHEAPEST ITEM $5,000,000!
SALE!
WHAT?!
5 MILLION SQUIDS!?!
JA! THAT'S WITH RAMPANT ROBOT TAX INCLUDED!
OK! I MAKE YOU DEAL!
GIVE ME YOUR BUTT AND I GIVE YOU RRREALLY SHARP DEATH SPOONS!
KILLING YOUR WAY TO Fame
SHARP SPOONS
SAVE THE WORLD... VS...SORE BUTT...
SURE! OK!
CHICKS LOVE DEATH! BUY A GUN! GET GIRLS!
KILLING YOUR WAY TO Fame
SALE!
CHAINSAW

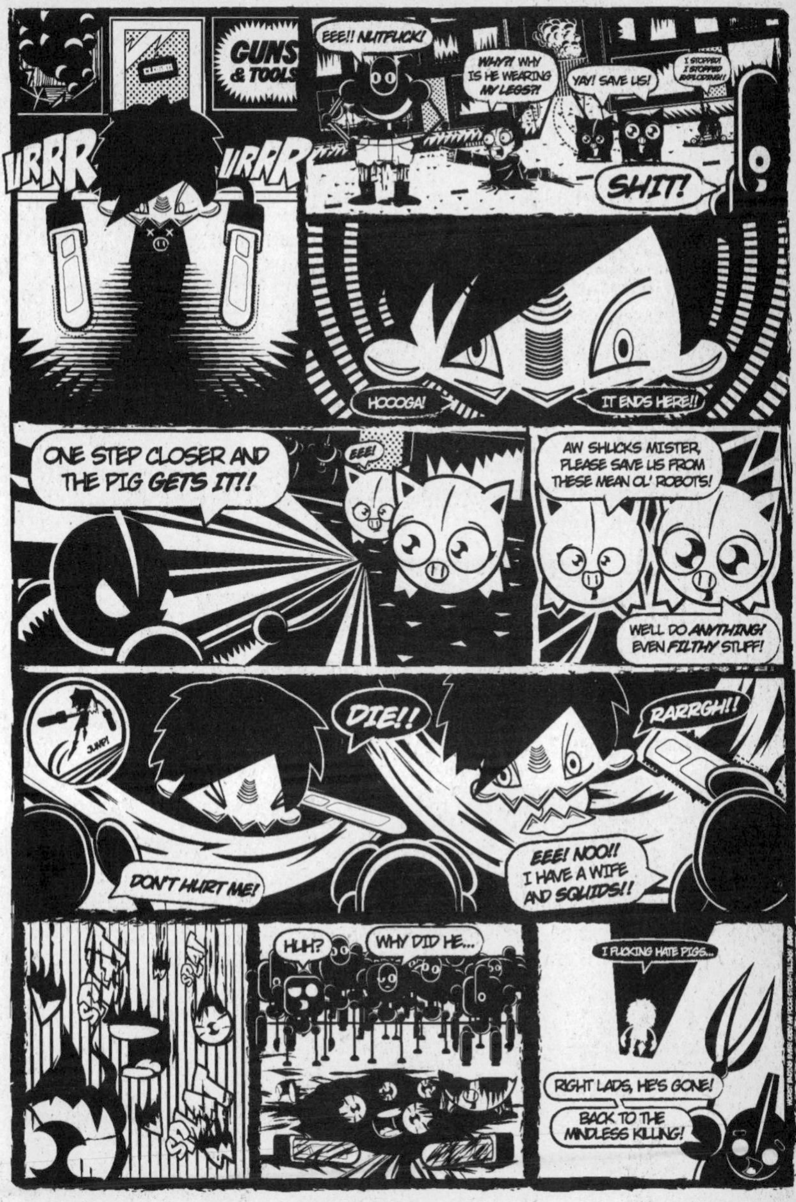
GUNS & TOOLS
URRR
URRR
EEE!! NUTFUCK!
WHY?! WHY IS HE WEARING MY LEGS?!
YAY! SAVE US!
I STOPPED! I STOPPED EXPLODING!!
SHIT!
HOOOGA!
IT ENDS HERE!!
ONE STEP CLOSER AND THE PIG GETS IT!!
EEE!
AW SHUCKS MISTER, PLEASE SAVE US FROM THESE MEAN OL' ROBOTS!
WE'LL DO ANYTHING! EVEN FILTHY STUFF!
DIE!!
RARRGH!!
DON'T HURT ME!
EEE! NOO!! I HAVE A WIFE AND SQUIDS!!
HUH?
WHY DID HE...
I FUCKING HATE PIGS...
RIGHT LADS, HE'S GONE!
BACK TO THE MINDLESS KILLING!

BY JEREMY GOAD / MYSPACE.COM/STEALTHEBANANA,
WRITTEN BY MATT DELACRUZ / MYSPACE.COM/WOXNTOX

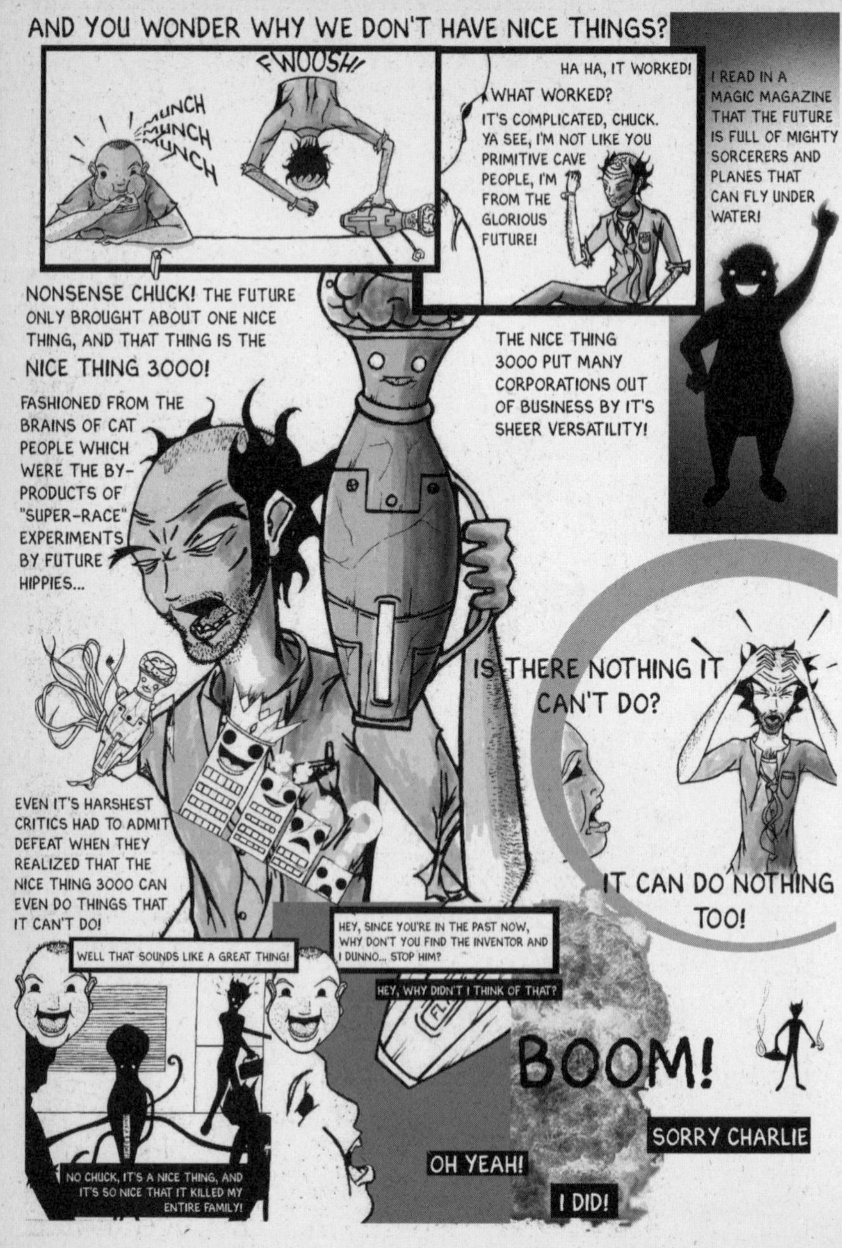
AND YOU WONDER WHY WE DON'T HAVE NICE THINGS?
MUNCH MUNCH MUNCH
FWOOSH!
HA HA, IT WORKED!
WHAT WORKED?
IT'S COMPLICATED, CHUCK. YA SEE, I'M NOT LIKE YOU PRIMITIVE CAVE PEOPLE, I'M FROM THE GLORIOUS FUTURE!
I READ IN A MAGIC MAGAZINE THAT THE FUTURE IS FULL OF MIGHTY SORCERERS AND PLANES THAT CAN FLY UNDER WATER!
NONSENSE CHUCK! THE FUTURE ONLY BROUGHT ABOUT ONE NICE THING, AND THAT THING IS THE NICE THING 3000!
THE NICE THING 3000 PUT MANY CORPORATIONS OUT OF BUSINESS BY IT'S SHEER VERSATILITY!
FASHIONED FROM THE BRAINS OF CAT PEOPLE WHICH WERE THE BY-PRODUCTS OF "SUPER-RACE" EXPERIMENTS BY FUTURE HIPPIES...
IS THERE NOTHING IT CAN'T DO?
EVEN IT'S HARSHEST CRITICS HAD TO ADMIT DEFEAT WHEN THEY REALIZED THAT THE NICE THING 3000 CAN EVEN DO THINGS THAT IT CAN'T DO!
IT CAN DO NOTHING TOO!
WELL THAT SOUNDS LIKE A GREAT THING!
NO CHUCK, IT'S A NICE THING, AND IT'S SO NICE THAT IT KILLED MY ENTIRE FAMILY!
HEY, SINCE YOU'RE IN THE PAST NOW, WHY DON'T YOU FIND THE INVENTOR AND I DUNNO... STOP HIM?
HEY, WHY DIDN'T I THINK OF THAT?
OH YEAH!
I DID!
BOOM!
SORRY CHARLIE

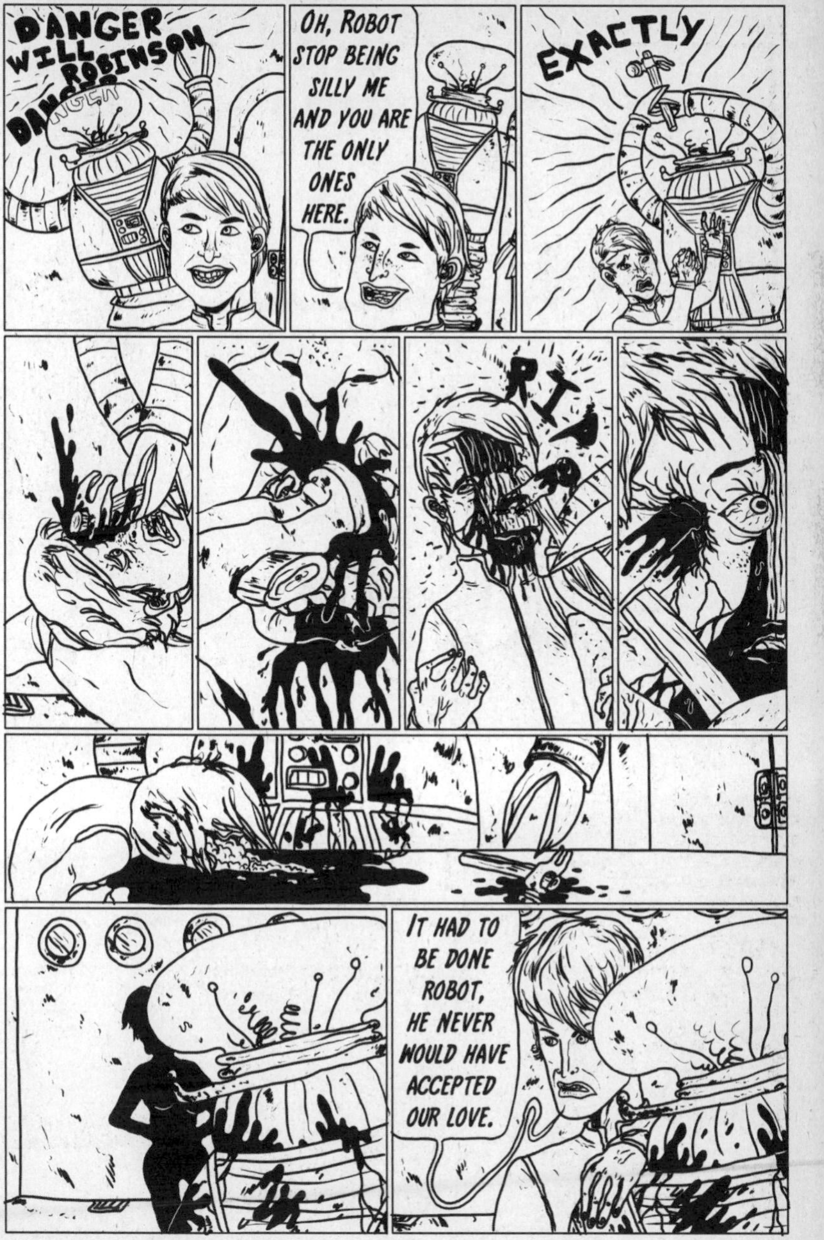
DANGER WILL ROBINSON DANGER
OH, ROBOT STOP BEING SILLY ME AND YOU ARE THE ONLY ONES HERE.
EXACTLY
RI
IT HAD TO BE DONE ROBOT, HE NEVER WOULD HAVE ACCEPTED OUR LOVE.

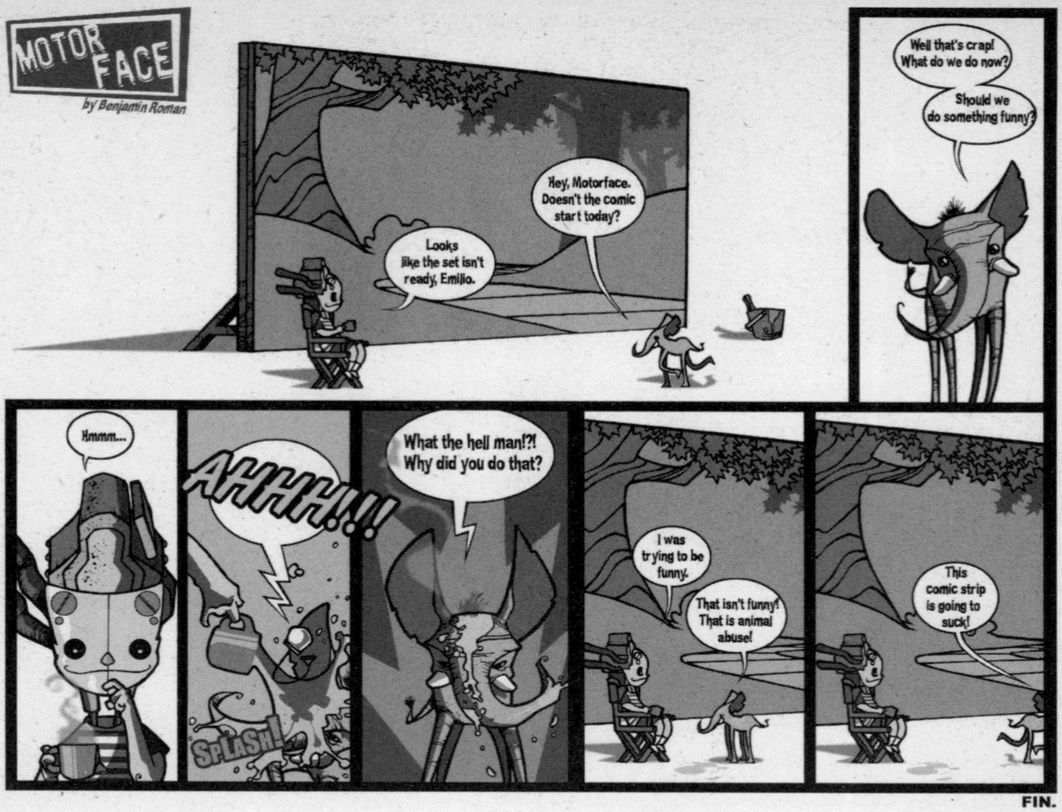
MOTOR FACE
by Benjamin Roman
Looks like the set isn't ready, Emilio.
Hey, Motorface. Doesn't the comic start today?
Well that's crap! What do we do now?
Should we do something funny?
Hmmm...
AHHH!!!!
SPLASH!
What the hell man!?! Why did you do that?
I was trying to be funny.
That isn't funny! That is animal abuse!
This comic strip is going to suck!
FIN.

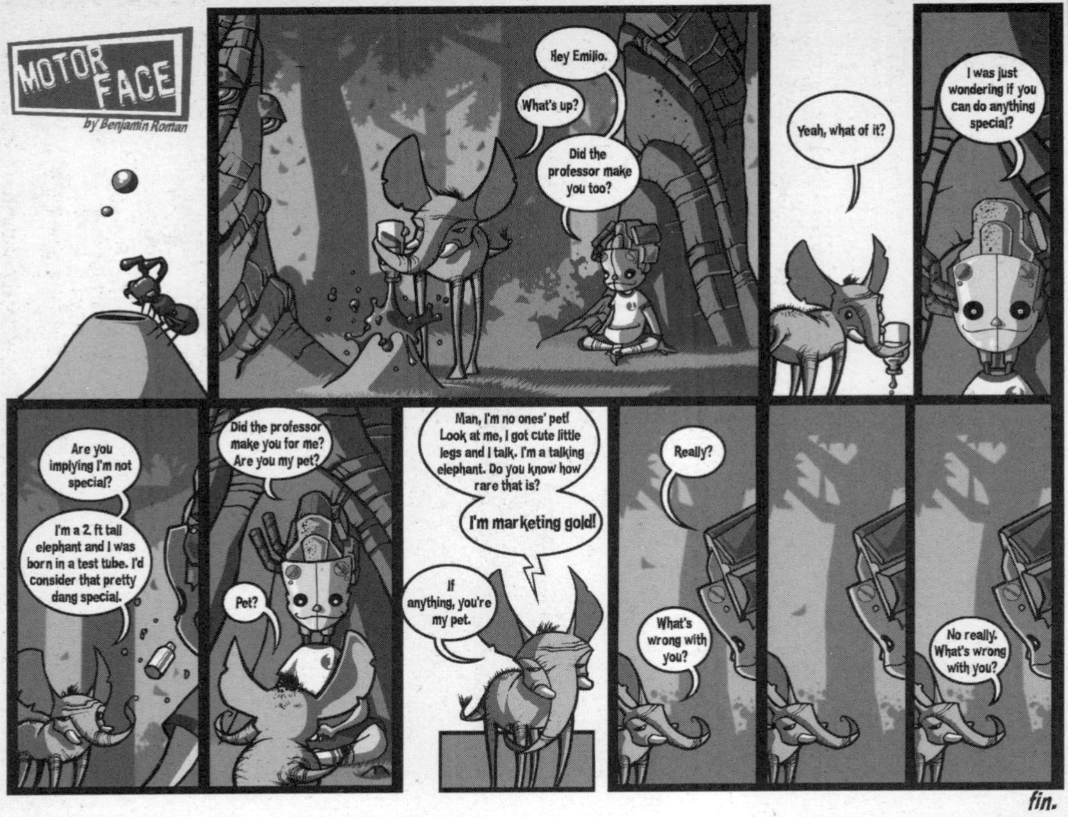
MOTOR FACE
by Benjamin Roman
Hey Emilio.
What's up?
Did the professor make you too?
Yeah, what of it?
I was just wondering if you can do anything special?
Are you implying I'm not special?
I'm a 2 ft tall elephant and I was born in a test tube. I'd consider that pretty dang special.
Did the professor make you for me? Are you my pet?
Pet?
Man, I'm no ones' pet! Look at me, I got cute little legs and I talk. I'm a talking elephant. Do you know how rare that is?
I'm marketing gold!
If anything, you're my pet.
Really?
What's wrong with you?
No really. What's wrong with you?
fin.

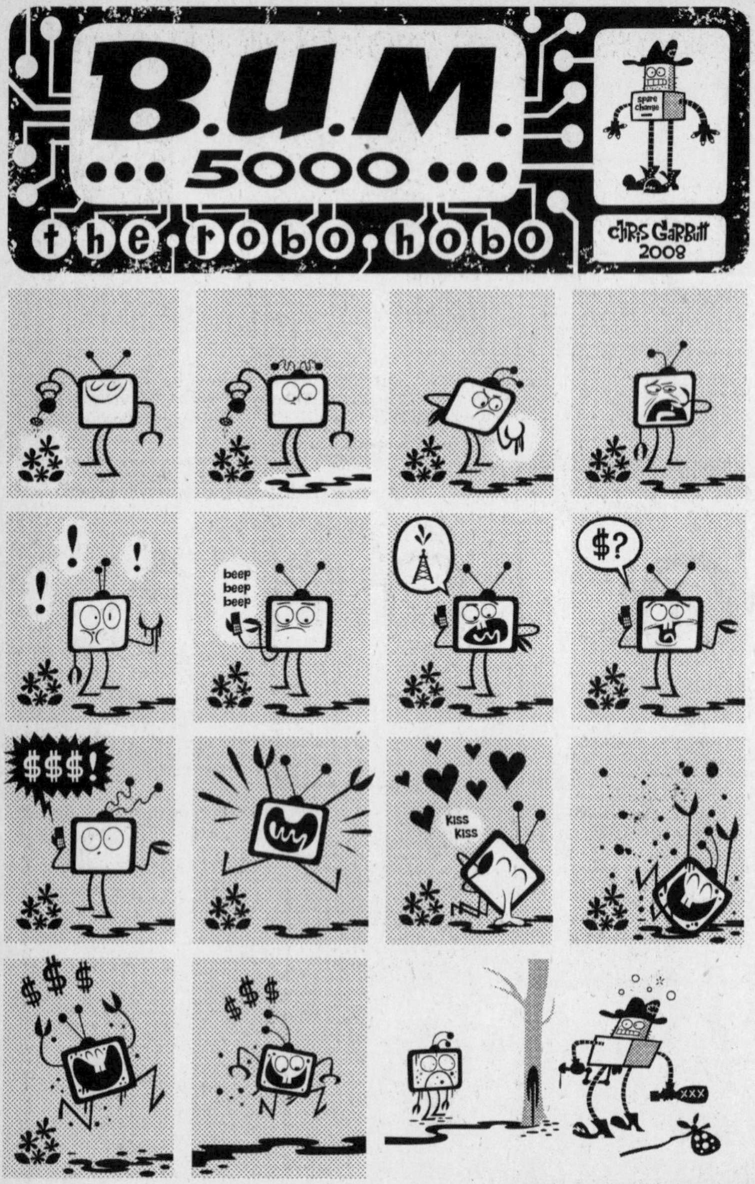
B.U.M.
5000
the robo hobo
spare change
CHRIS GARBUTT
2008
!
!
!
beep
beep
beep
$?
$$$!
KISS
KISS
$$$
$$$
XXX

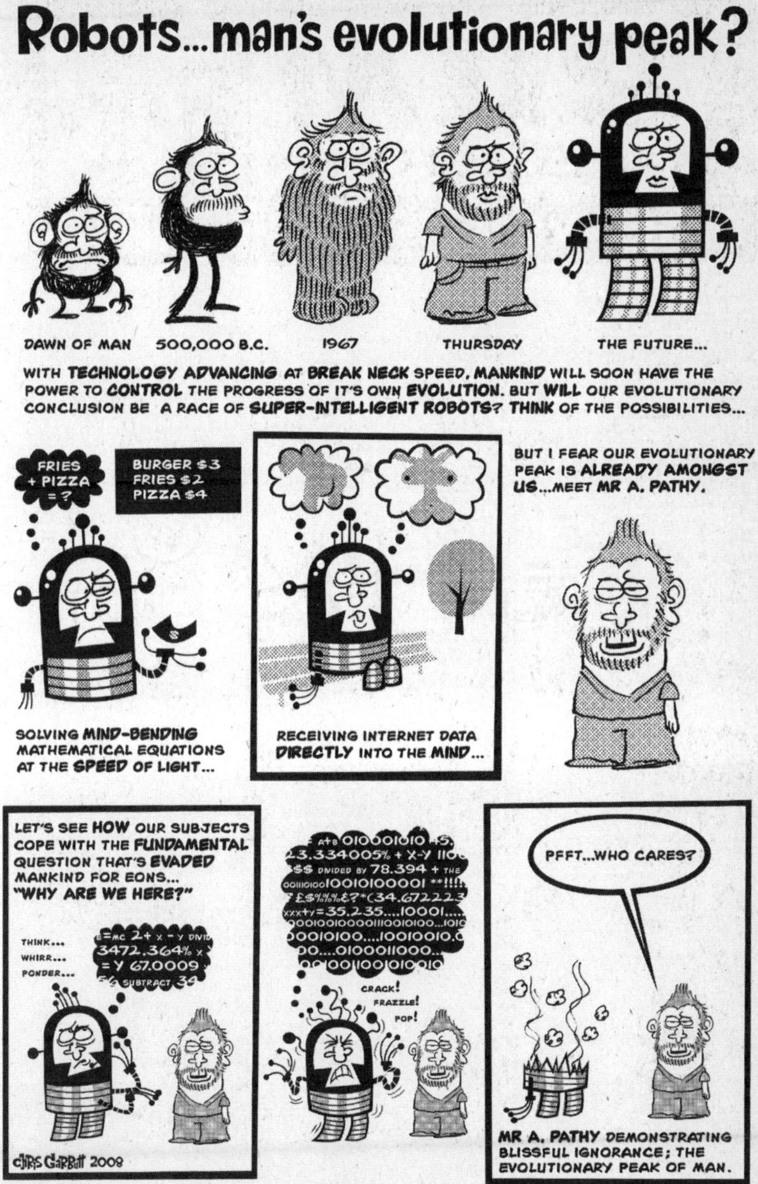
Robots...man's evolutionary peak?
DAWN OF MAN
500,000 B.C.
1967
THURSDAY
THE FUTURE...
WITH TECHNOLOGY ADVANCING AT BREAK NECK SPEED, MANKIND WILL SOON HAVE THE POWER TO CONTROL THE PROGRESS OF IT'S OWN EVOLUTION. BUT WILL OUR EVOLUTIONARY CONCLUSION BE A RACE OF SUPER-INTELLIGENT ROBOTS? THINK OF THE POSSIBILITIES...
FRIES + PIZZA = ?
BURGER $3
FRIES $2
PIZZA $4
SOLVING MIND-BENDING MATHEMATICAL EQUATIONS AT THE SPEED OF LIGHT...
RECEIVING INTERNET DATA DIRECTLY INTO THE MIND...
BUT I FEAR OUR EVOLUTIONARY PEAK IS ALREADY AMONGST US...MEET MR A. PATHY.
LET'S SEE HOW OUR SUBJECTS COPE WITH THE FUNDAMENTAL QUESTION THAT'S EVADED MANKIND FOR EONS... "WHY ARE WE HERE?"
THINK...
WHIRR...
PONDER...
3472.364%
= Y 67.0009
SUBTRACT
$$ DIVIDED BY 78.394 + THE
CRACK!
FRAZZLE!
POP!
CHRIS GARBUTT 2008
PFFT...WHO CARES?
MR A. PATHY DEMONSTRATING BLISSFUL IGNORANCE; THE EVOLUTIONARY PEAK OF MAN.

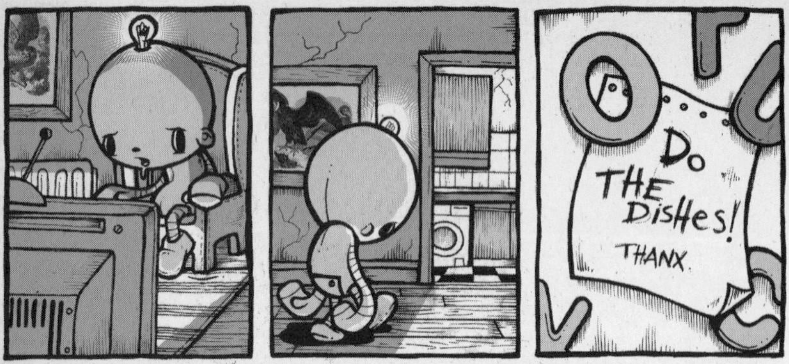
Do THE DisHes!
THANX

rust:

or a short comic strip about the perils of robot ownership, including the development of robot emotions and dish washing

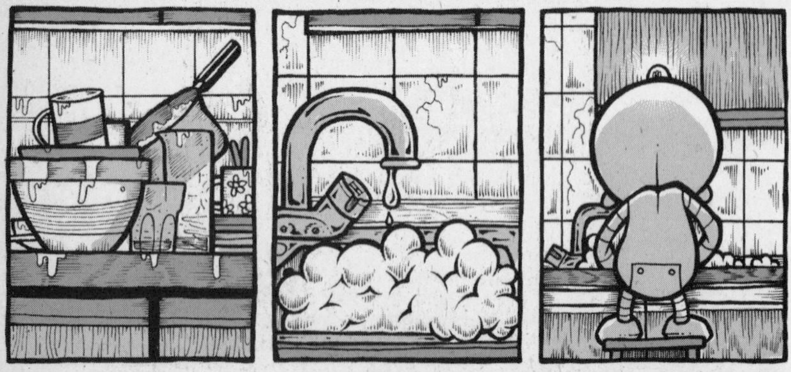

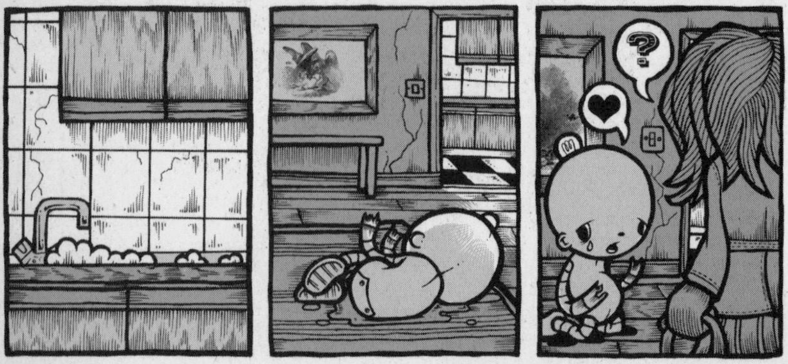
?

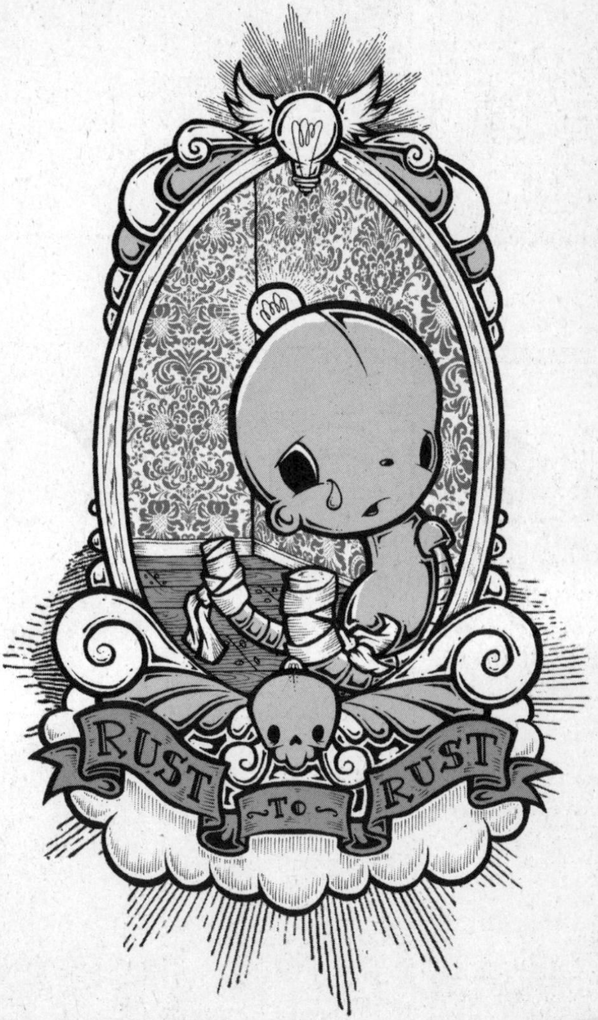
RUST
TO
RUST

BY ANDY MAHONEY / SUICIDAL-COW.DEVIANTART.COM

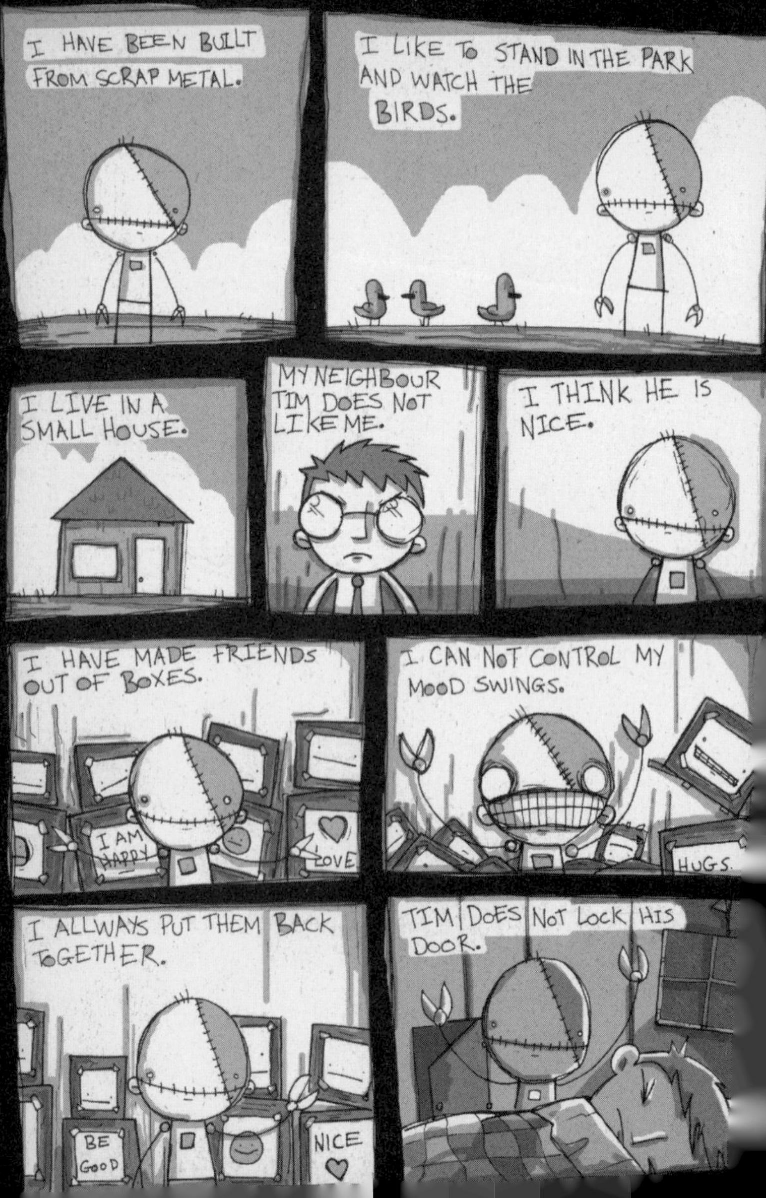
I HAVE BEEN BUILT FROM SCRAP METAL.
I LIKE TO STAND IN THE PARK AND WATCH THE BIRDS.
I LIVE IN A SMALL HOUSE.
MY NEIGHBOUR TIM DOES NOT LIKE ME.
I THINK HE IS NICE.
I HAVE MADE FRIENDS OUT OF BOXES.
I AM HAPPY
LOVE
I CAN NOT CONTROL MY MOOD SWINGS.
HUGS.
I ALLWAYS PUT THEM BACK TOGETHER.
BE GOOD
NICE
TIM DOES NOT LOCK HIS DOOR.

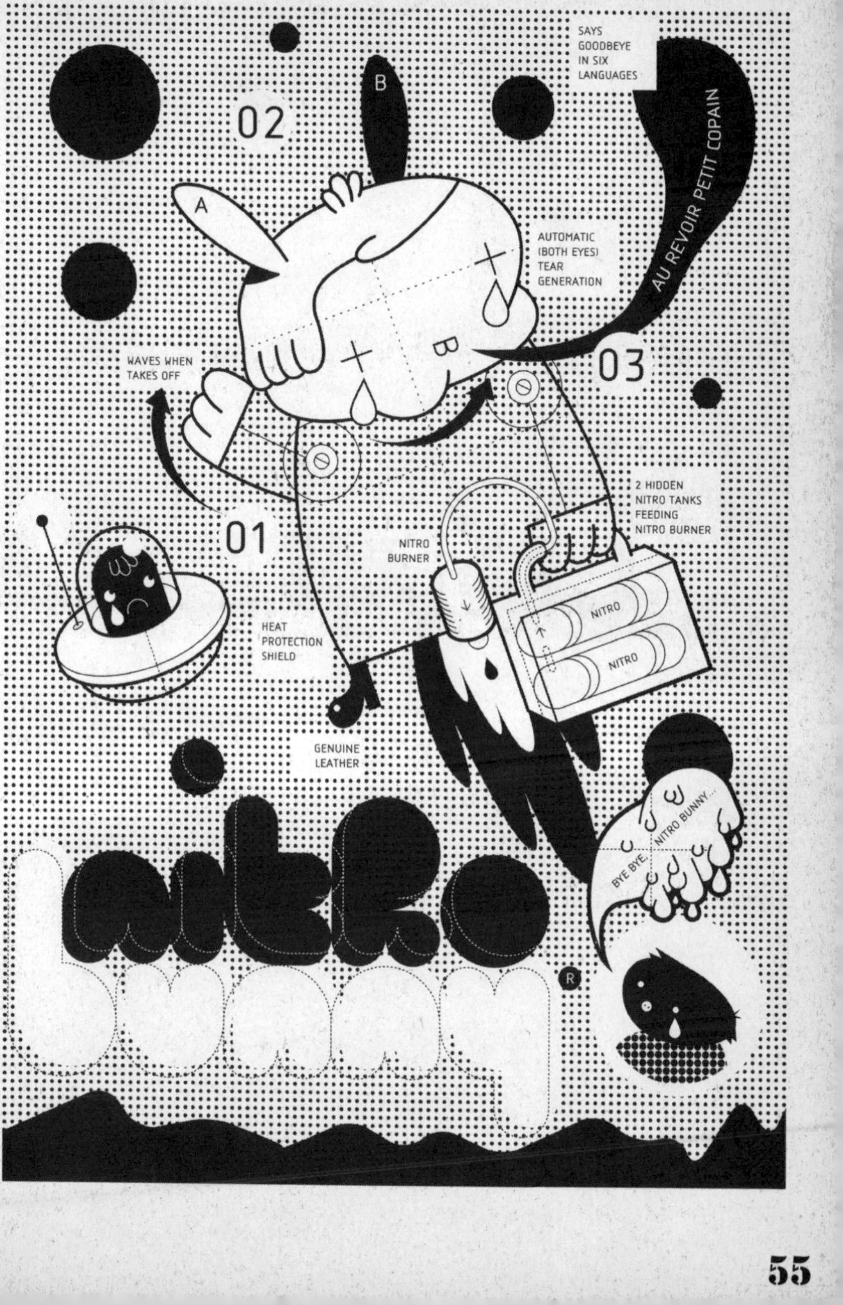
SAYS GOODBEYE IN SIX LANGUAGES
AU REVOIR PETIT COPAIN
02
A
B
AUTOMATIC (BOTH EYES) TEAR GENERATION
WAVES WHEN TAKES OFF
03
2 HIDDEN NITRO TANKS FEEDING NITRO BURNER
01
NITRO BURNER
NITRO
NITRO
HEAT PROTECTION SHIELD
GENUINE LEATHER
BYE BYE, NITRO BUNNY...
R

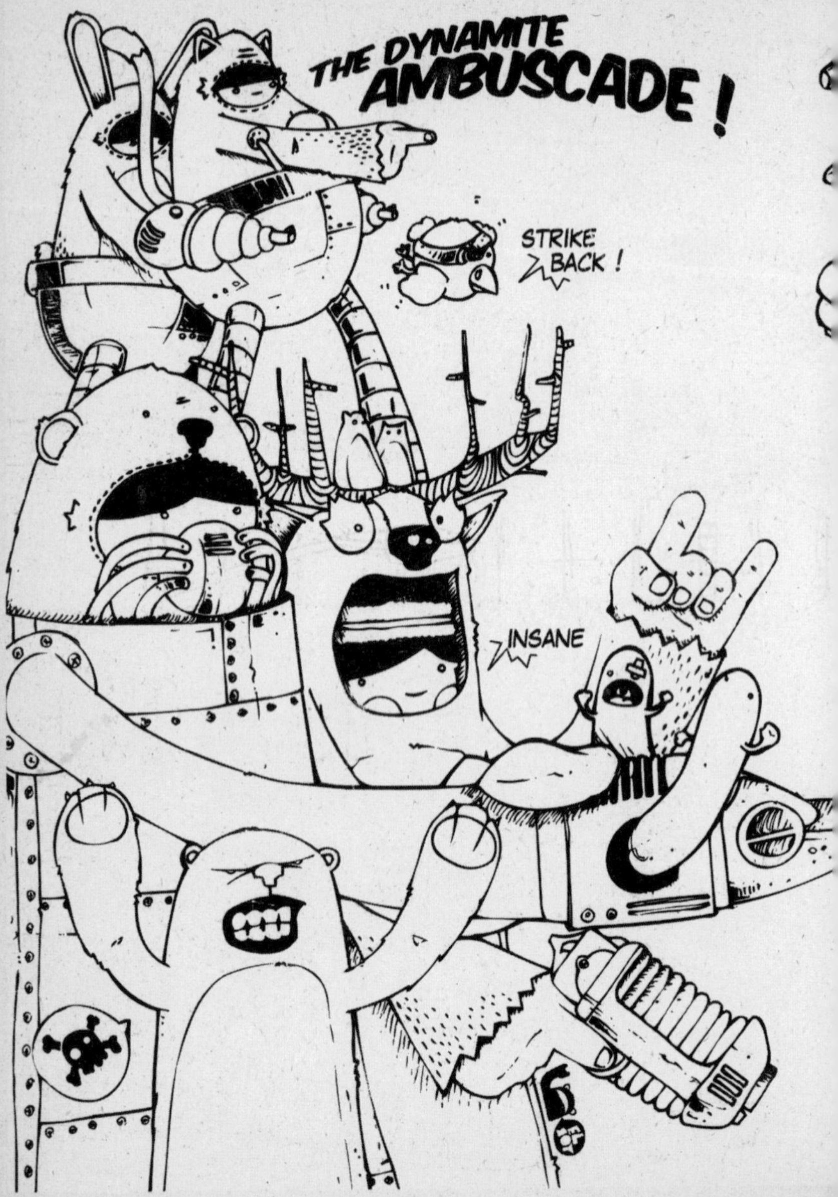
THE DYNAMITE AMBUSCADE !
STRIKE BACK !
INSANE

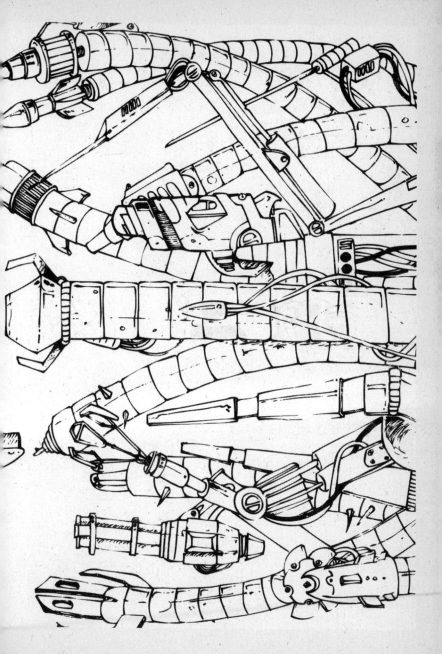

Illustrated Narratives of an Historical Nature

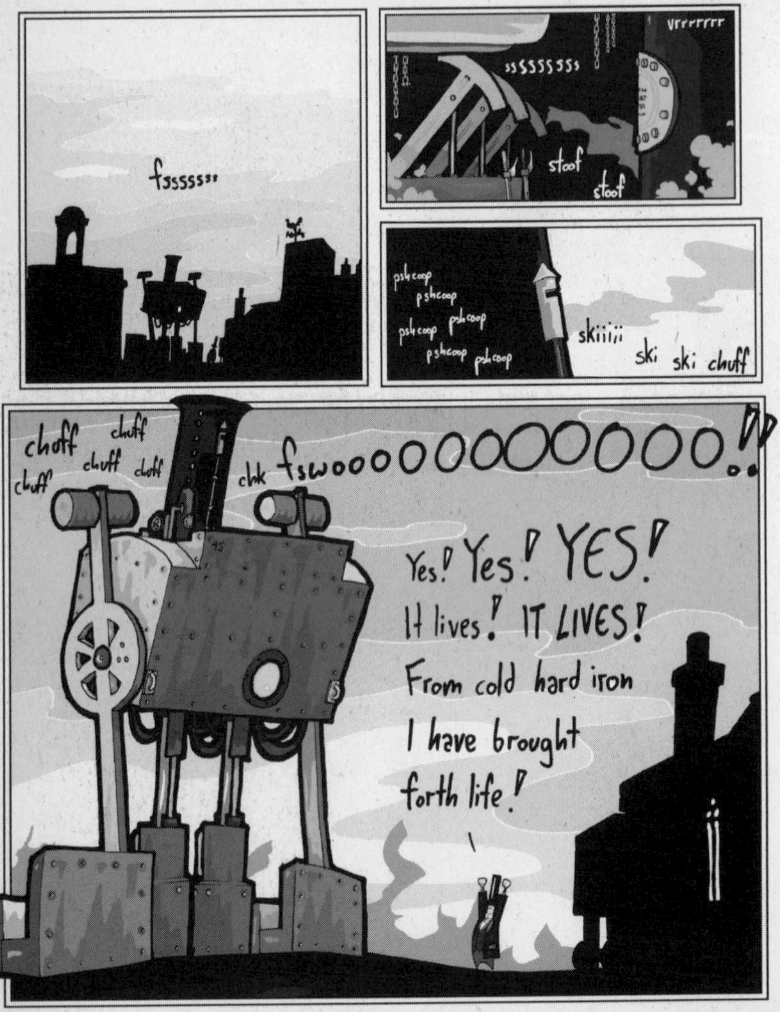
fssssss
sssssssss
vrrrrrrr
stoof
stoof
pshcoop
pshcoop
pshcoop
pshcoop
pshcoop
pshcoop
skiiiii
ski
ski
chuff
chuff
chuff
chuff
chuff
chuff
chk
fswoooOOOOOOOOO!!
Yes! Yes! YES!
It lives! IT LIVES!
From cold hard iron
I have brought
forth life!

Plate 1 of 2

Patent No. 233675 *G. D. Banyard* *26th February 2007*

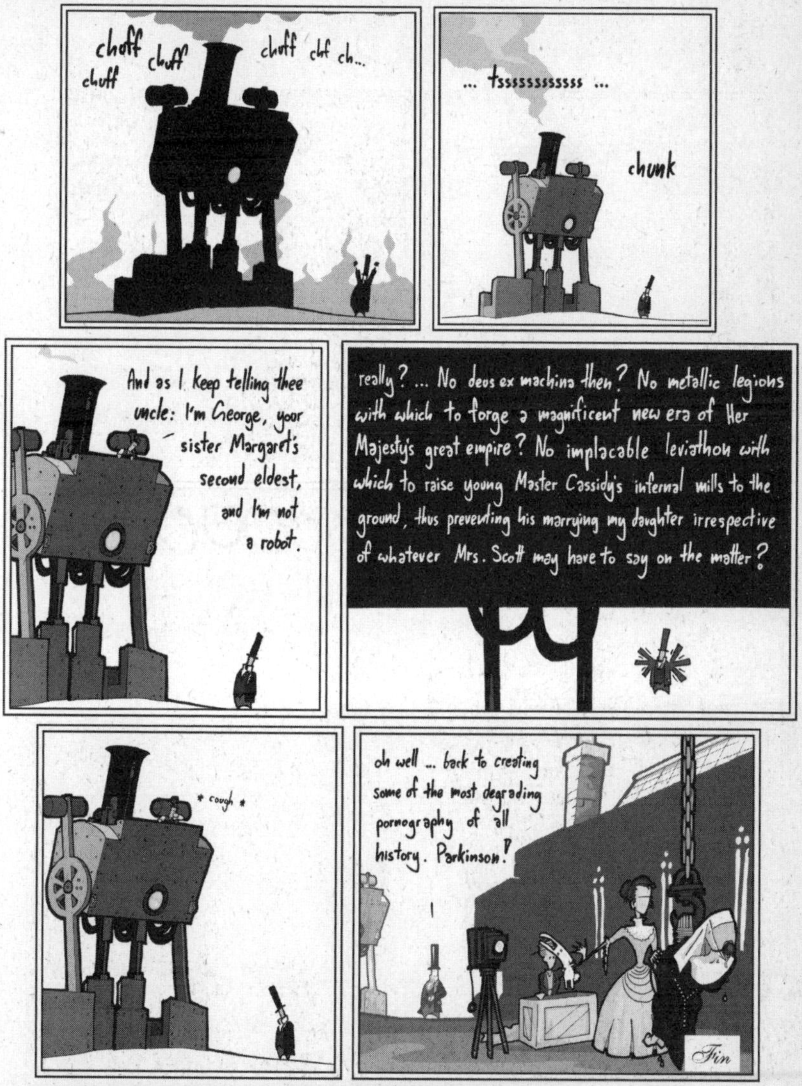
chuff
chuff
chuff
chuff chf ch...
... tssssssssssss ...
chunk
And as I keep telling thee uncle: I'm George, your sister Margaret's second eldest, and I'm not a robot.
really? ... No deus ex machina then? No metallic legions with which to forge a magnificent new era of Her Majesty's great empire? No implacable leviathon with which to raise young Master Cassidy's infernal mills to the ground, thus preventing his marrying my daughter irrespective of whatever Mrs. Scott may have to say on the matter?
* cough *
oh well ... back to creating some of the most degrading pornography of all history. Parkinson!
!
Fin

Inventor: *Plate 2 of 2* *Witness:*

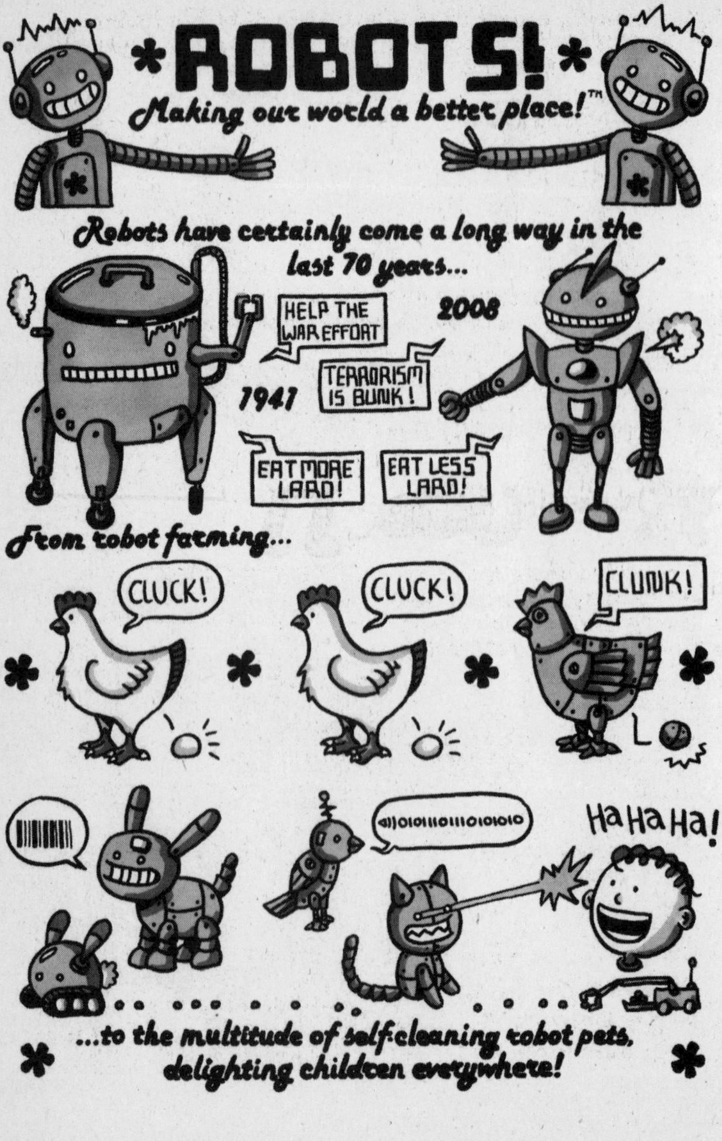
ROBOTS!
Making our world a better place!™
Robots have certainly come a long way in the last 70 years...
HELP THE WAR EFFORT
TERRORISM IS BUNK!
1941
2008
EAT MORE LARD!
EAT LESS LARD!
From robot farming...
CLUCK!
CLUCK!
CLUNK!
01011101110101010
HaHaHa!
...to the multitude of self-cleaning robot pets, delighting children everywhere!

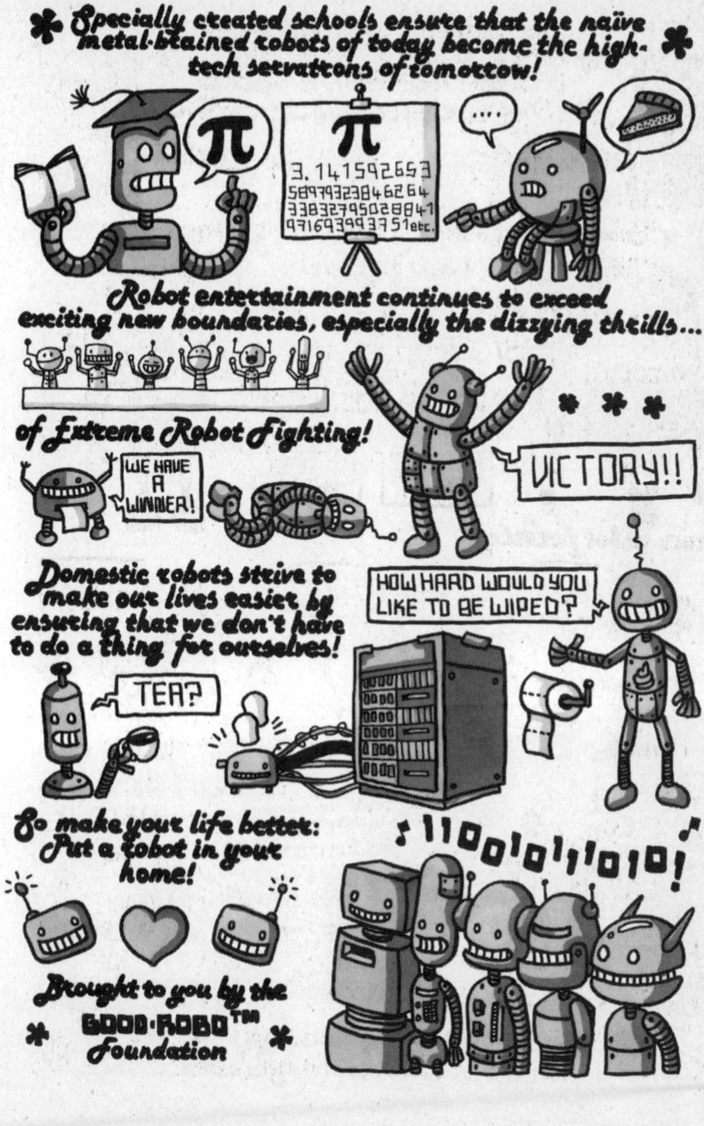
Specially created schools ensure that the naïve metal-brained robots of today become the high-tech servants of tomorrow!
π
π
3.141592653
58979323846264
33832795028841
9716939937 51etc.
....
Robot entertainment continues to exceed exciting new boundaries, especially the dizzying thrills...
of Extreme Robot Fighting!
WE HAVE A WINNER!
VICTORY!!
Domestic robots strive to make our lives easier by ensuring that we don't have to do a thing for ourselves!
HOW HARD WOULD YOU LIKE TO BE WIPED?
TEA?
So make your life better: Put a robot in your home!
110010111010!
Brought to you by the
GOOD·ROBO™
Foundation

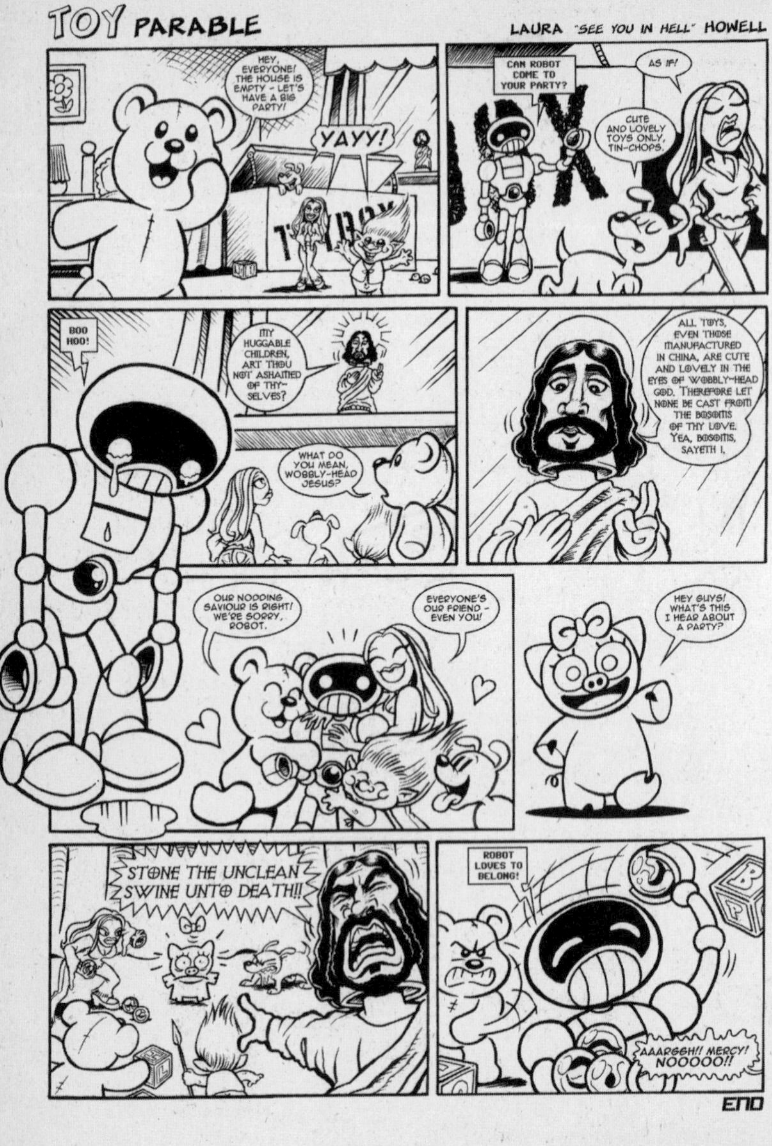
TOY PARABLE
LAURA "SEE YOU IN HELL" HOWELL
HEY, EVERYONE! THE HOUSE IS EMPTY - LET'S HAVE A BIG PARTY!
YAYY!
CAN ROBOT COME TO YOUR PARTY?
AS IF!
CUTE AND LOVELY TOYS ONLY, TIN-CHOPS.
BOO HOO!
MY HUGGABLE CHILDREN, ART THOU NOT ASHAMED OF THY-SELVES?
WHAT DO YOU MEAN, WOBBLY-HEAD JESUS?
ALL TOYS, EVEN THOSE MANUFACTURED IN CHINA, ARE CUTE AND LOVELY IN THE EYES OF WOBBLY-HEAD GOD. THEREFORE LET NONE BE CAST FROM THE BOSOMS OF THY LOVE. YEA, BOSOMS, SAYETH I.
OUR NODDING SAVIOUR IS RIGHT! WE'RE SORRY, ROBOT.
EVERYONE'S OUR FRIEND - EVEN YOU!
HEY GUYS! WHAT'S THIS I HEAR ABOUT A PARTY?
STONE THE UNCLEAN SWINE UNTO DEATH!!
ROBOT LOVES TO BELONG!
AAARGGH!! MERCY! NOOOOO!!
END

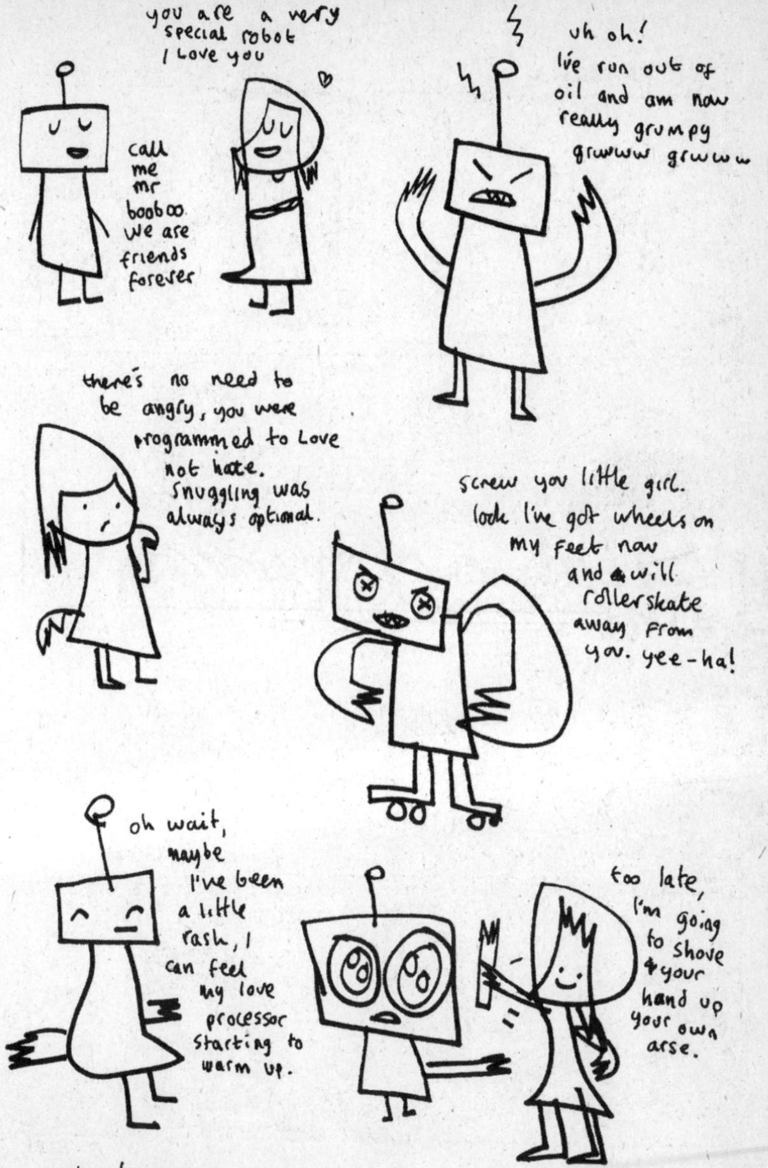
you are a very special robot I love you
call me mr booboo. we are friends forever
uh oh! I've run out of oil and am now really grumpy grwww grwww
there's no need to be angry, you were programmed to love not hate. Snuggling was always optional.
screw you little girl. look I've got wheels on my feet now and will rollerskate away from you. yee-ha!
oh wait, maybe I've been a little rash, I can feel my love processor starting to warm up.
too late, I'm going to shove your hand up your own arse.
Jon burgerman - 2007.

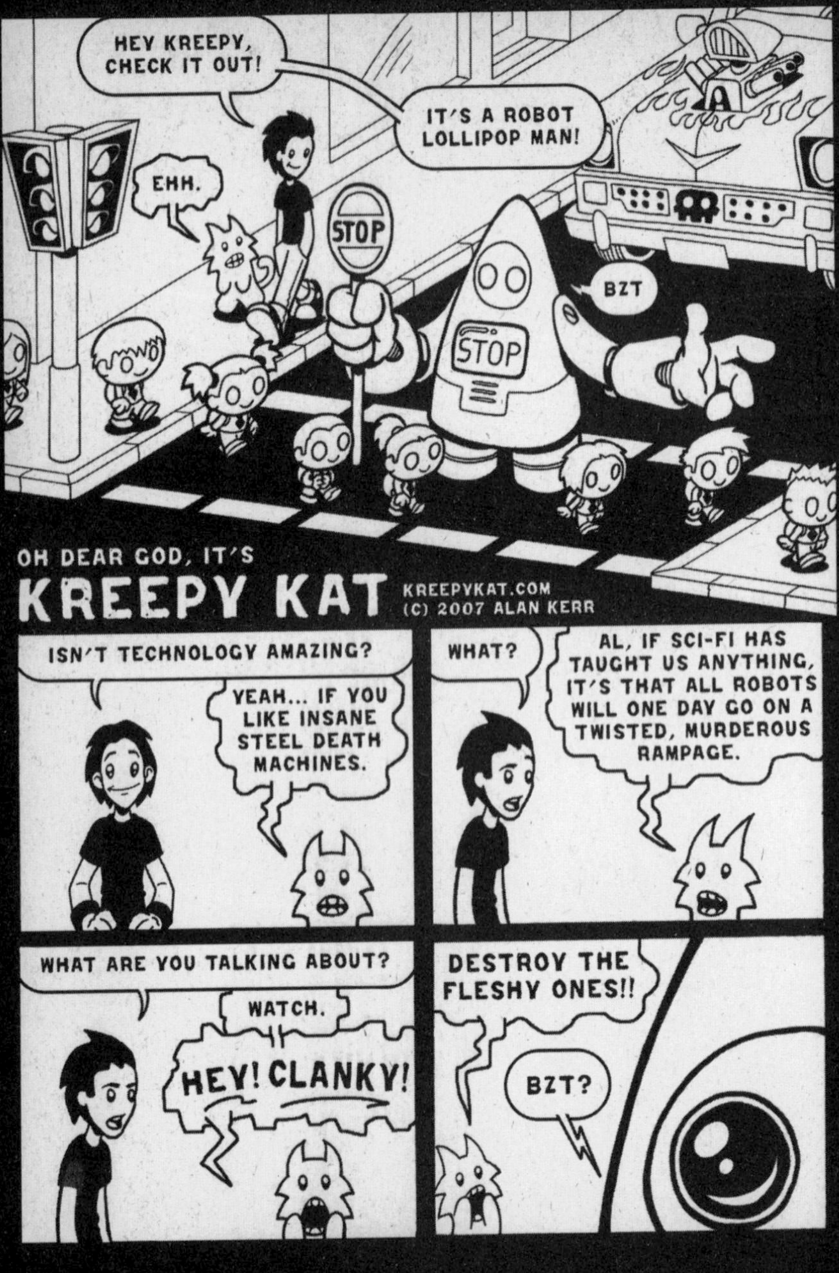
HEY KREEPY, CHECK IT OUT!
IT'S A ROBOT LOLLIPOP MAN!
EHH.
STOP
STOP
BZT
OH DEAR GOD, IT'S
KREEPY KAT
KREEPYKAT.COM
(C) 2007 ALAN KERR
ISN'T TECHNOLOGY AMAZING?
YEAH... IF YOU LIKE INSANE STEEL DEATH MACHINES.
WHAT?
AL, IF SCI-FI HAS TAUGHT US ANYTHING, IT'S THAT ALL ROBOTS WILL ONE DAY GO ON A TWISTED, MURDEROUS RAMPAGE.
WHAT ARE YOU TALKING ABOUT?
WATCH.
HEY! CLANKY!
DESTROY THE FLESHY ONES!!
BZT?

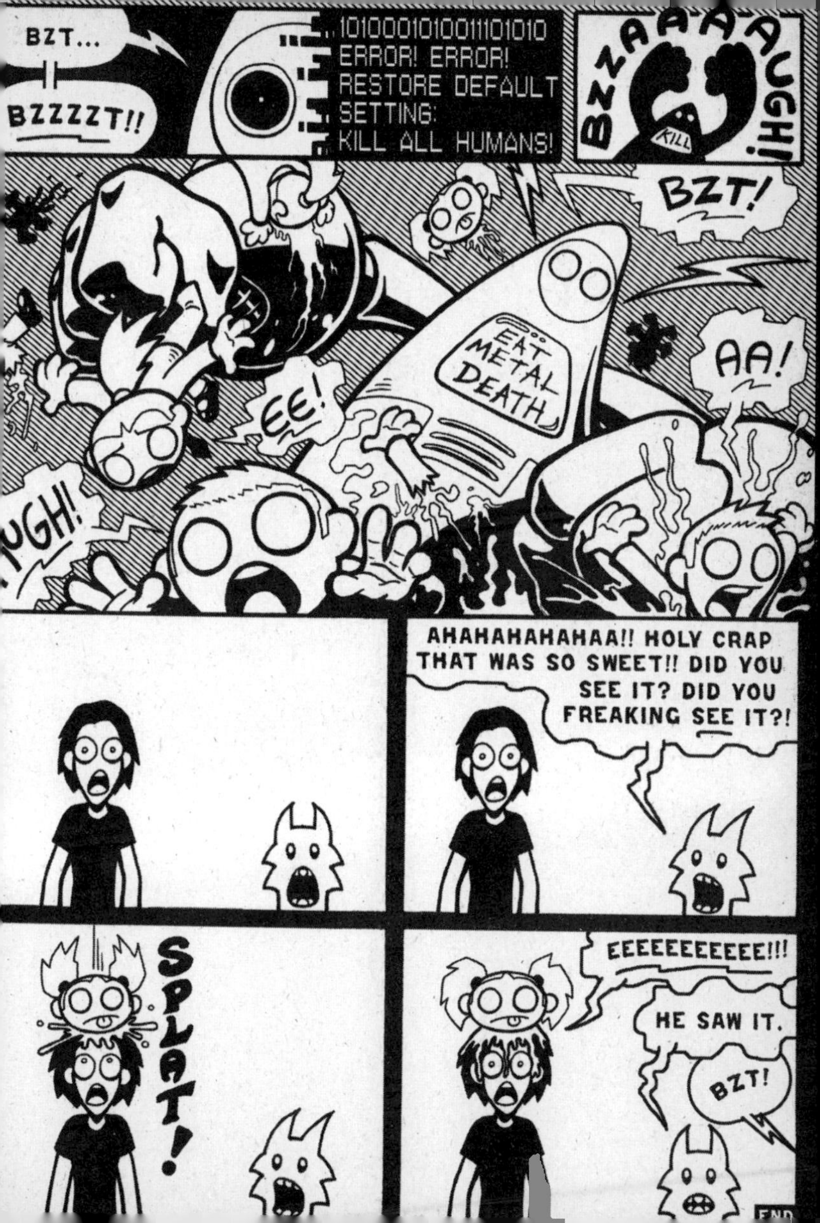
BZT...
BZZZZT!!
1010001010011101010
ERROR! ERROR!
RESTORE DEFAULT
SETTING:
KILL ALL HUMANS!
BZZAAAAAUGH!
KILL
BZT!
EAT METAL DEATH
AA!
EE!
UGH!
AHAHAHAHAHAA!! HOLY CRAP THAT WAS SO SWEET!! DID YOU SEE IT? DID YOU FREAKING SEE IT?!
SPLAT!
EEEEEEEEEEE!!!
HE SAW IT.
BZT!
END

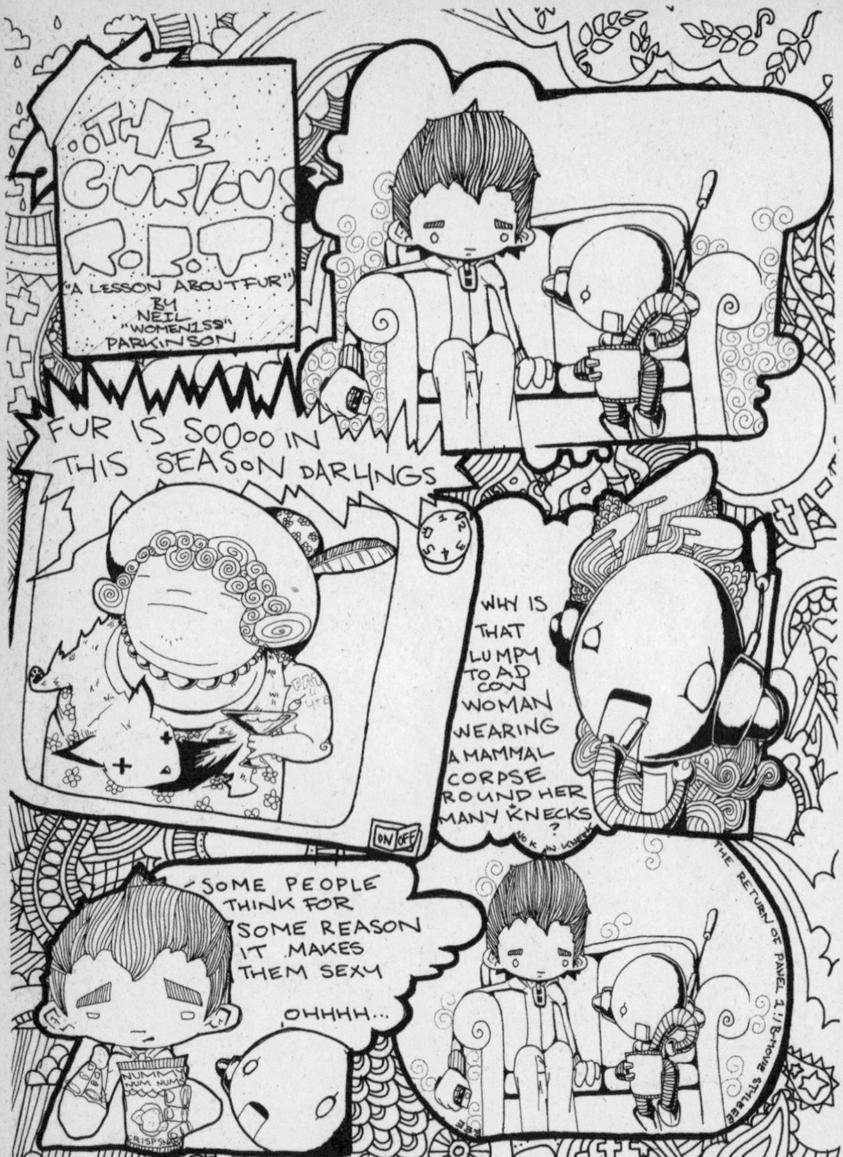
THE CURIOUS R.O.B.O.T
"A LESSON ABOUT FUR"
BY NEIL "WOMEN1SS" PARKINSON
FUR IS SOOoo IN THIS SEASON DARLYNGS
WHY IS THAT LUMPY TO AD CON WOMAN WEARING A MAMMAL CORPSE ROUND HER MANY KNECKS?
NO K IN KNECK
ON OFF
SOME PEOPLE THINK FOR SOME REASON IT MAKES THEM SEXY
OHHHH...
NUMMY NUM NUMS CRISPS
THE RETURN OF PANEL 1!! B-MOVIE STYLEEE

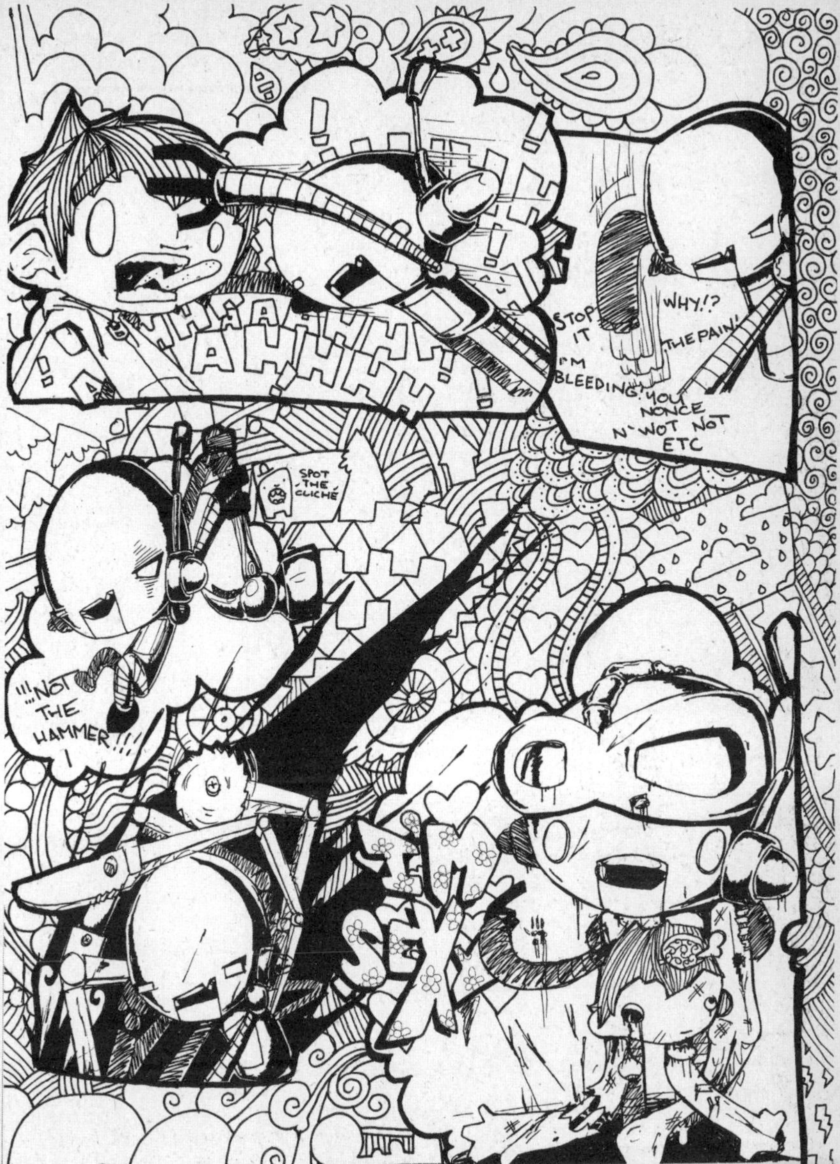
AHHHH! AHHHHHH!
STOP IT
I'M BLEEDING!
WHY!?
THE PAIN!
YOU NONCE N' WOT NOT ETC
SPOT THE CLICHÉ
!!!...NOT THE HAMMER!!!!
SEX
FACTS :- IF YOU WEAR FUR, WORK IN THE FUR TRADE, ENDORSE OR AGREE WITH THE TRADE OF DEAD CREATURES FOR PLEASURE YOU ARE EVIL & I HATE YOU.

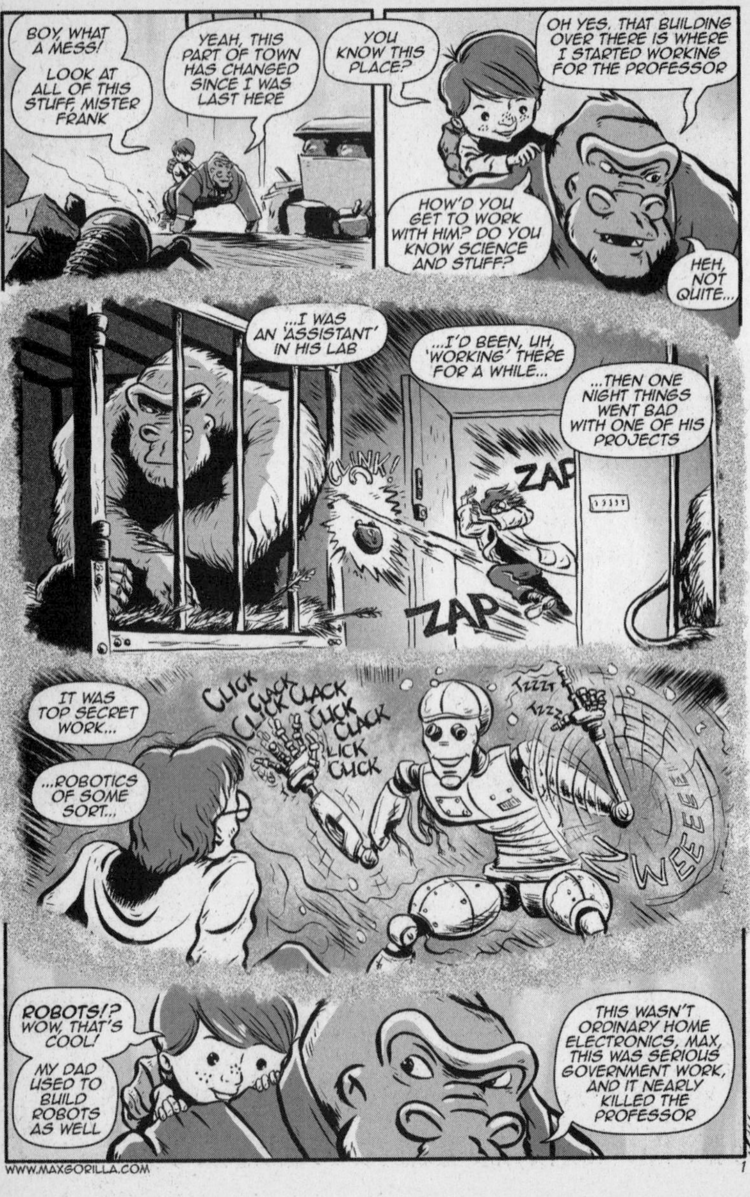
BOY, WHAT A MESS! LOOK AT ALL OF THIS STUFF, MISTER FRANK
YEAH, THIS PART OF TOWN HAS CHANGED SINCE I WAS LAST HERE
YOU KNOW THIS PLACE?
OH YES. THAT BUILDING OVER THERE IS WHERE I STARTED WORKING FOR THE PROFESSOR
HOW'D YOU GET TO WORK WITH HIM? DO YOU KNOW SCIENCE AND STUFF?
HEH, NOT QUITE...
...I WAS AN 'ASSISTANT' IN HIS LAB
...I'D BEEN, UH, 'WORKING' THERE FOR A WHILE...
...THEN ONE NIGHT THINGS WENT BAD WITH ONE OF HIS PROJECTS
CLUNK!
ZAP
ZAP
IT WAS TOP SECRET WORK...
...ROBOTICS OF SOME SORT...
CLICK CLACK CLICK CLACK CLICK CLACK LICK CLICK
TZZZT TZZZ
WEEEEE
ROBOTS!? WOW, THAT'S COOL!
MY DAD USED TO BUILD ROBOTS AS WELL
THIS WASN'T ORDINARY HOME ELECTRONICS, MAX, THIS WAS SERIOUS GOVERNMENT WORK, AND IT NEARLY KILLED THE PROFESSOR
12.2007
WWW.MAXGORILLA.COM
1

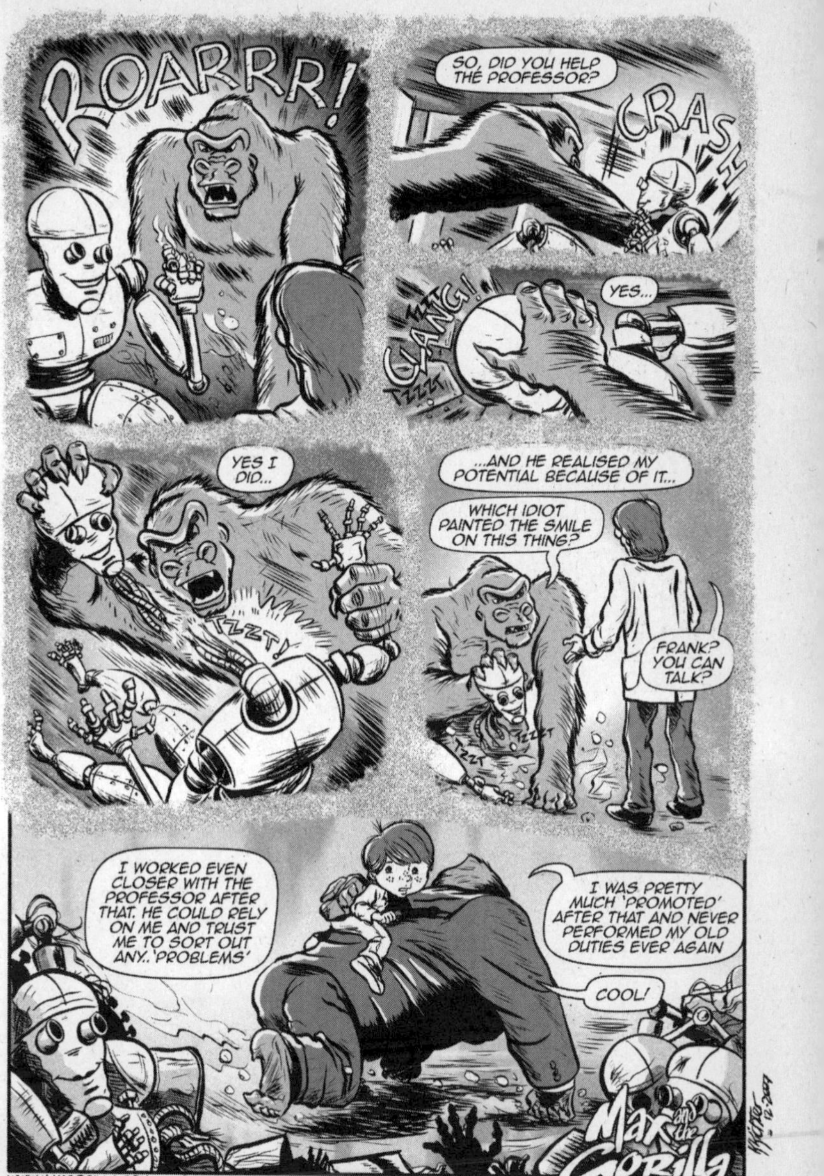
ROARRR!
SO, DID YOU HELP THE PROFESSOR?
CRASH
YES...
GANG!
TZZZT
YES I DID...
TZZZT!
...AND HE REALISED MY POTENTIAL BECAUSE OF IT...
WHICH IDIOT PAINTED THE SMILE ON THIS THING?
FRANK? YOU CAN TALK?
TZZZT
TZZZT
I WORKED EVEN CLOSER WITH THE PROFESSOR AFTER THAT. HE COULD RELY ON ME AND TRUST ME TO SORT OUT ANY.. 'PROBLEMS'
I WAS PRETTY MUCH 'PROMOTED' AFTER THAT AND NEVER PERFORMED MY OLD DUTIES EVER AGAIN
COOL!
WWW.MAXGORILLA.COM
Max and the Gorilla Goon Squad
2

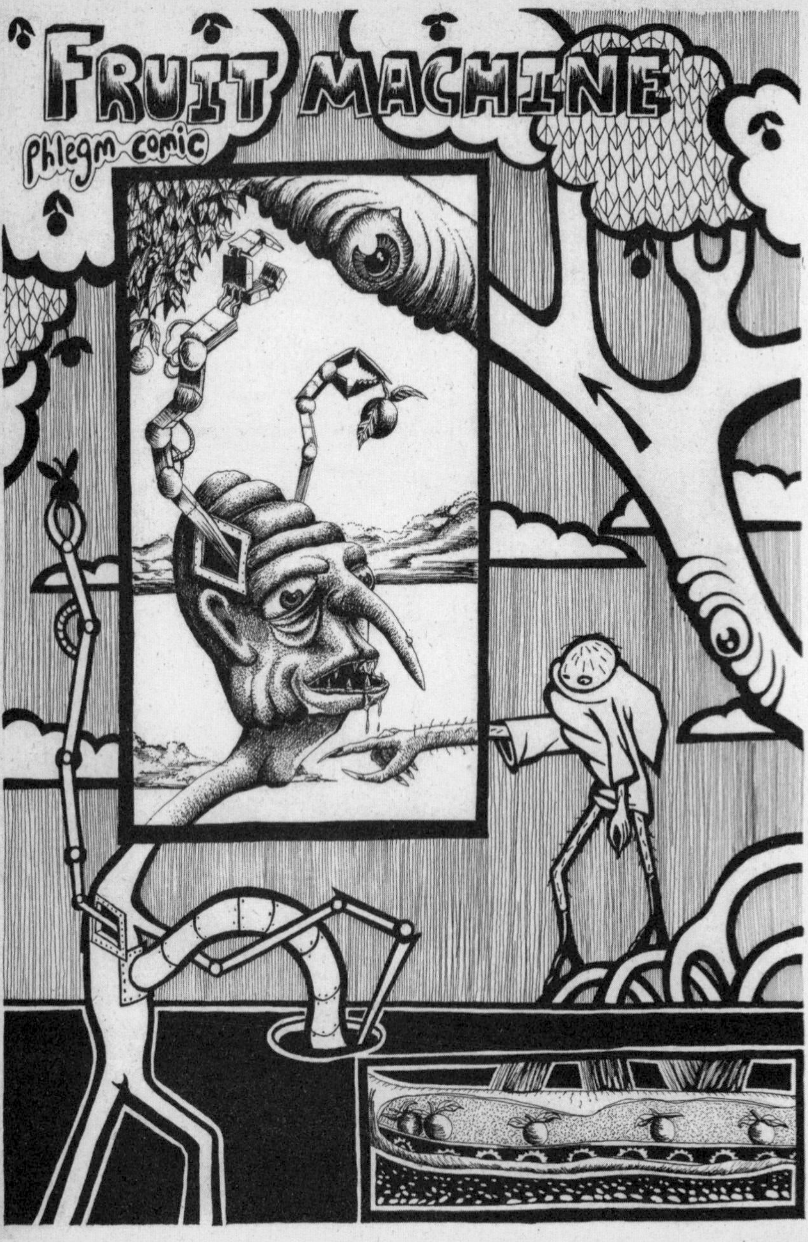
FRUIT MACHINE
phlegm comic

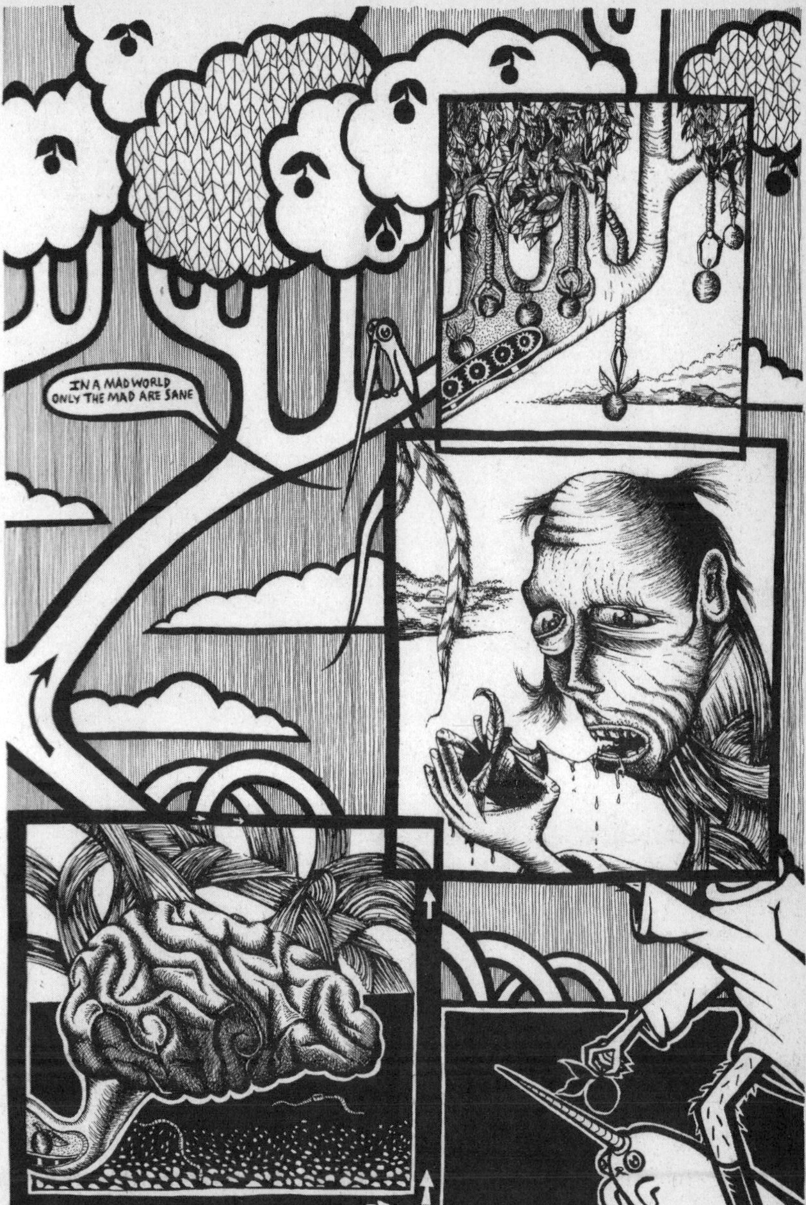
IN A MAD WORLD
ONLY THE MAD ARE SANE

BY OKTUS / MYSPACE.COM/OKTUS, DELKOGRAPHIK.COM

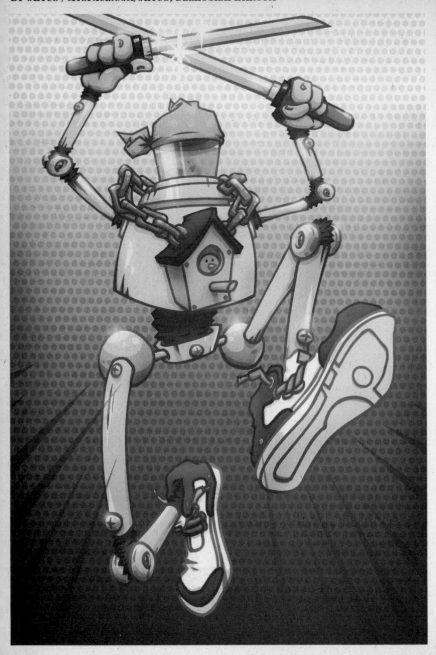

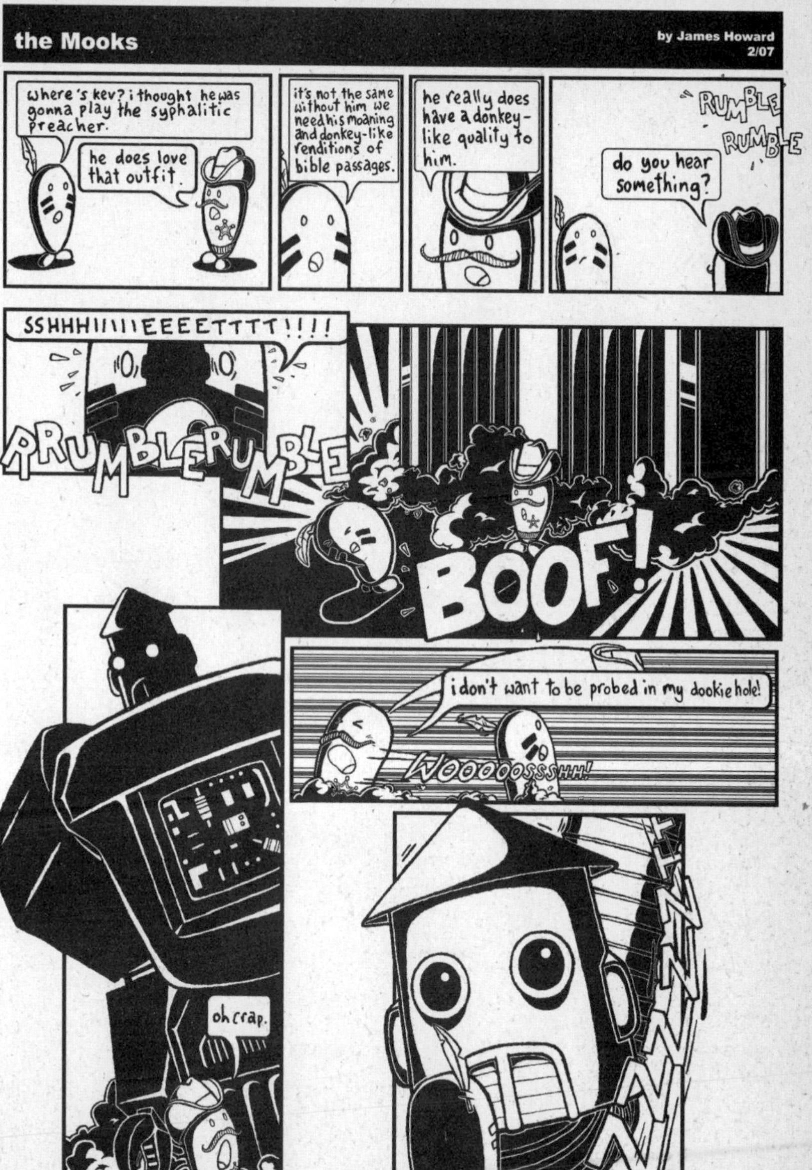
the Mooks
by James Howard
2/07
where's kev? i thought he was gonna play the syphalitic preacher.
he does love that outfit.
it's not the same without him we need his moaning and donkey-like renditions of bible passages.
he really does have a donkey-like quality to him.
RUMBLE
RUMBLE
do you hear something?
SSHHHIIIIIIEEEETTTTT!!!!
RRUMBLERUMBLE
BOOF!
i don't want to be probed in my dookie hole!
WOOOOOOSSSHHH!
oh crap.

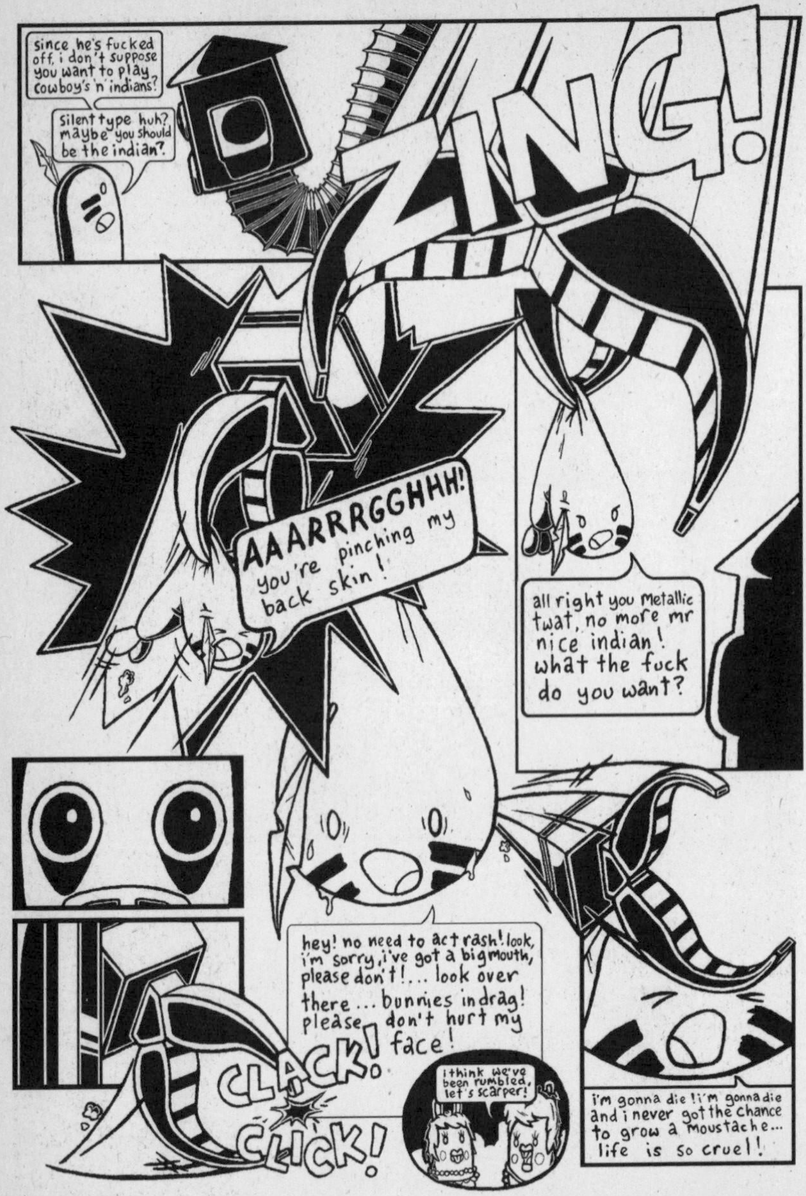
since he's fucked off, i don't suppose you want to play cowboy's 'n' indians?
silent type huh? maybe you should be the indian?
ZING!
AAARRRGGHHH! you're pinching my back skin!
all right you metallic twat, no more mr nice indian! what the fuck do you want?
hey! no need to act rash! look, i'm sorry, i've got a big mouth, please don't!... look over there... bunnies in drag! please, don't hurt my face!
CLACK! CLICK!
i think we've been rumbled, let's scarper!
i'm gonna die! i'm gonna die and i never got the chance to grow a moustache... life is so cruel!

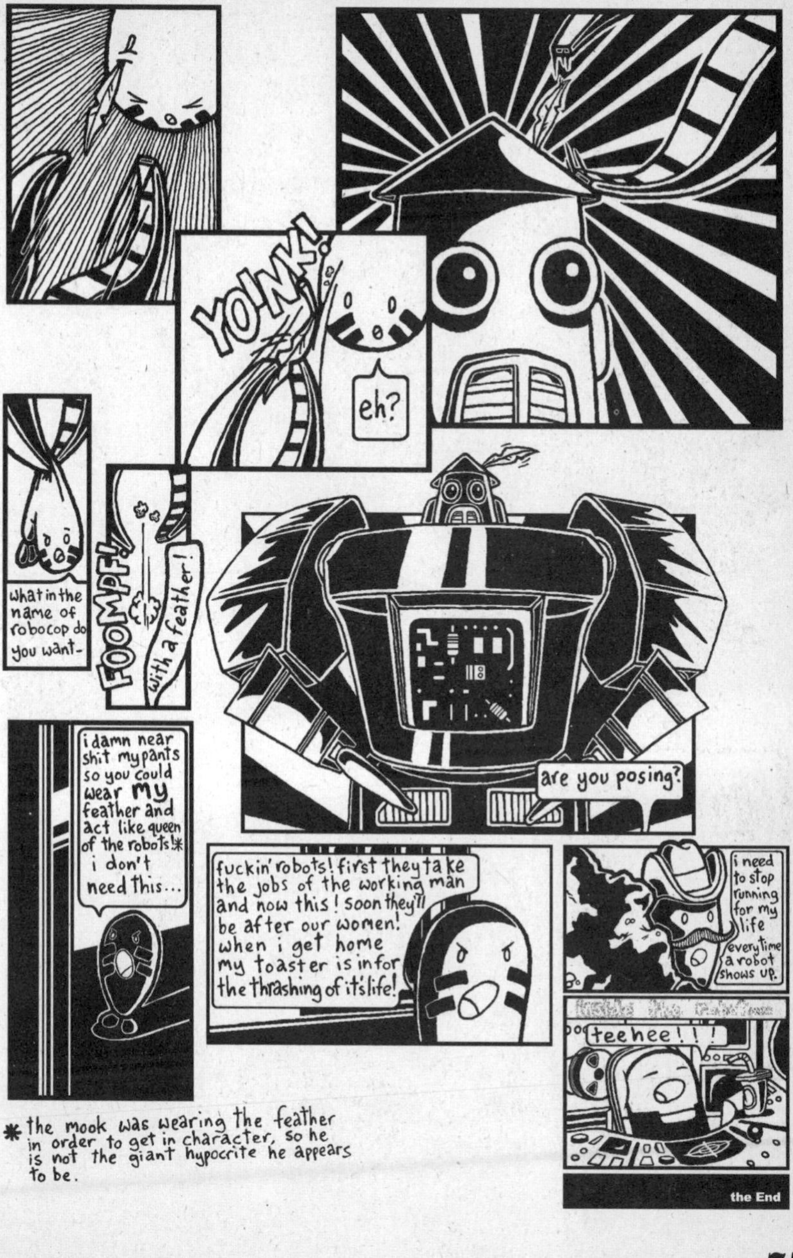
YOINK!
eh?
what in the name of robocop do you want-
FOOMPF!
with a feather!
are you posing?
i damn near shit my pants so you could wear my feather and act like queen of the robots!*
i don't need this...
fuckin' robots! first they take the jobs of the working man and now this! soon they'll be after our women! when i get home my toaster is in for the thrashing of it's life!
i need to stop running for my life every time a robot shows up.
teehee!!!
the End
* the mook was wearing the feather in order to get in character, so he is not the giant hypocrite he appears to be.

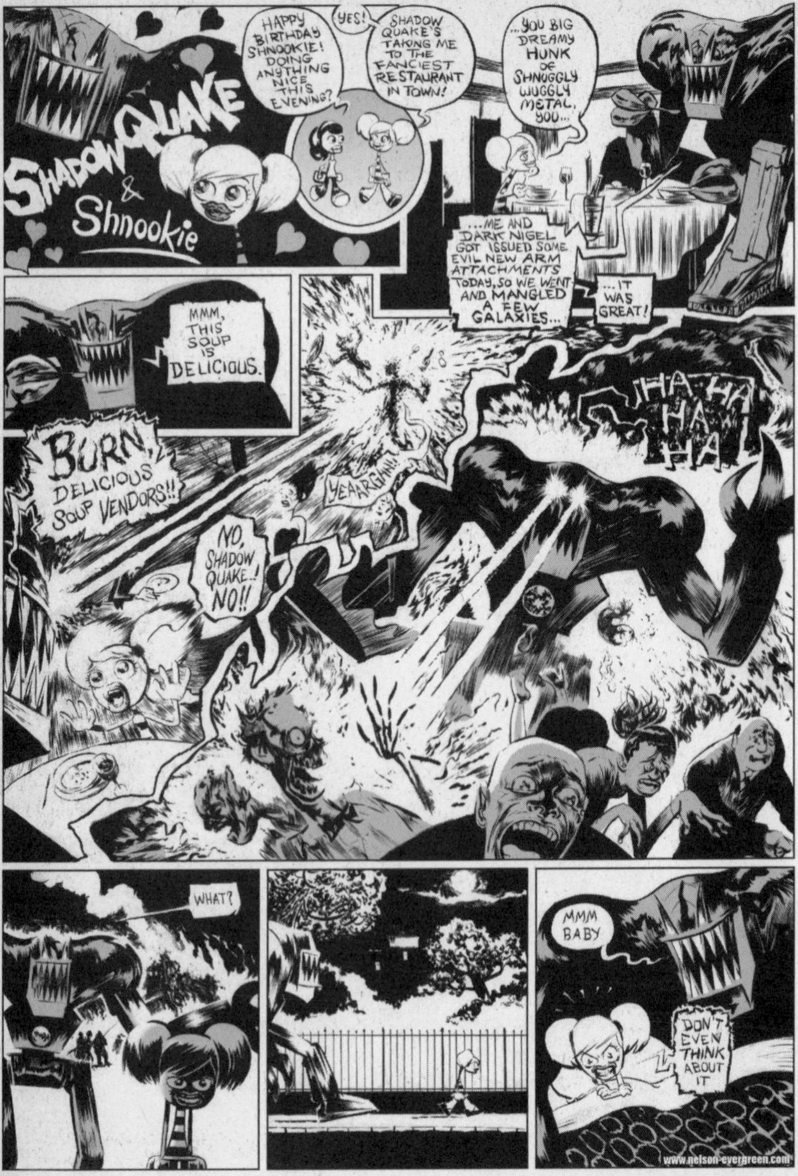
SHADOWQUAKE & Shnookie
HAPPY BIRTHDAY SHNOOKIE! DOING ANYTHING NICE THIS EVENING?
YES!
SHADOW QUAKE'S TAKING ME TO THE FANCIEST RESTAURANT IN TOWN!
...YOU BIG DREAMY HUNK OF SHNUGGLY WUGGLY METAL, YOU...
...ME AND DARK NIGEL GOT ISSUED SOME EVIL NEW ARM ATTACHMENTS TODAY, SO WE WENT AND MANGLED A FEW GALAXIES...
...IT WAS GREAT!
MMM, THIS SOUP IS DELICIOUS.
BURN, DELICIOUS SOUP VENDORS!!
HA HA HA HA
YEAARGH!!
NO, SHADOW QUAKE..! NO!!
WHAT?
MMM BABY
DON'T EVEN THINK ABOUT IT
www.nelson-evergreen.com

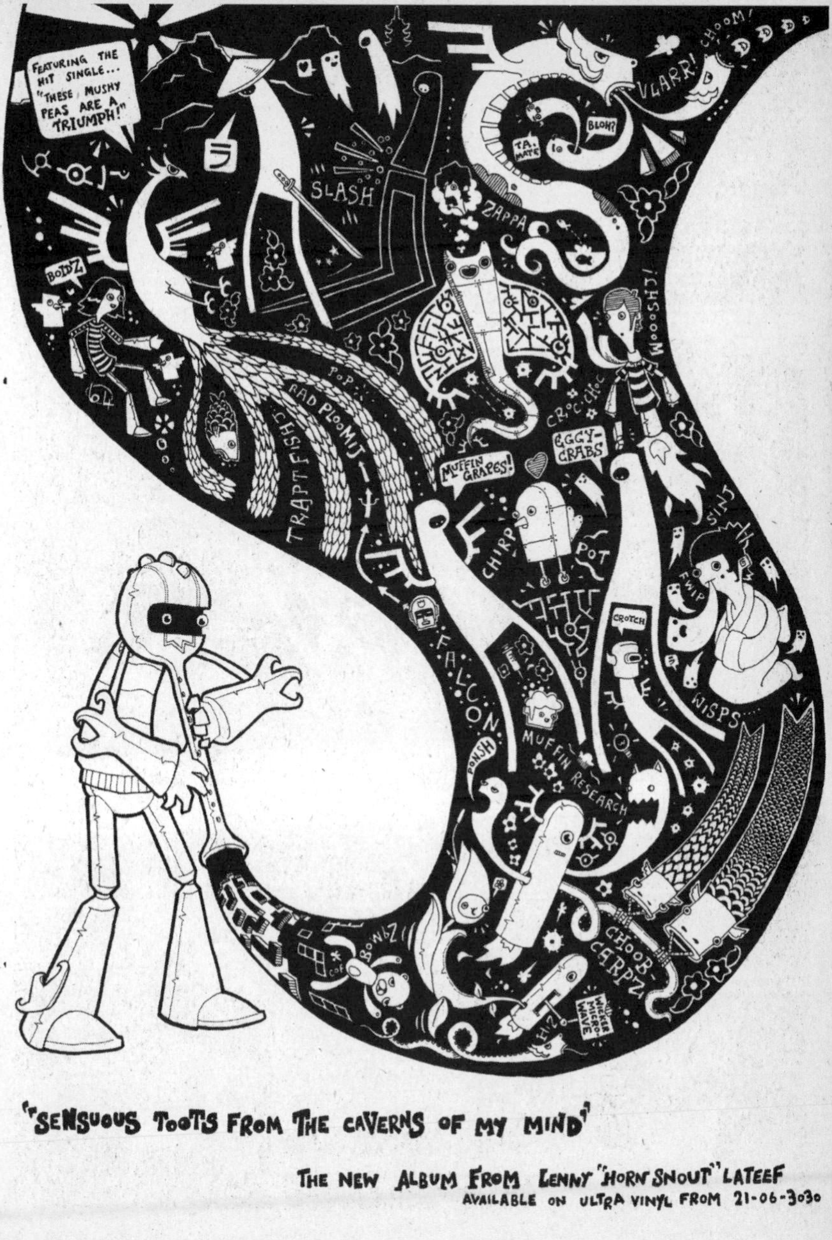
FEATURING THE HIT SINGLE... "THESE, MUSHY PEAS ARE A TRIUMPH!"
SLASH
VLARR!
CHOOM!
BLOH?
TA. MATE
ZAPPA
BOIDZ
WOOOSHJ!
POP
RAD
PLOOMIJ
TRAPTFISH
CROC-CHOC
EGGY-CRABS
MUFFIN GRAPES!
CHIRP
POT
SINJ
FWIP
CROTCH
FALCON
WISPS
MUFFIN RESEARCH
PONSH
BOWBZ
CHOOB-CARPZ
WICKER MICRO-WAVE
"SENSUOUS TOOTS FROM THE CAVERNS OF MY MIND"
THE NEW ALBUM FROM LENNY "HORN SNOUT" LATEEF
AVAILABLE ON ULTRA VINYL FROM 21-06-3030

I've been lonely lately.

So very lonely.

Things haven't been the same since the crewmen died.

Scurvy.

It ate their bodies.

Towards the end they'd all try to steal from my citrus pile.

Stay away from my fruits!!

Walter, please, my gums... They're spongy. So very spongy.

THE ISLAND OF MISFIT ROBOTS

PATT KELLEY ©2007

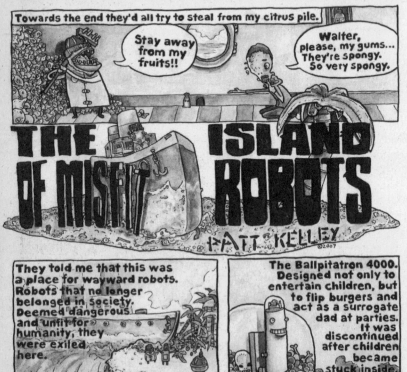

They told me that this was a place for wayward robots. Robots that no longer belonged in society. Deemed dangerous and unfit for humanity, they were exiled here.

I've met so many new friends.

The Ballpitatron 4000. Designed not only to entertain children, but to flip burgers and act as a surrogate dad at parties. It was discontinued after children became stuck inside.

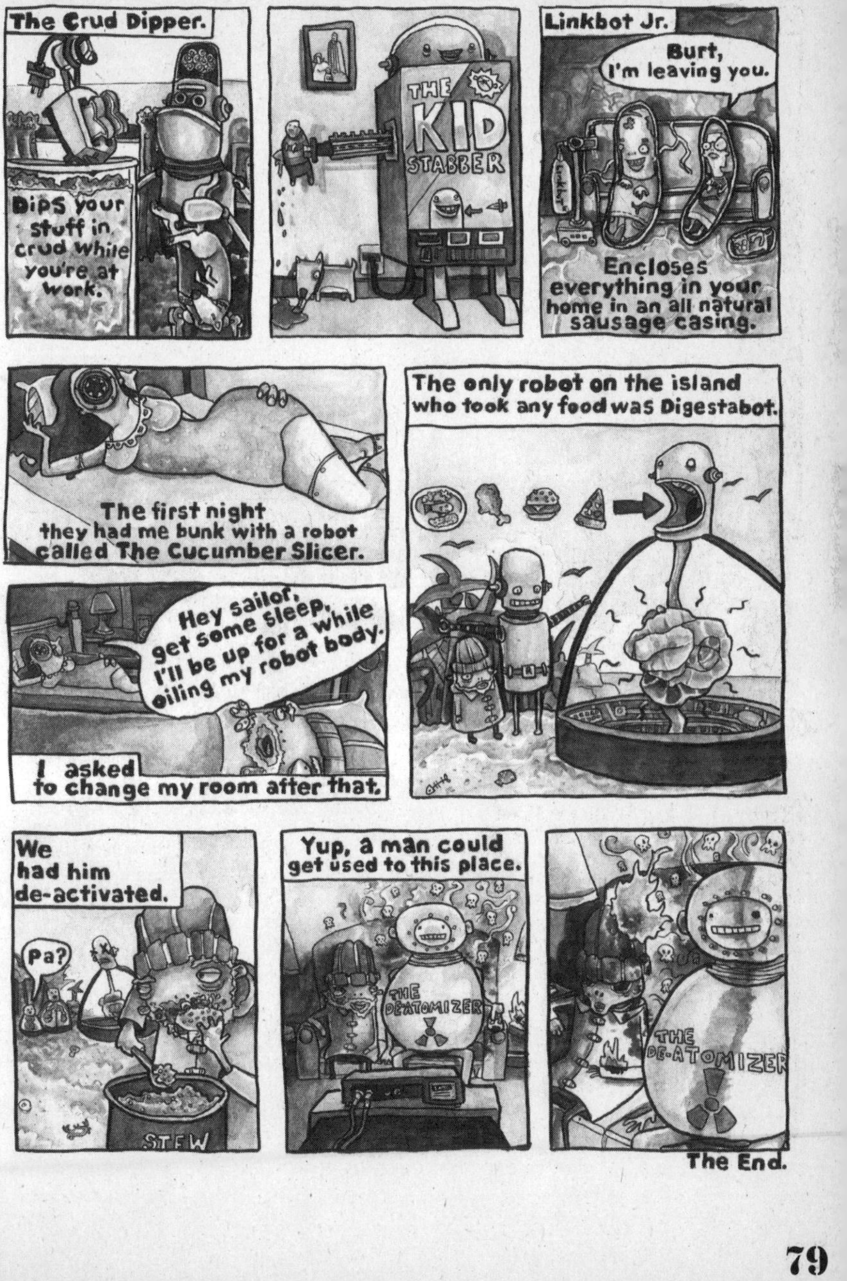
The Crud Dipper.
Dips your stuff in crud while you're at work.
THE KID STABBER
Linkbot Jr.
Burt, I'm leaving you.
Encloses everything in your home in an all natural sausage casing.
The first night they had me bunk with a robot called The Cucumber Slicer.
Hey sailor, get some sleep, I'll be up for a while oiling my robot body.
I asked to change my room after that.
The only robot on the island who took any food was Digestabot.
We had him de-activated.
Pa?
STEW
Yup, a man could get used to this place.
THE DEATOMIZER
THE DE-ATOMIZER
The End.

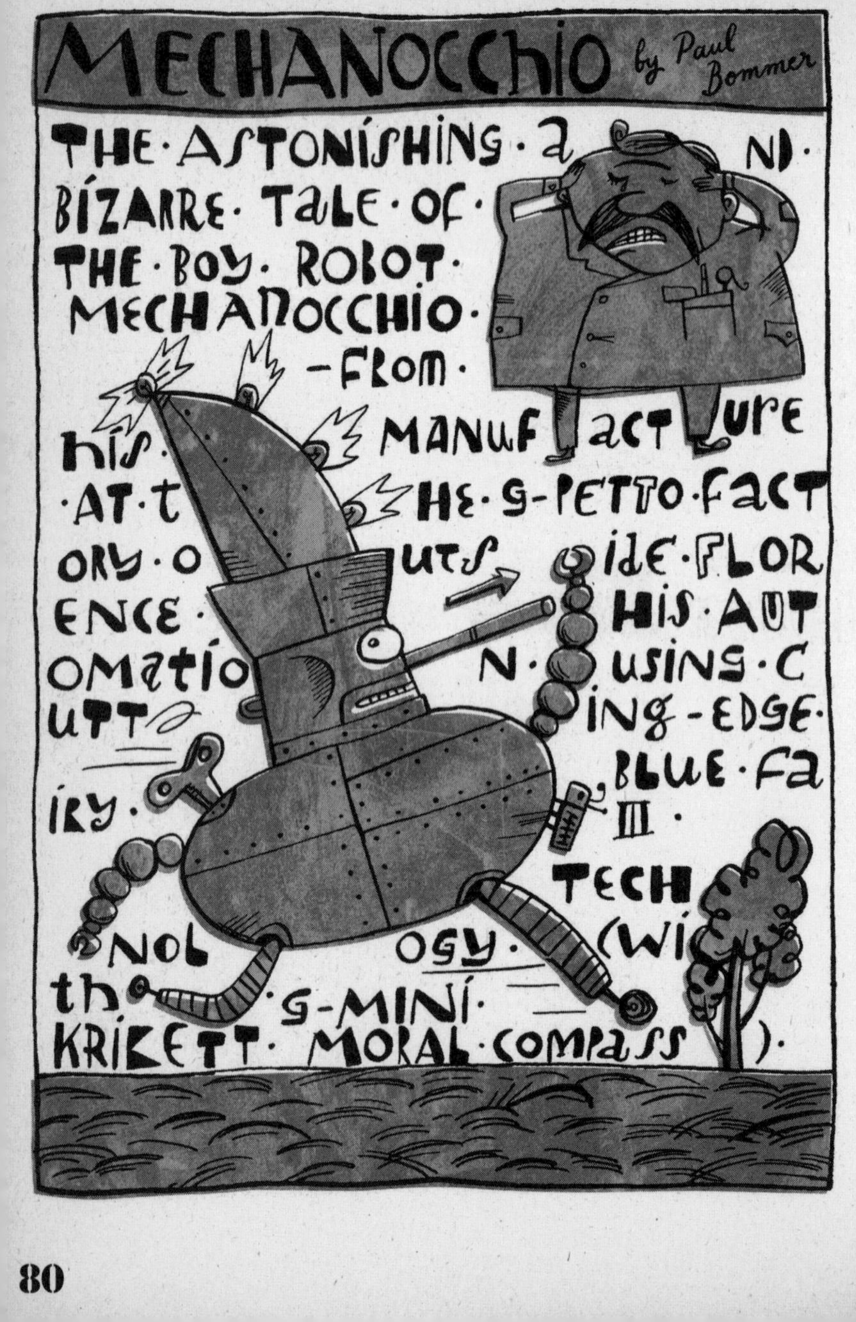

MECHANOCCHIO
by Paul Bommer
THE·ASTONISHING·A ND·
BIZARRE·TALE·OF·
THE·BOY·ROBOT·
MECHANOCCHIO·
-FROM·
HIS· MANUF ACT URE
·AT·T HE·G-PETTO·FACT
ORY·O UTS IDE·FLOR
ENCE· HIS·AUT
OMATIO N· USING·C
UTT ING-EDGE·
BLUE·FA
IRY· III·
TECH
NOL OGY· (WI
TH ·G-MINI·
KRIKETT· MORAL·COMPASS).

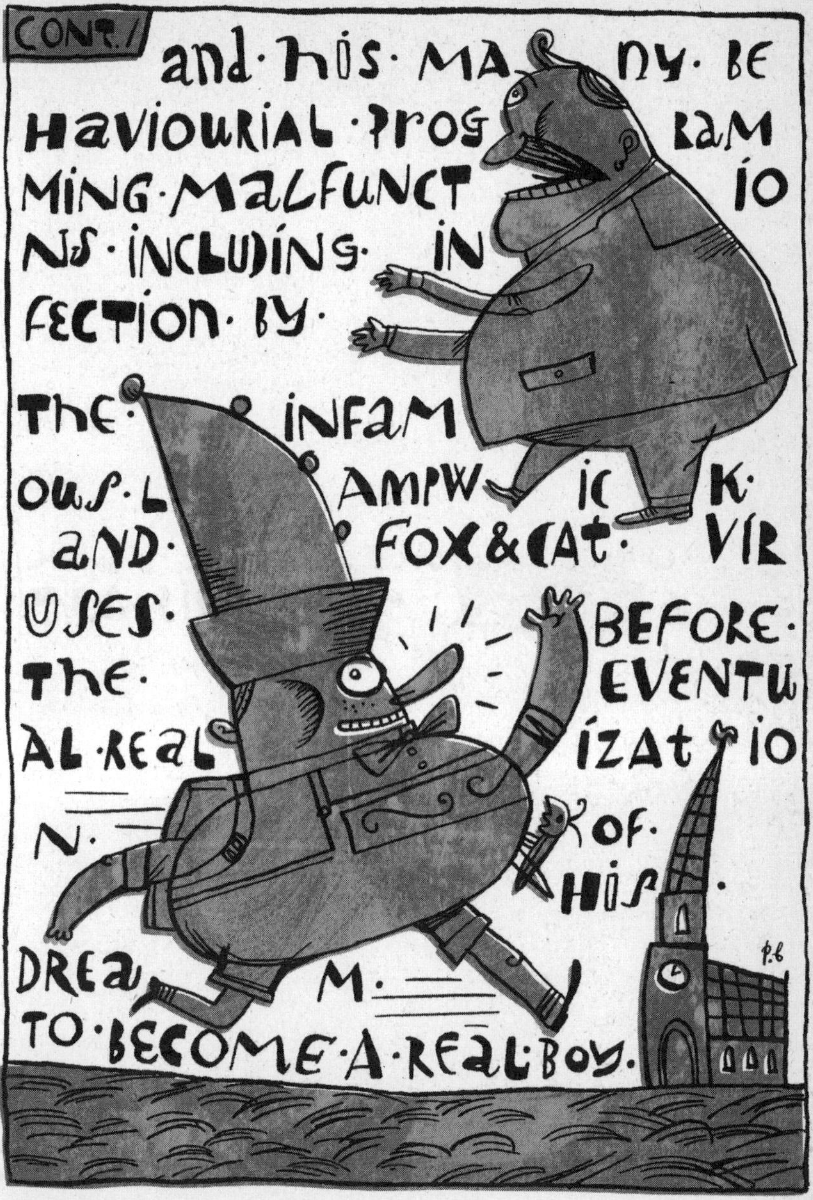
CONT./
and·his·MANY·BE
HAVIOURIAL·PROGRAM
MING·MALFUNCTIO
NS·INCLUDING·IN
FECTION·BY·
THE·INFAM
OUS·LAMPWICK·
AND·FOX&CAT·VIR
USES·BEFORE·
THE·EVENTU
AL·REALIZATIO
N·OF·
HIS·
DREAM·
TO·BECOME·A·REAL·BOY.

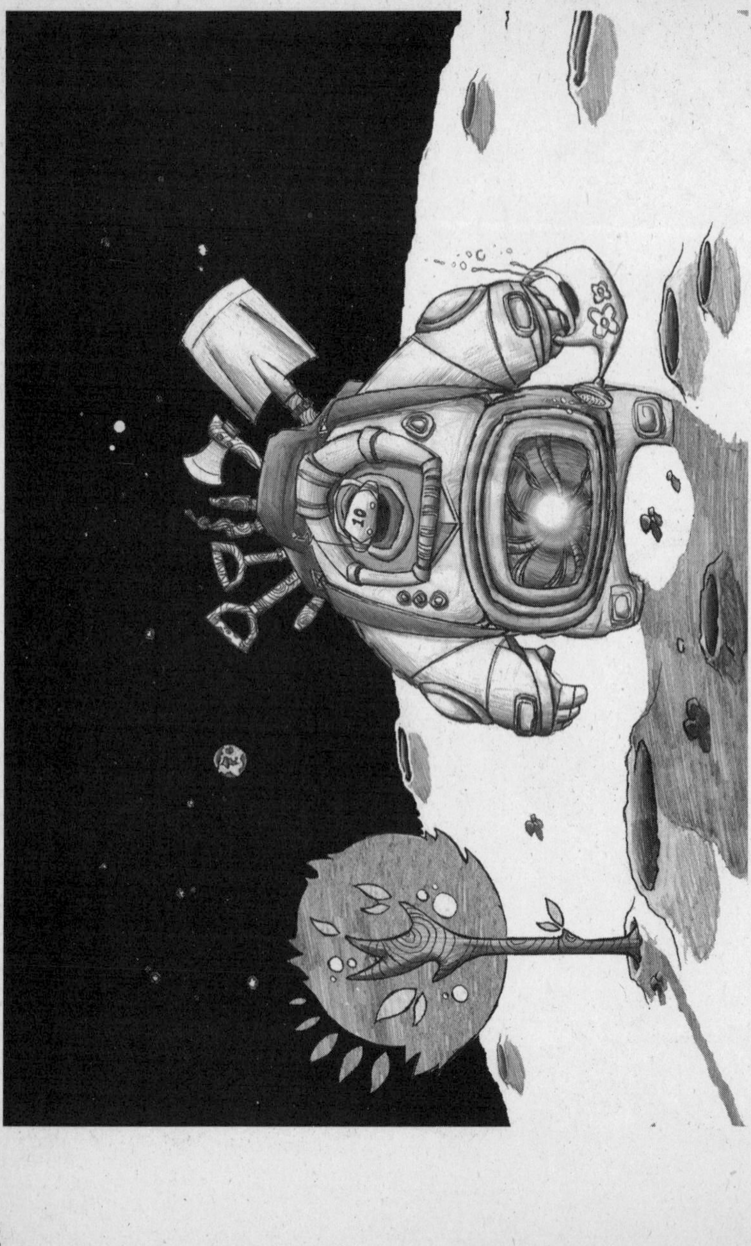

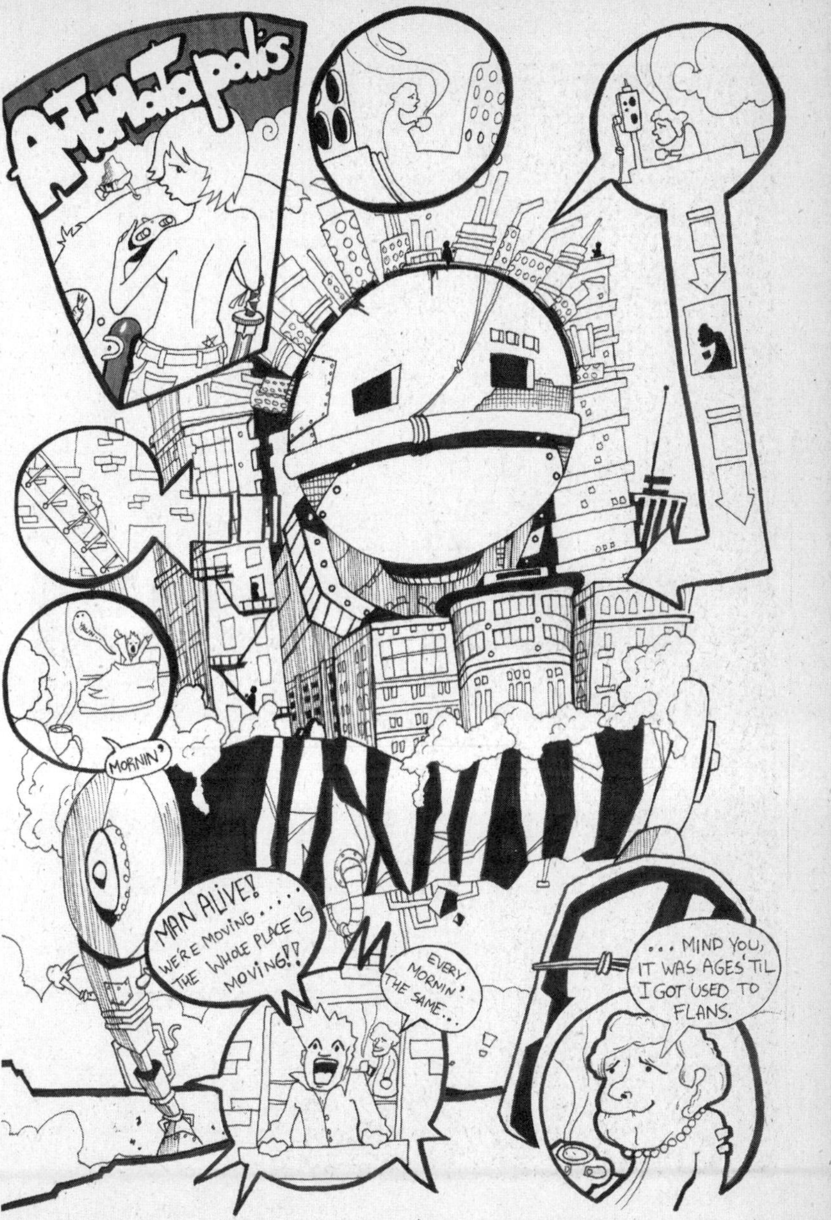
AuToMaTapolis
MORNIN'
MAN ALIVE! WE'RE MOVING..... THE WHOLE PLACE IS MOVING!!
EVERY MORNIN' THE SAME...
... MIND YOU, IT WAS AGES 'TIL I GOT USED TO FLANS.

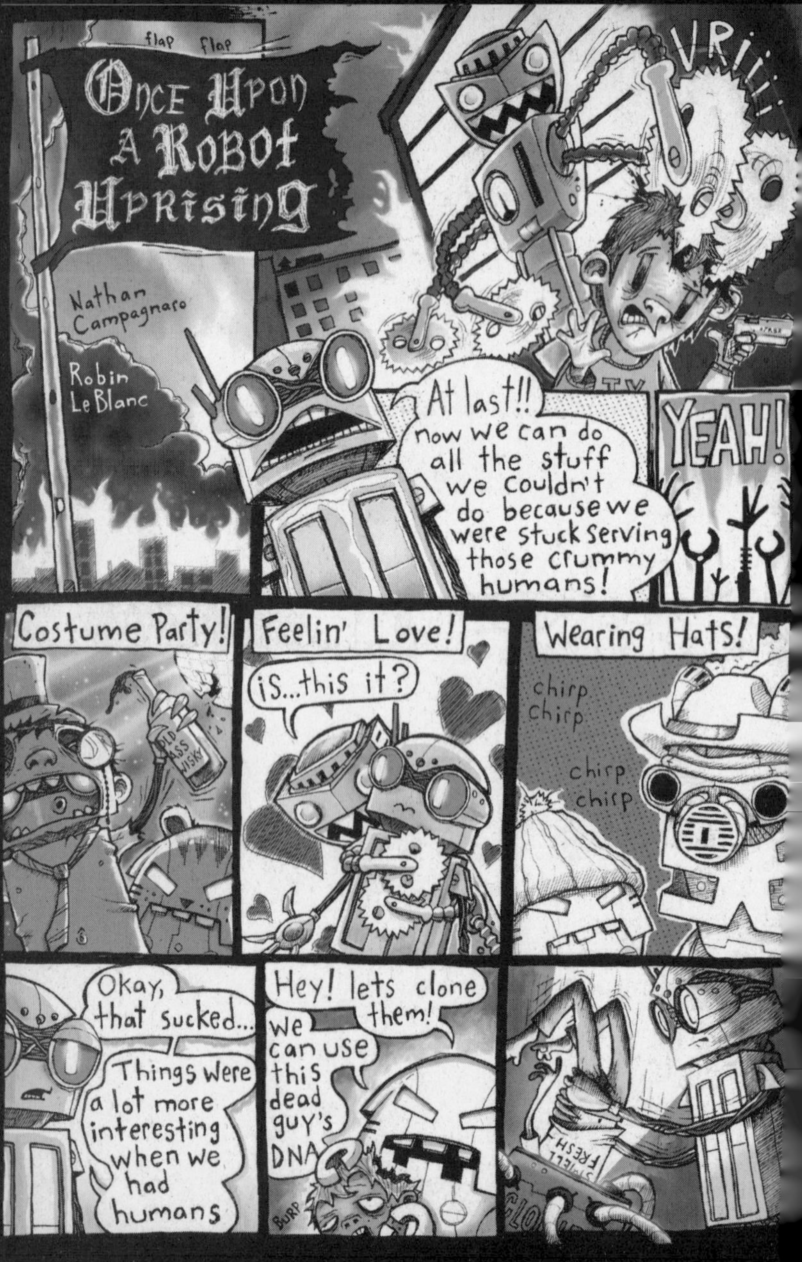
flap flap
Once Upon A Robot Uprising
Nathan Campagnaro
Robin Le Blanc
VRiii!
At last!! now we can do all the stuff we couldn't do because we were stuck serving those crummy humans!
YEAH!
Costume Party!
OLD ASS WISKY
Feelin' Love!
is...this it?
Wearing Hats!
chirp chirp
chirp chirp
Okay, that sucked...
Things were a lot more interesting when we had humans
Hey! lets clone them!
we can use this dead guy's DNA
BURP
SMELL FRESH

BY ROBIN LEBLANC AND NATHAN CAMPAGNARO / MYSPACE.COM/BANANAFA

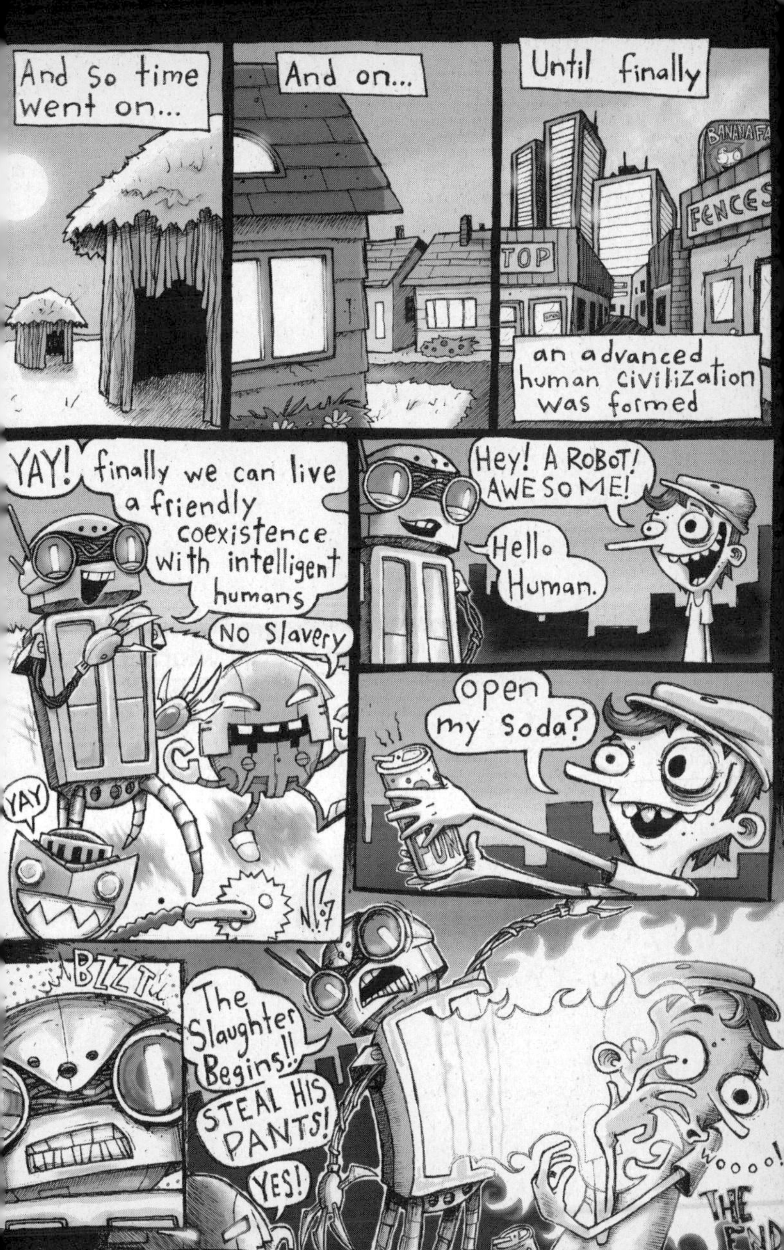
And so time went on...
And on...
Until finally
TOP
FENCES
an advanced human civilization was formed
YAY! finally we can live a friendly coexistence with intelligent humans
No Slavery
YAY
Hey! A ROBOT! AWESOME!
Hello Human.
open my soda?
FUN
BZZT
The Slaughter Begins!!
STEAL HIS PANTS!
YES!
Woooo!
THE END

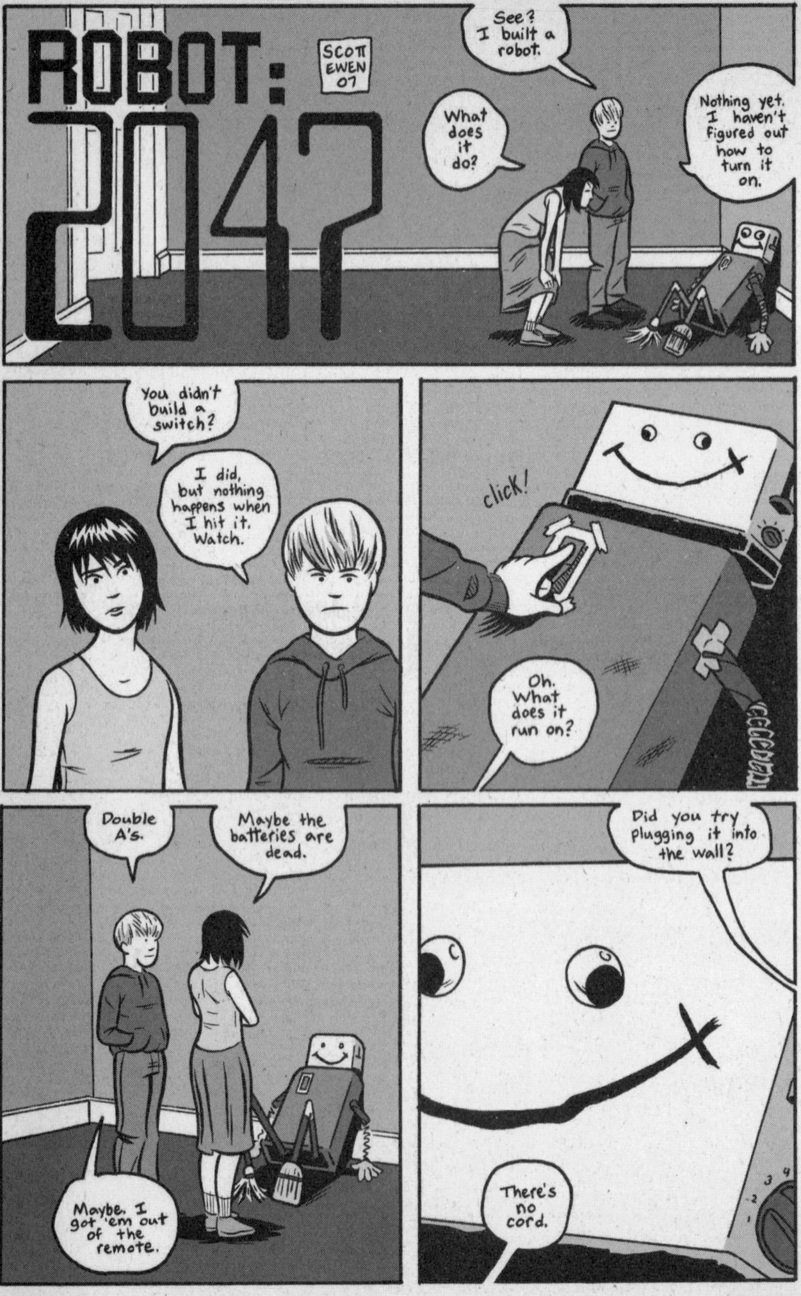
ROBOT: 2047
SCOTT EWEN 07
See? I built a robot.
What does it do?
Nothing yet. I haven't figured out how to turn it on.
You didn't build a switch?
I did, but nothing happens when I hit it. Watch.
click!
Oh. What does it run on?
Double A's.
Maybe the batteries are dead.
Maybe. I got 'em out of the remote.
Did you try plugging it into the wall?
There's no cord.

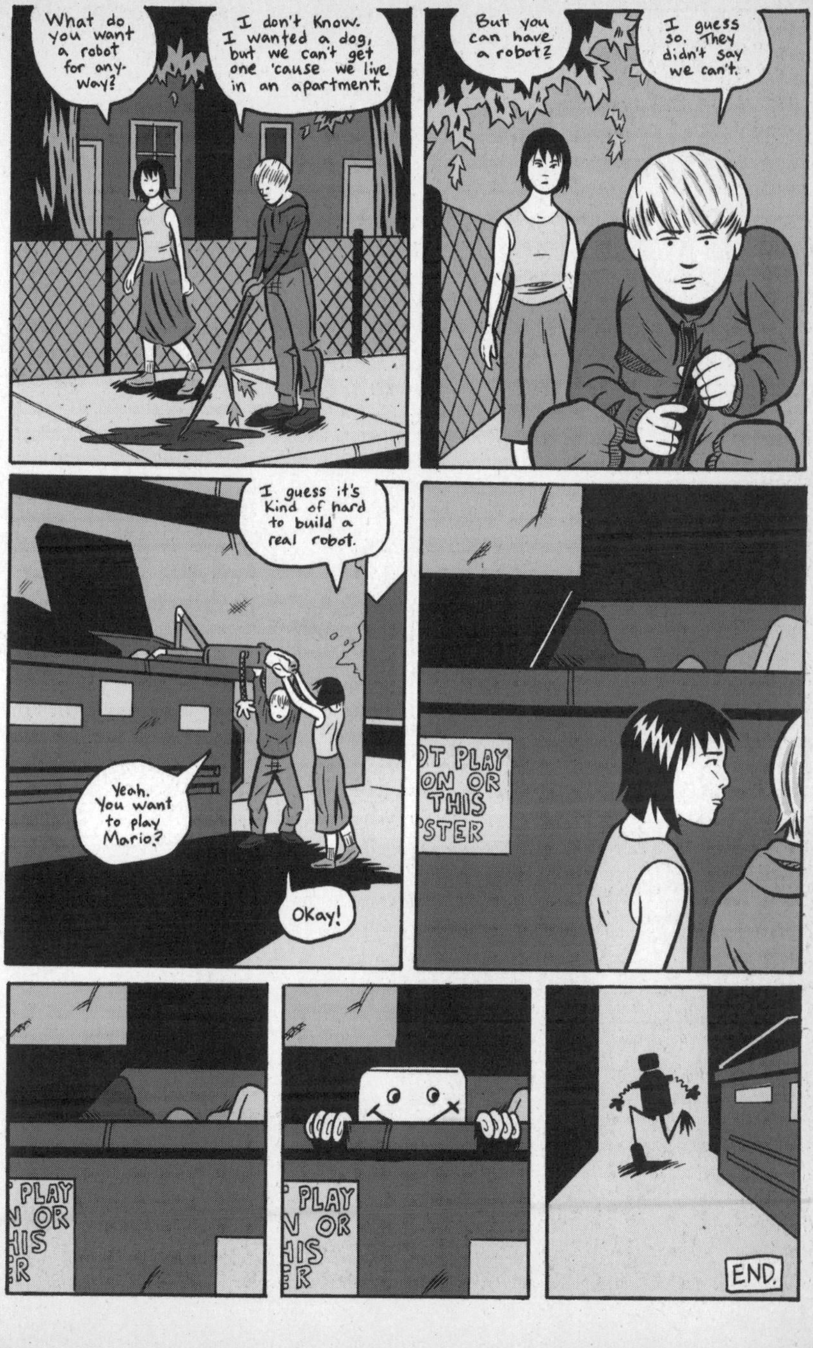
What do you want a robot for any-way?
I don't know. I wanted a dog, but we can't get one 'cause we live in an apartment.
But you can have a robot?
I guess so. They didn't say we can't.
I guess it's kind of hard to build a real robot.
Yeah. You want to play Mario?
Okay!
OT PLAY
ON OR
THIS
PSTER
END.

ROBOTS HATE....

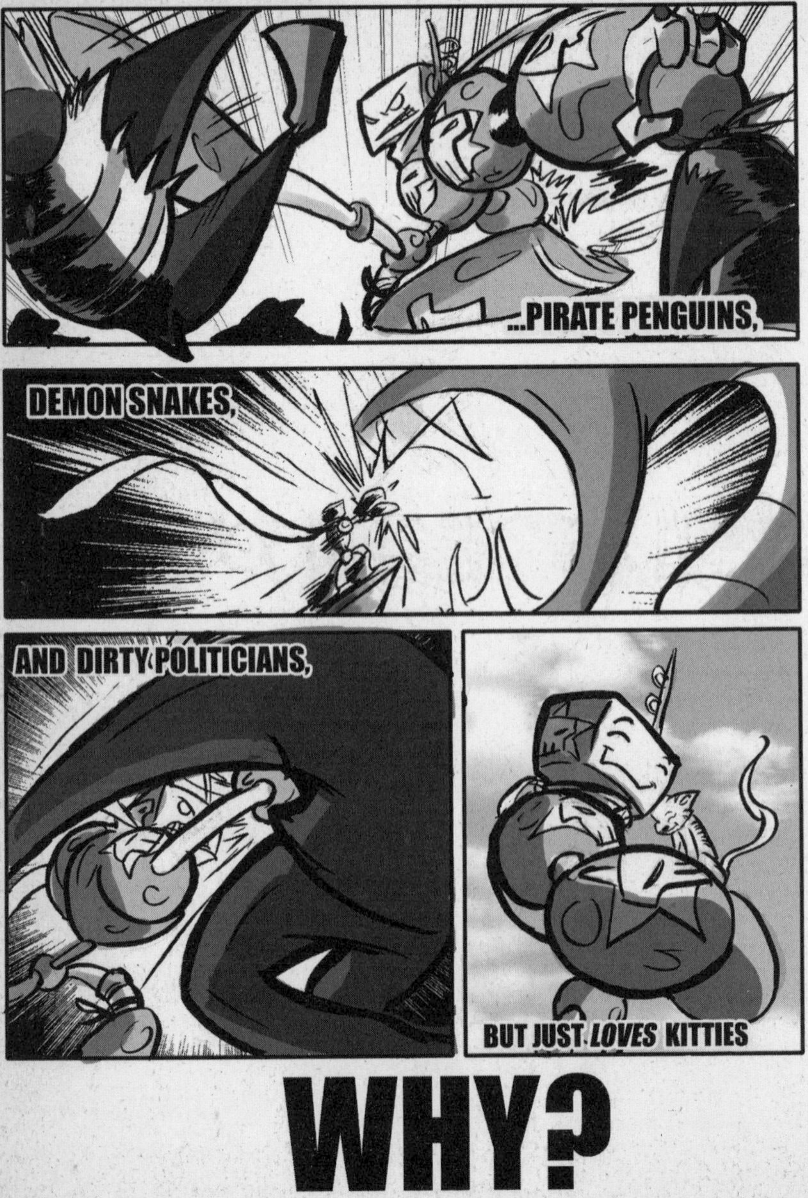
...PIRATE PENGUINS,
DEMON SNAKES,
AND DIRTY POLITICIANS,
BUT JUST *LOVES* KITTIES

WHY?

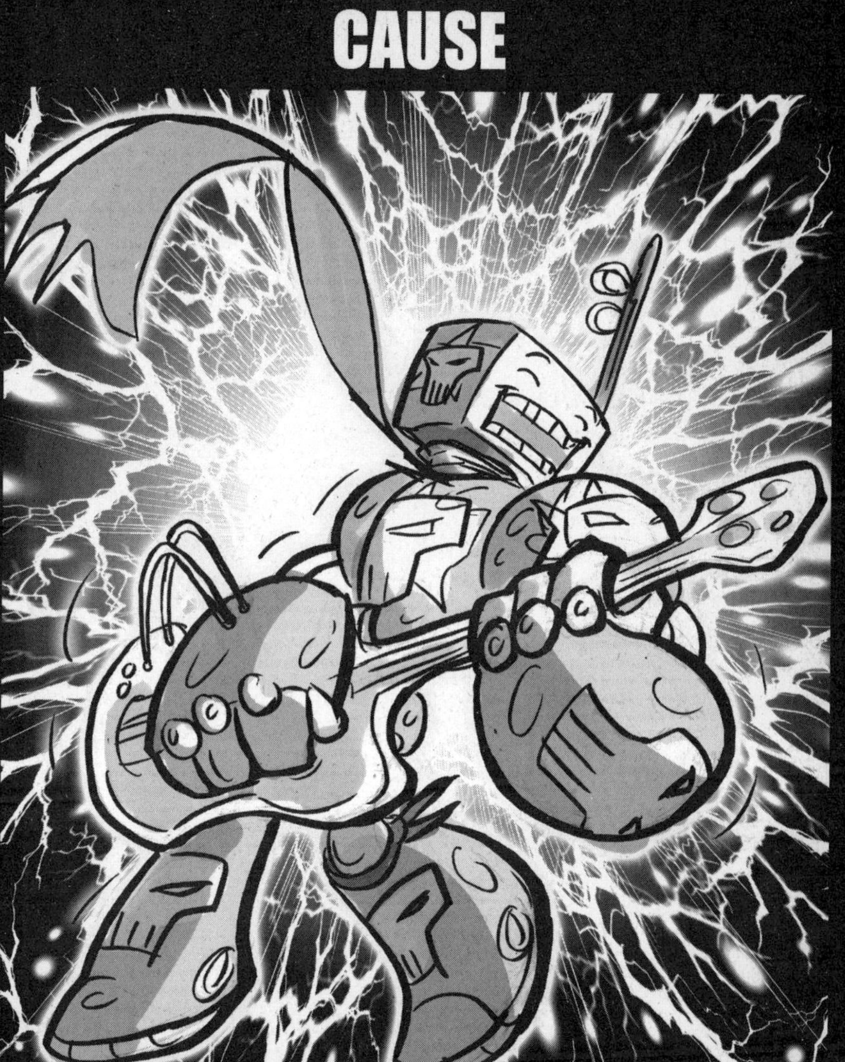
CAUSE
ROBOTS ROCK!!!!
by: rashad doucet http://kross29.deviantart.com

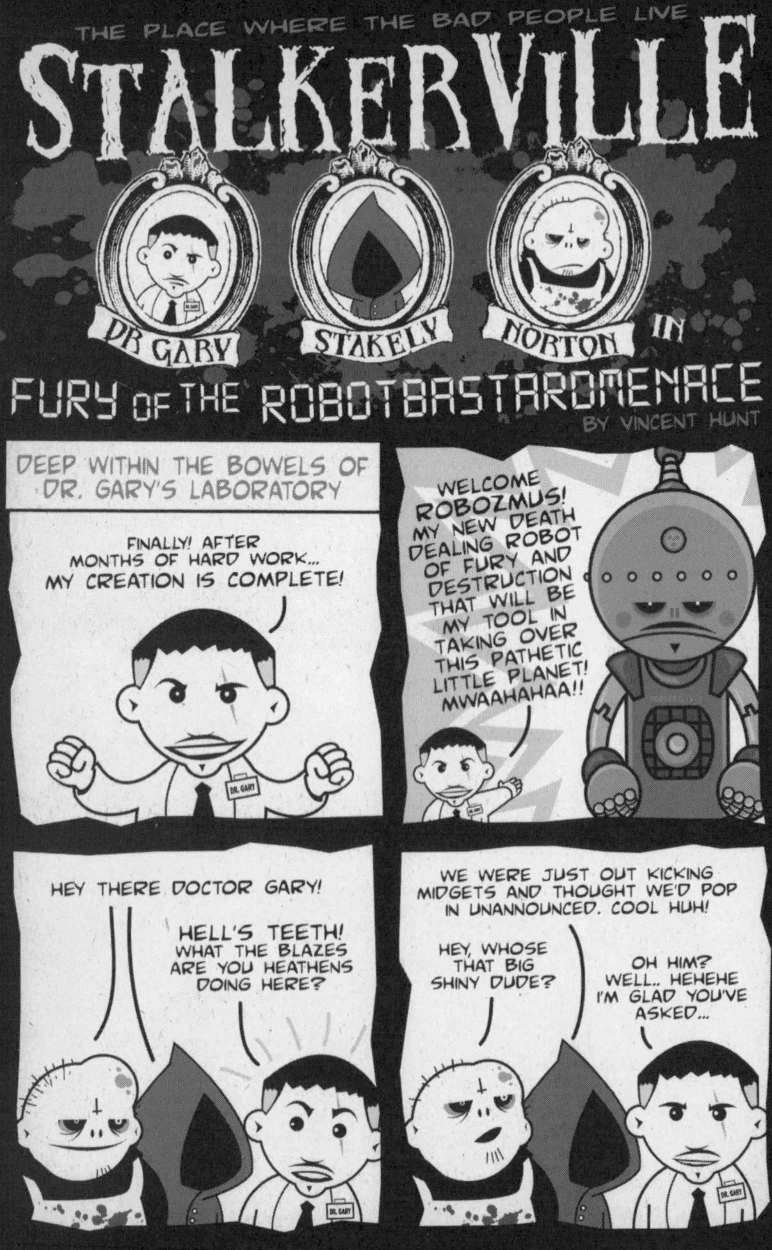
THE PLACE WHERE THE BAD PEOPLE LIVE
STALKERVILLE
DR GARY
STAKELY
NORTON
IN
FURY OF THE ROBOTBASTARDMENACE
BY VINCENT HUNT
DEEP WITHIN THE BOWELS OF DR. GARY'S LABORATORY
FINALLY! AFTER MONTHS OF HARD WORK... MY CREATION IS COMPLETE!
WELCOME ROBOZMUS! MY NEW DEATH DEALING ROBOT OF FURY AND DESTRUCTION THAT WILL BE MY TOOL IN TAKING OVER THIS PATHETIC LITTLE PLANET! MWAAHAHAA!!
HEY THERE DOCTOR GARY!
HELL'S TEETH! WHAT THE BLAZES ARE YOU HEATHENS DOING HERE?
WE WERE JUST OUT KICKING MIDGETS AND THOUGHT WE'D POP IN UNANNOUNCED. COOL HUH!
HEY, WHOSE THAT BIG SHINY DUDE?
OH HIM? WELL.. HEHEHE I'M GLAD YOU'VE ASKED...

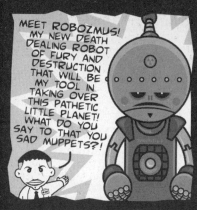

MEET ROBOZMUS! MY NEW DEATH DEALING ROBOT OF FURY AND DESTRUCTION THAT WILL BE MY TOOL IN TAKING OVER THIS PATHETIC LITTLE PLANET! WHAT DO YOU SAY TO THAT YOU SAD MUPPETS?!

UM... ACTUALLY, IT LOOKS A LITTLE... CAMP TO ME.

CAMP? CAMP?! HOW DARE YOU SPOUT SUCH MINDLESS, IGNORANT DRIVEL YOU SAD POTATO-BRAINED MONGALOIDS! YOU'LL BE LAUGHING ON THE OTHER SIDES OF YOUR UGLY BASTARD FACES WHEN ROBOZMUS BRINGS FIRE, PAIN AND TERRIFYING DESTRUCTION RAINING DOWN UPON EVERY MAN, WOMAN AND CHILD WHO DARES TO STAND IN MY WAY. MARK MY WORDS, TODAY IS THE DAY I RULE THE WORLD. JUST YOU WAIT AND SEE...

SOME TIME LATER...

HEY DOC... WHY IS YOUR ROBOT VIOLENTLY DRY HUMPING THAT BUILDING?

KHANG! KHANG! KHANG! KHANG! KHANG!

DEAR GOD WHY WONT IT SWITCH OFF?! WHY WONT IT SWITCH OFF?!

THE END

91

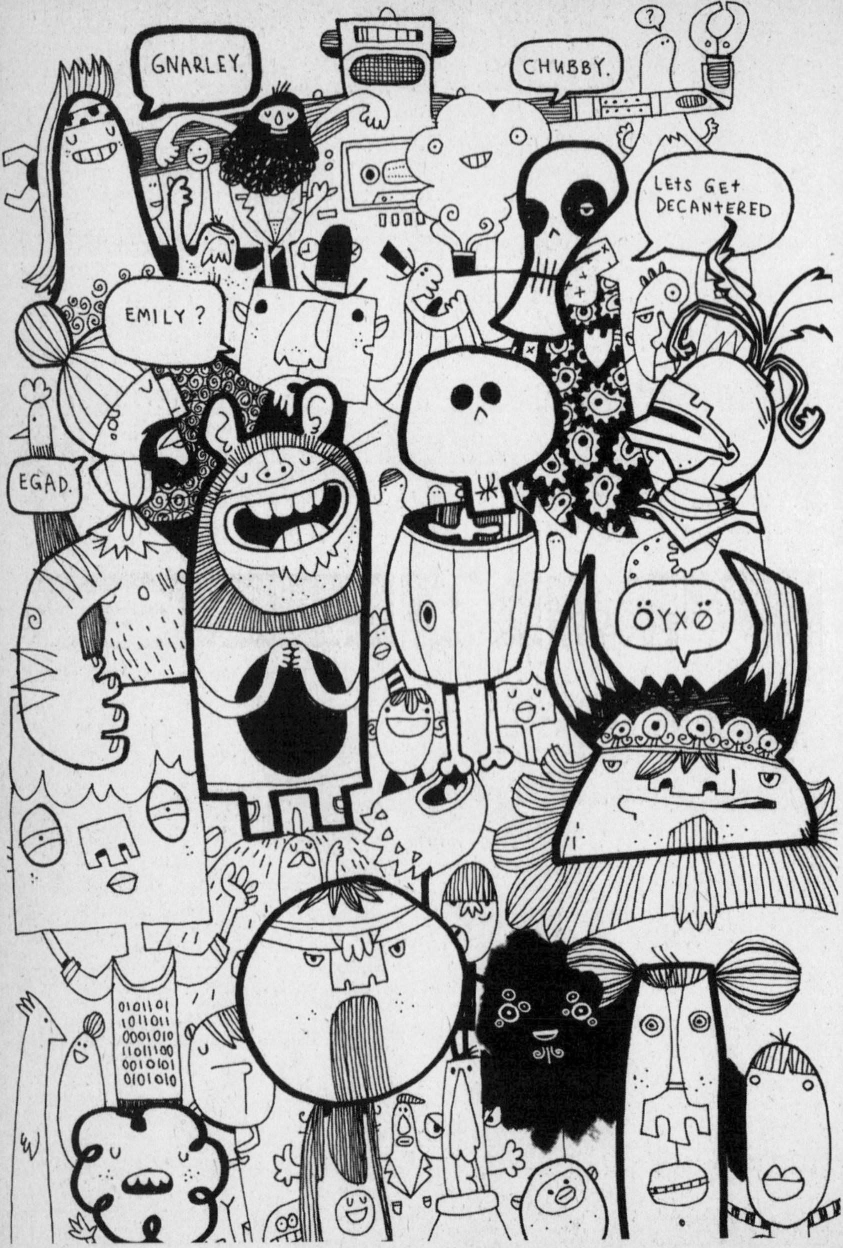
GNARLEY.
CHUBBY.
Lets Get DECANTERED
EMILY ?
EGAD.
ÖYXØ
01011 01
10101011
0001010
11011100
0010101
0101010

CHANG AND ENG IN New York New York

BY SONNY LIEW

CHANG AND ENG ARRIVE ON DISTANT SHORES...

WHERE THEY SUDDENLY REALISE THEY KNOW... KUNG-FU!!

WOAH!

THEY SOON FIND THEMSELVES WORKING IN A *CHINESE RESTAURANT.*

MEANWHILE A VILLAINOUS SORT WITH EITHER AN (A) *ORIENTAL* (B) *BRITISH* OR (C) *EAST EUROPEAN* ACCENT IS BUSY HATCHING NEFARIOUS PLANS...

...INVOLVING A *GIANT ROBOT* CAPABLE OF UTTER AND WANTON DESTRUCTION.

MUA HA HA HA HA

AN UNUSUALLY ATTRACTIVE MEMBER OF THE OPPOSITE SEX SOMEHOW GETS INVOLVED.

AS DOES A WISE-CRACKING INDIVIDUAL OF EITHER CAUCASIAN OR AFRO-AMERICAN DESCENT...

WHAT DO YOU GET WHEN YOU STEAM ROLL TWO CHINESE GUYS?

GRRRR

IT EMERGES THAT SOME *VILLAINOUS LACKEYS* KNOW KUNG-FU TOO.

A CLIMATIC BATTLE TAKES PLACE INVOLVING OUR PROTAGONISTS.

YAR!

HI-YAA!!

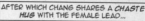

AFTER WHICH CHANG SHARES A *CHASTE HUG* WITH THE FEMALE LEAD...

YOU GO YELLOW AT YOUR PERIL!

...'COS ASIAN GUYS NEVER GET TO KISS THE GIRL.

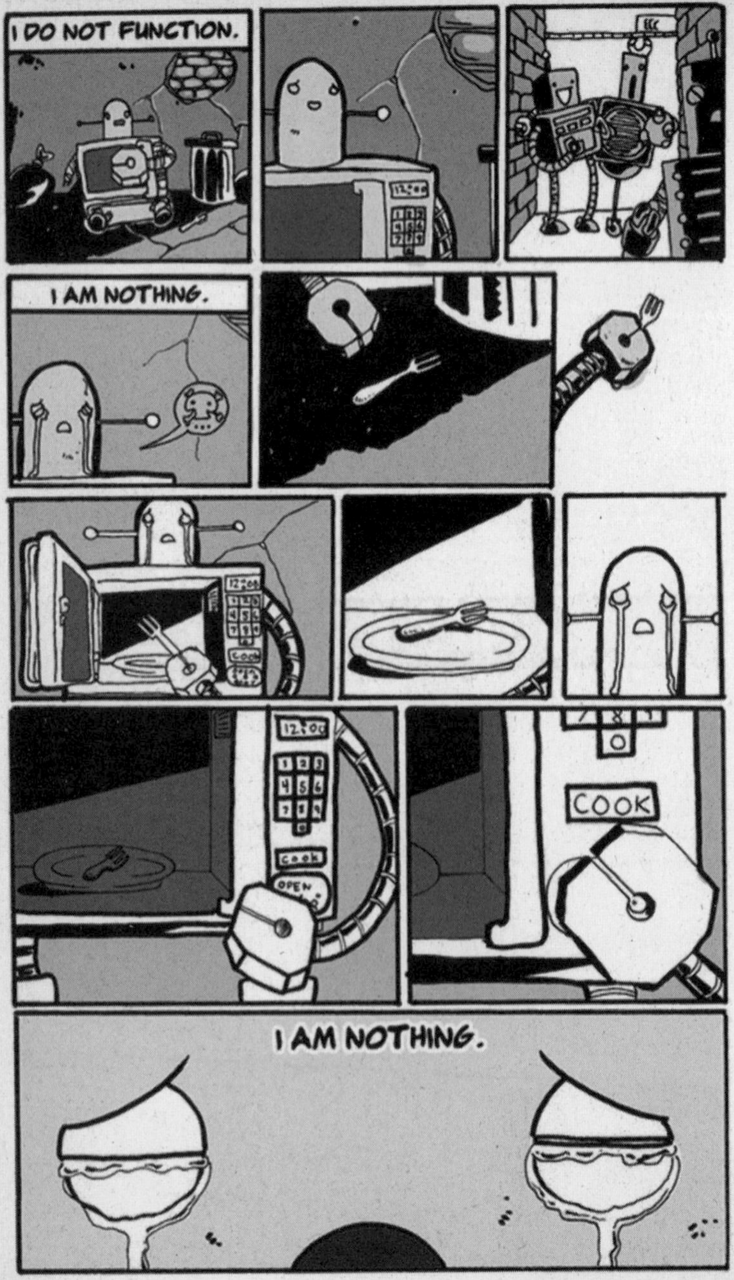
I DO NOT FUNCTION.
I AM NOTHING.
COOK
I AM NOTHING.

BY SHANE MCCAULLEY / HAVENTECH.COSMICDEATHRAY.COM

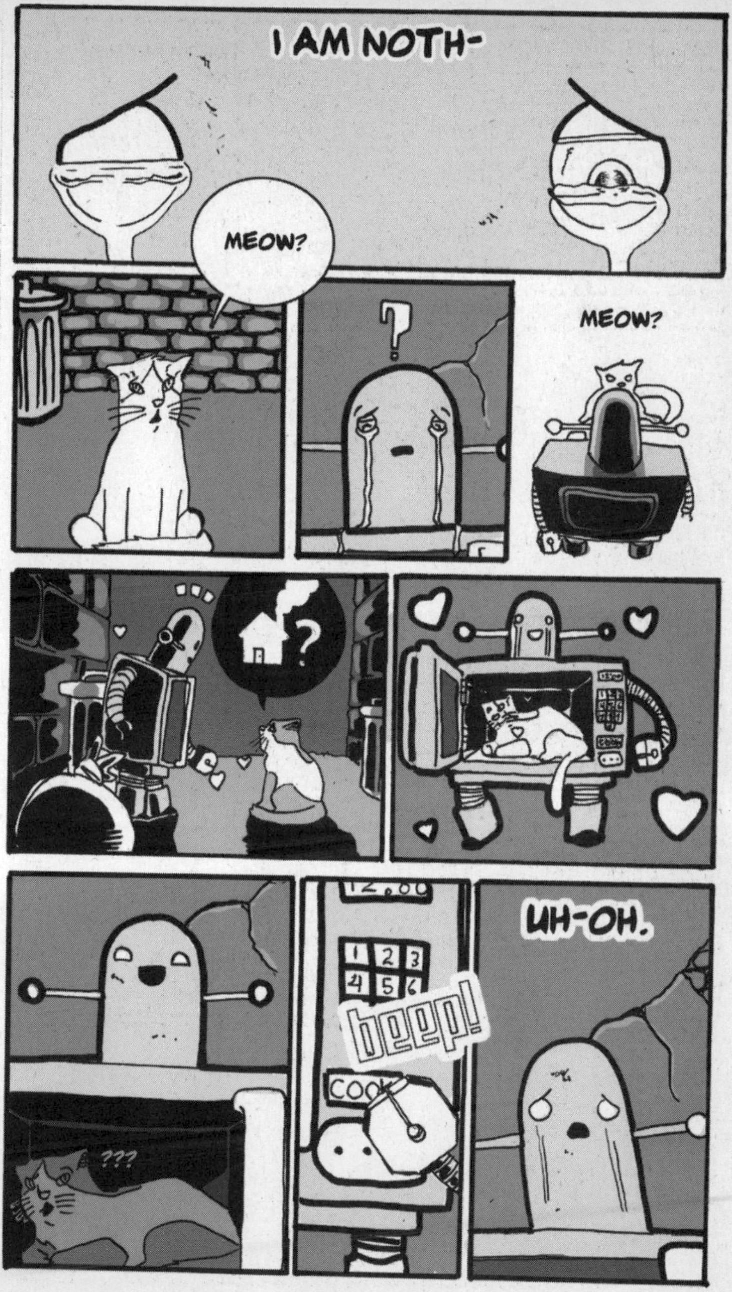

I AM NOTH-
MEOW?
?
MEOW?
?
beep!
???
UH-OH.

"OFFICE BITCH"

BY T.J. KIRSCH

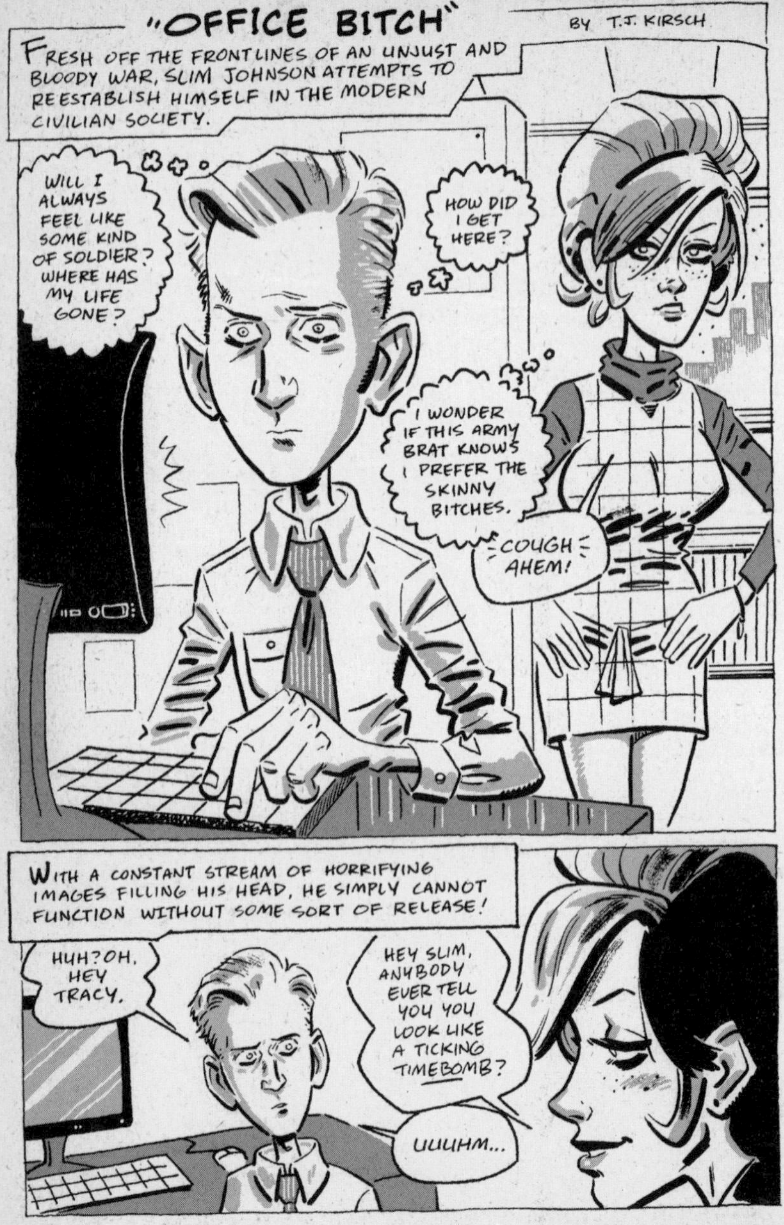
FRESH OFF THE FRONTLINES OF AN UNJUST AND BLOODY WAR, SLIM JOHNSON ATTEMPTS TO REESTABLISH HIMSELF IN THE MODERN CIVILIAN SOCIETY.
WILL I ALWAYS FEEL LIKE SOME KIND OF SOLDIER? WHERE HAS MY LIFE GONE?
HOW DID I GET HERE?
I WONDER IF THIS ARMY BRAT KNOWS I PREFER THE SKINNY BITCHES.
COUGH AHEM!
WITH A CONSTANT STREAM OF HORRIFYING IMAGES FILLING HIS HEAD, HE SIMPLY CANNOT FUNCTION WITHOUT SOME SORT OF RELEASE!
HEY SLIM, ANYBODY EVER TELL YOU YOU LOOK LIKE A TICKING TIMEBOMB?
HUH? OH. HEY TRACY.
UUUHM...

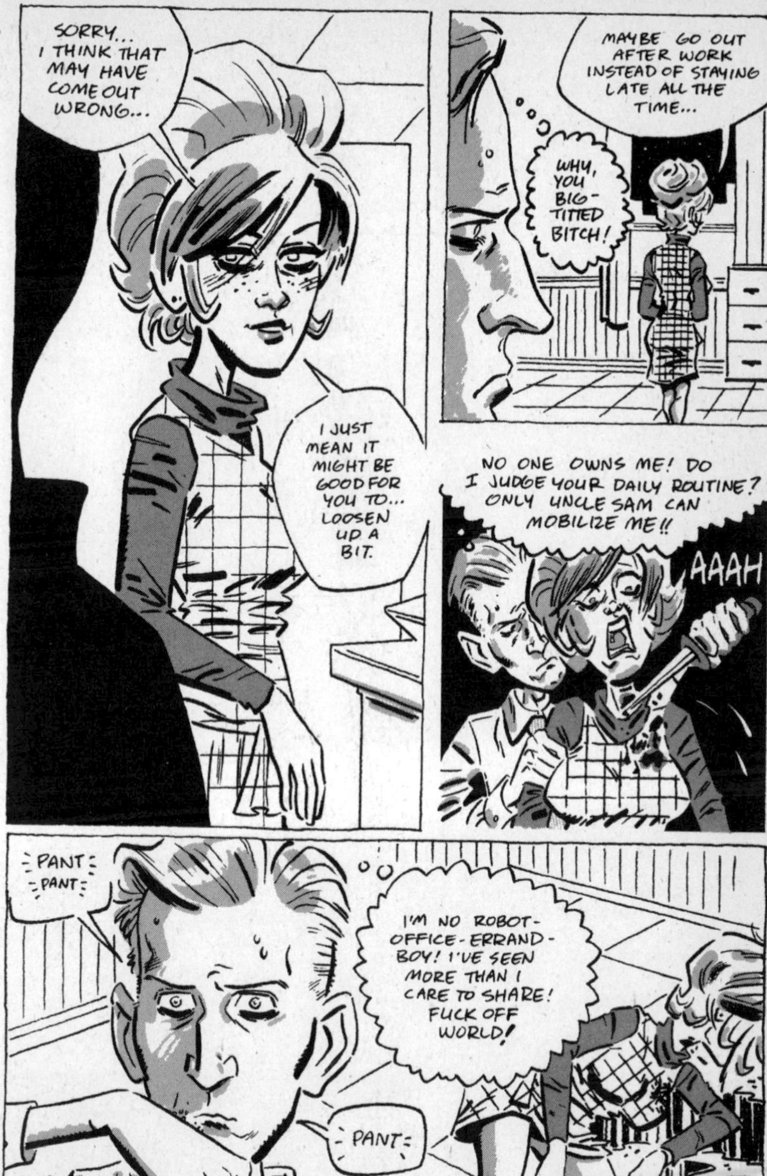
SORRY... I THINK THAT MAY HAVE COME OUT WRONG...
I JUST MEAN IT MIGHT BE GOOD FOR YOU TO... LOOSEN UP A BIT.
MAYBE GO OUT AFTER WORK INSTEAD OF STAYING LATE ALL THE TIME...
WHY, YOU BIG-TITTED BITCH!
NO ONE OWNS ME! DO I JUDGE YOUR DAILY ROUTINE? ONLY UNCLE SAM CAN MOBILIZE ME!!
AAAH
PANT PANT
I'M NO ROBOT-OFFICE-ERRAND-BOY! I'VE SEEN MORE THAN I CARE TO SHARE! FUCK OFF WORLD!
PANT
THE END!

BY SHAKINO / NIKKISTU.CO.UK

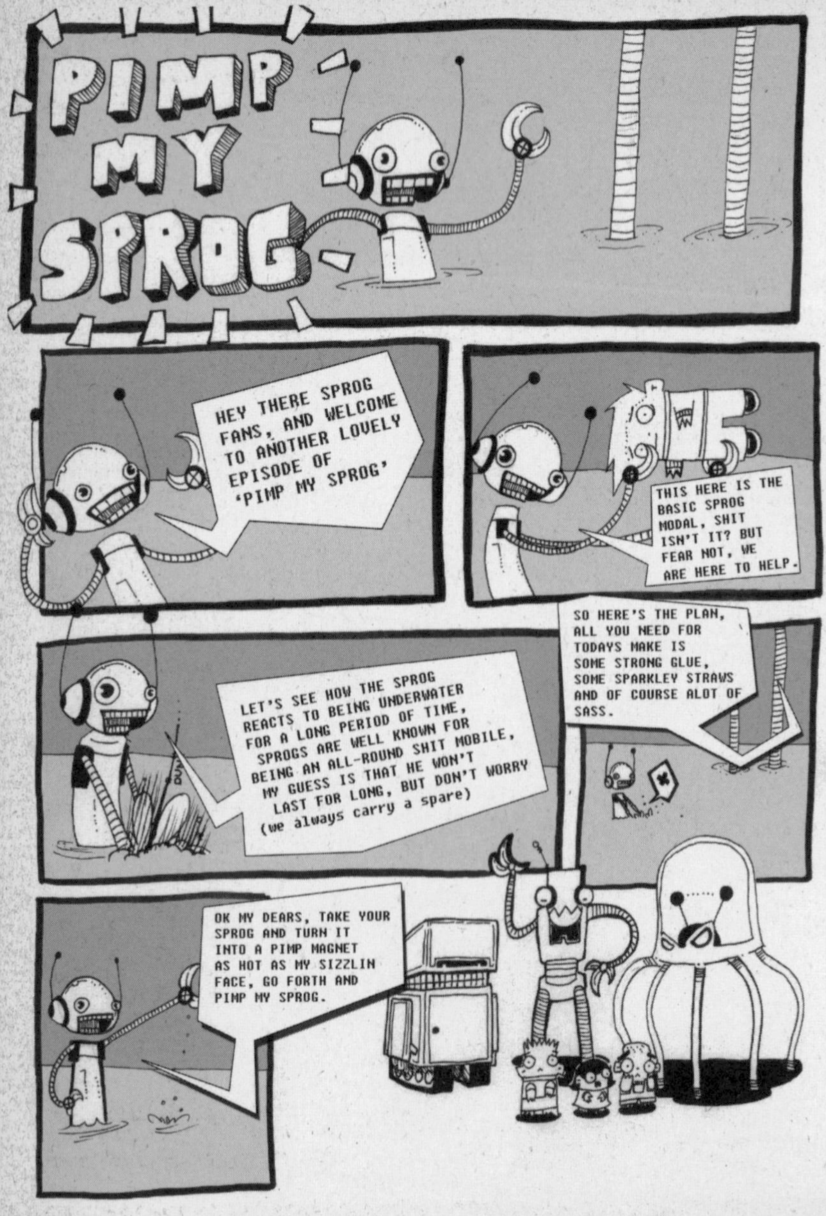
PIMP MY SPROG
HEY THERE SPROG FANS, AND WELCOME TO ANOTHER LOVELY EPISODE OF 'PIMP MY SPROG'
THIS HERE IS THE BASIC SPROG MODAL, SHIT ISN'T IT? BUT FEAR NOT, WE ARE HERE TO HELP.
LET'S SEE HOW THE SPROG REACTS TO BEING UNDERWATER FOR A LONG PERIOD OF TIME, SPROGS ARE WELL KNOWN FOR BEING AN ALL-ROUND SHIT MOBILE, MY GUESS IS THAT HE WON'T LAST FOR LONG, BUT DON'T WORRY (we always carry a spare)
SO HERE'S THE PLAN, ALL YOU NEED FOR TODAYS MAKE IS SOME STRONG GLUE, SOME SPARKLEY STRAWS AND OF COURSE ALOT OF SASS.
OK MY DEARS, TAKE YOUR SPROG AND TURN IT INTO A PIMP MAGNET AS HOT AS MY SIZZLIN FACE, GO FORTH AND PIMP MY SPROG.

BY XANDER MYLES / MYSPACE.COM/SKETCH_BOOK

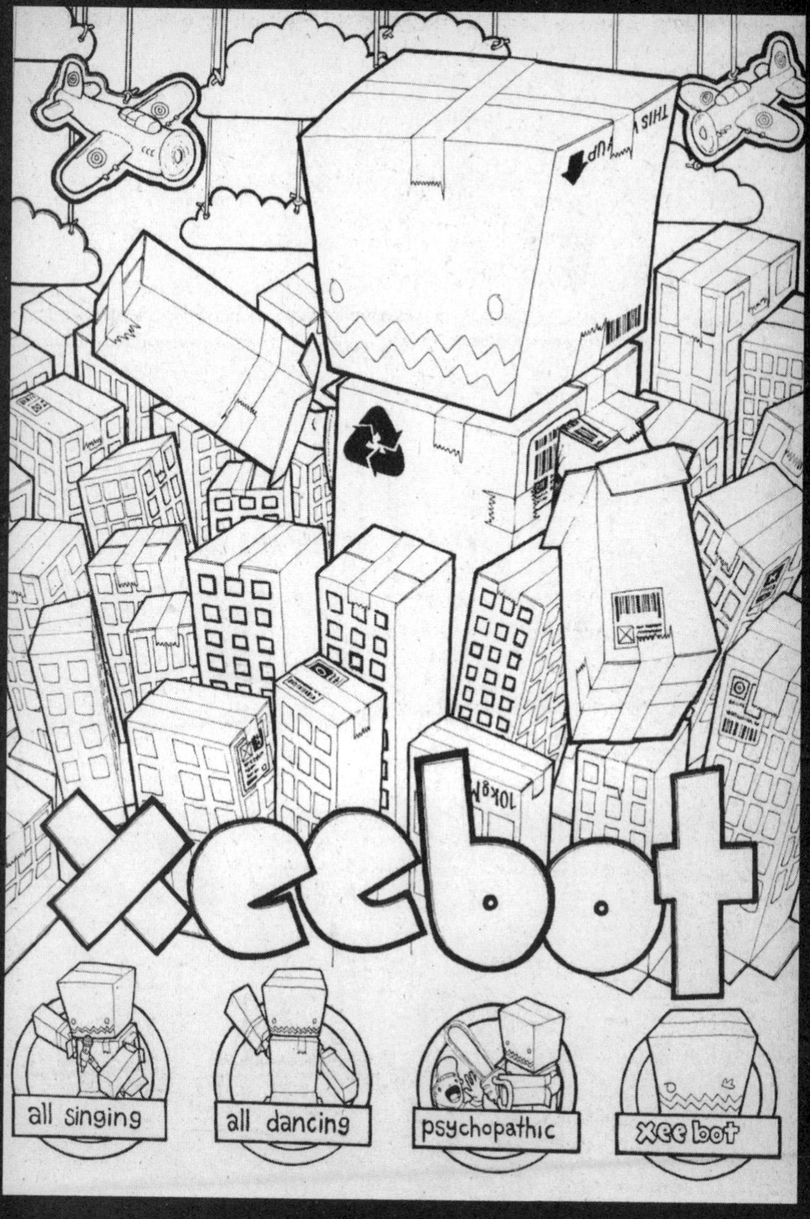
xeebot
all singing
all dancing
psychopathic
xee bot

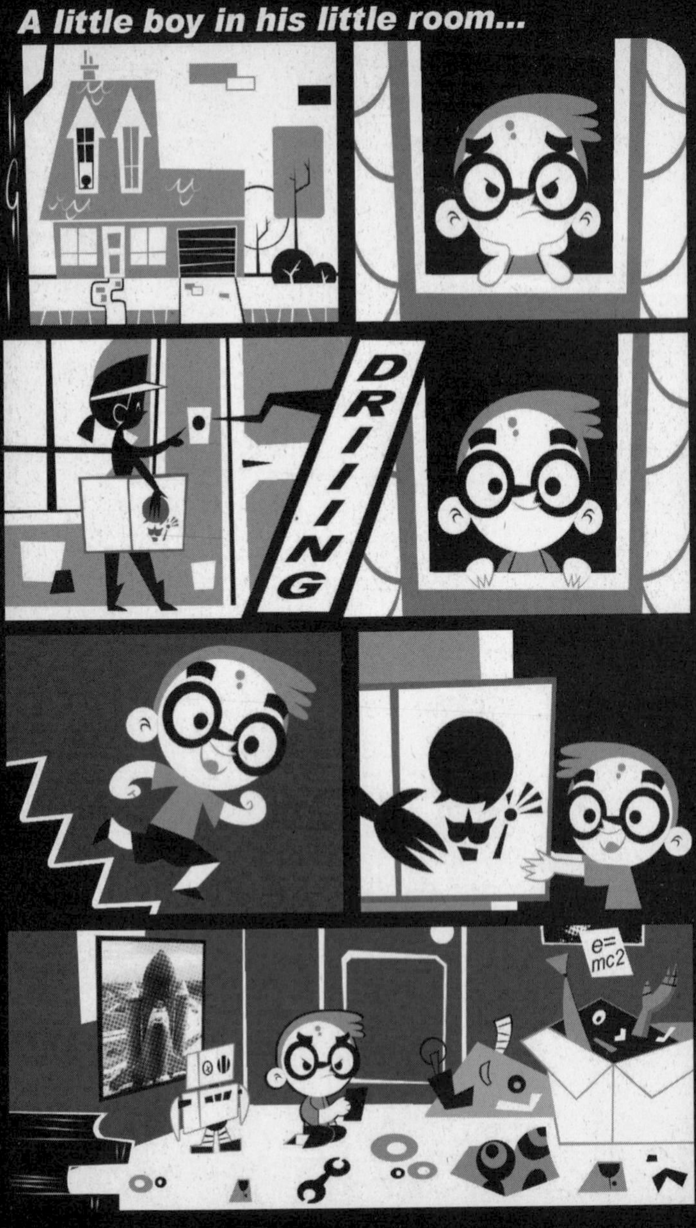
A little boy in his little room...
DRIIING
e=
mc2

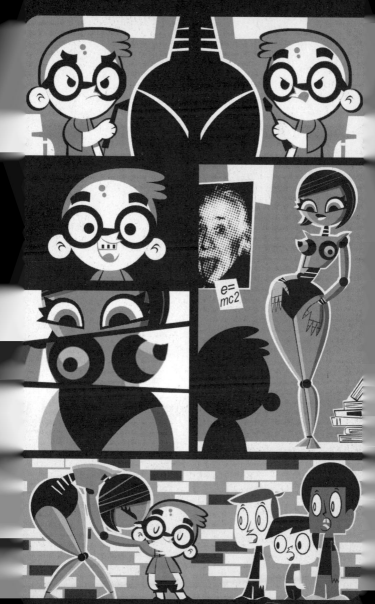

BY TANDOORI / TANDOORIDES

$e = mc^2$

Tandoori -2007

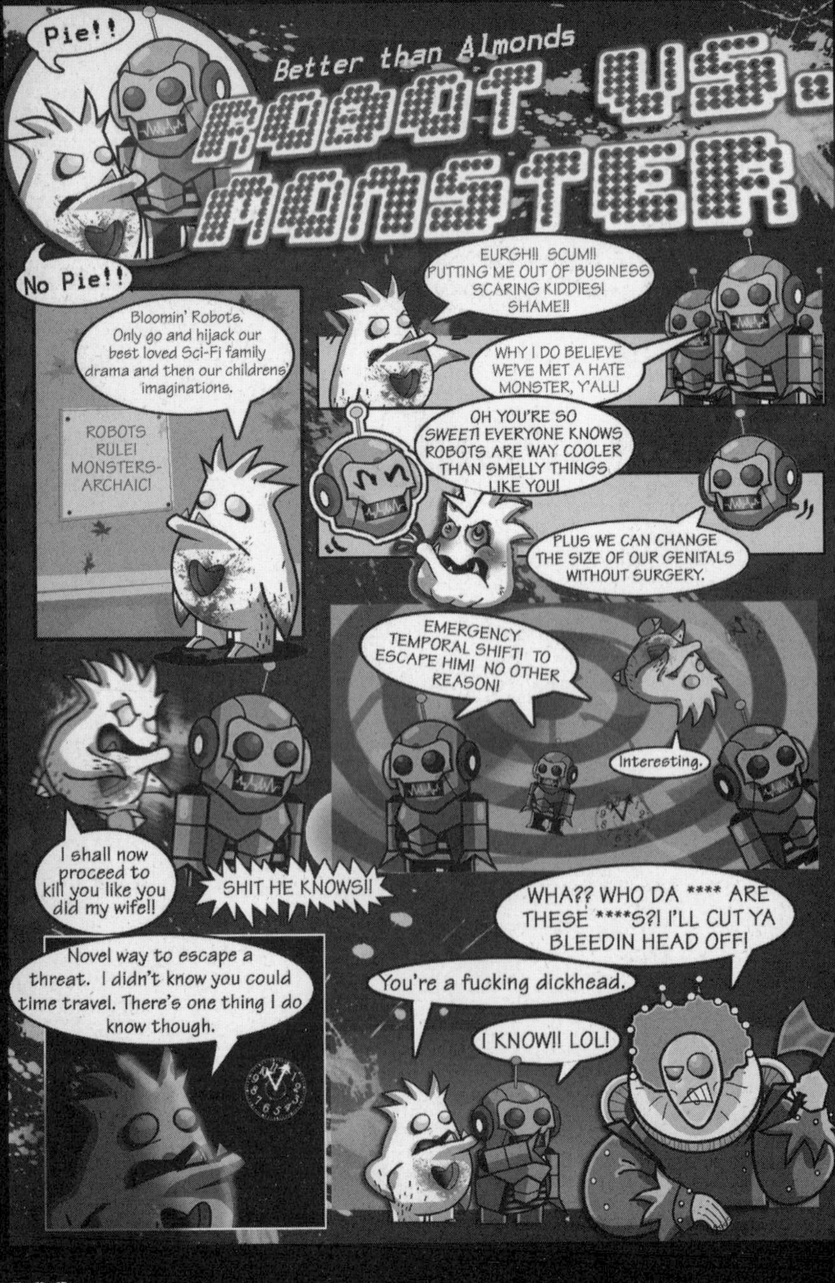
Pie!!
Better than Almonds
ROBOT VS. MONSTER
No Pie!!
Bloomin' Robots. Only go and hijack our best loved Sci-Fi family drama and then our childrens' imaginations.
ROBOTS RULE! MONSTERS-ARCHAIC!
EURGH!! SCUM!! PUTTING ME OUT OF BUSINESS SCARING KIDDIES! SHAME!!
WHY I DO BELIEVE WE'VE MET A HATE MONSTER, Y'ALL!
OH YOU'RE SO SWEET! EVERYONE KNOWS ROBOTS ARE WAY COOLER THAN SMELLY THINGS LIKE YOU!
PLUS WE CAN CHANGE THE SIZE OF OUR GENITALS WITHOUT SURGERY.
I shall now proceed to kill you like you did my wife!!
SHIT HE KNOWS!!
EMERGENCY TEMPORAL SHIFT! TO ESCAPE HIM! NO OTHER REASON!
Interesting.
Novel way to escape a threat. I didn't know you could time travel. There's one thing I do know though.
WHA?? WHO DA **** ARE THESE ****S?! I'LL CUT YA BLEEDIN HEAD OFF!
You're a fucking dickhead.
I KNOW!! LOL!

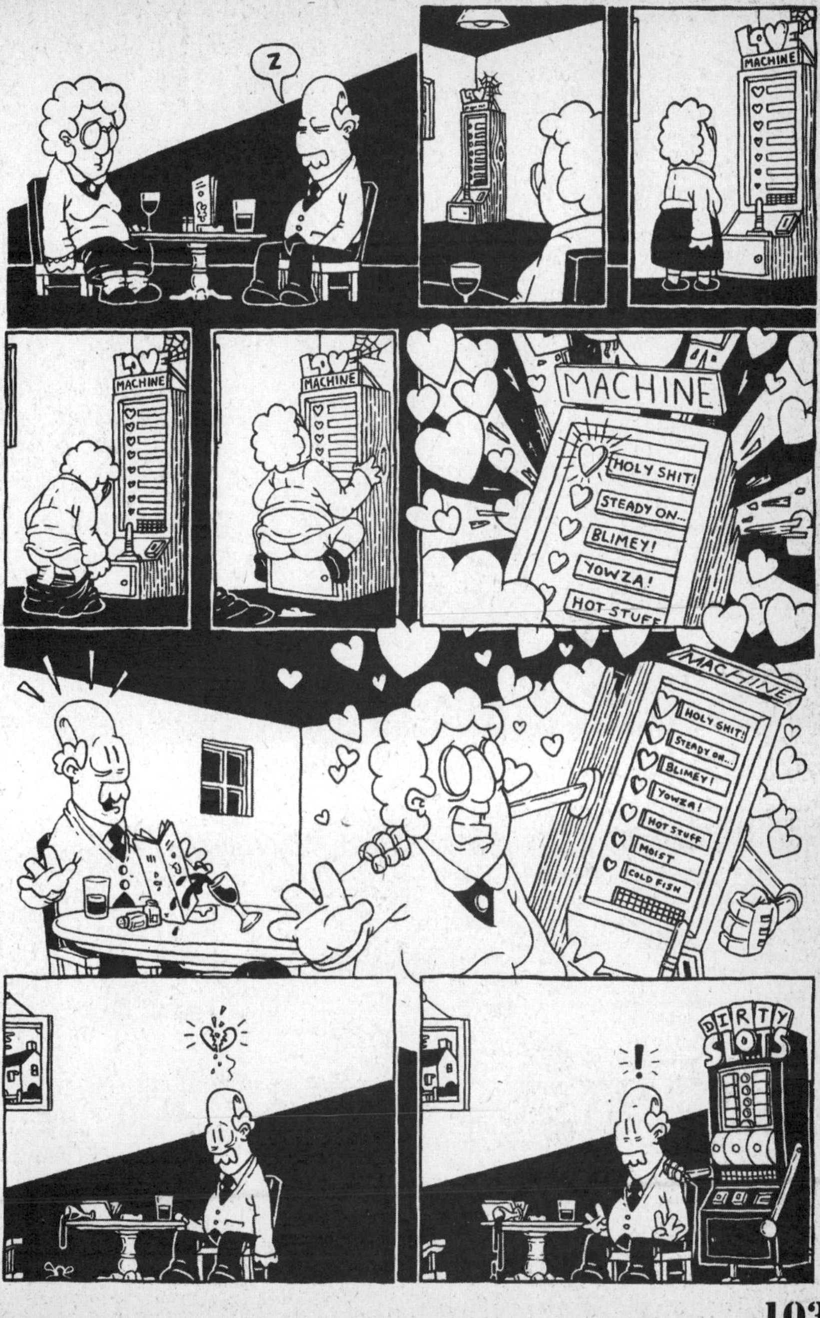
Z
LOVE
MACHINE
MACHINE
HOLY SHIT!
STEADY ON...
BLIMEY!
YOWZA!
HOT STUFF
MACHINE
HOLY SHIT!
STEADY ON...
BLIMEY!
YOWZA!
HOT STUFF
MOIST
COLD FISH
!
DIRTY
SLOTS

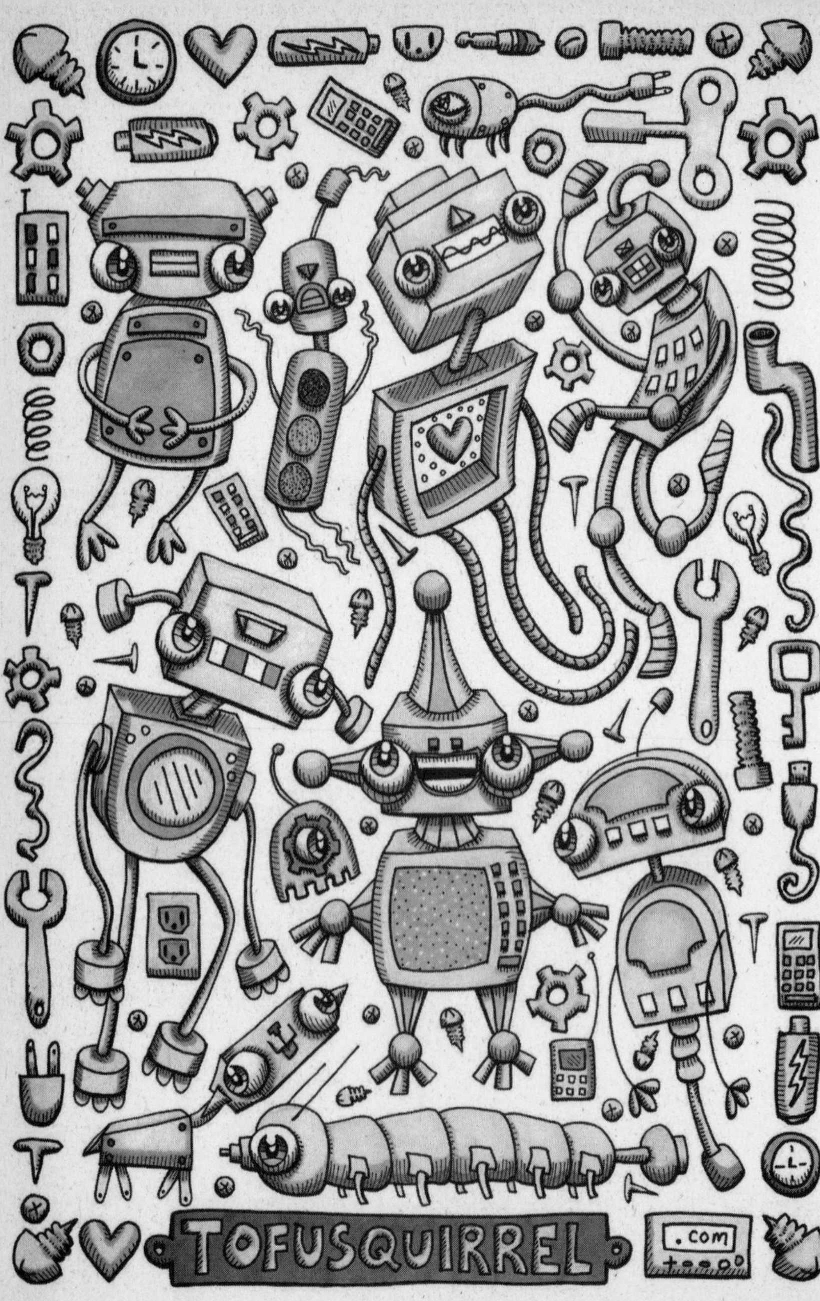
TOFUSQUIRREL
.com

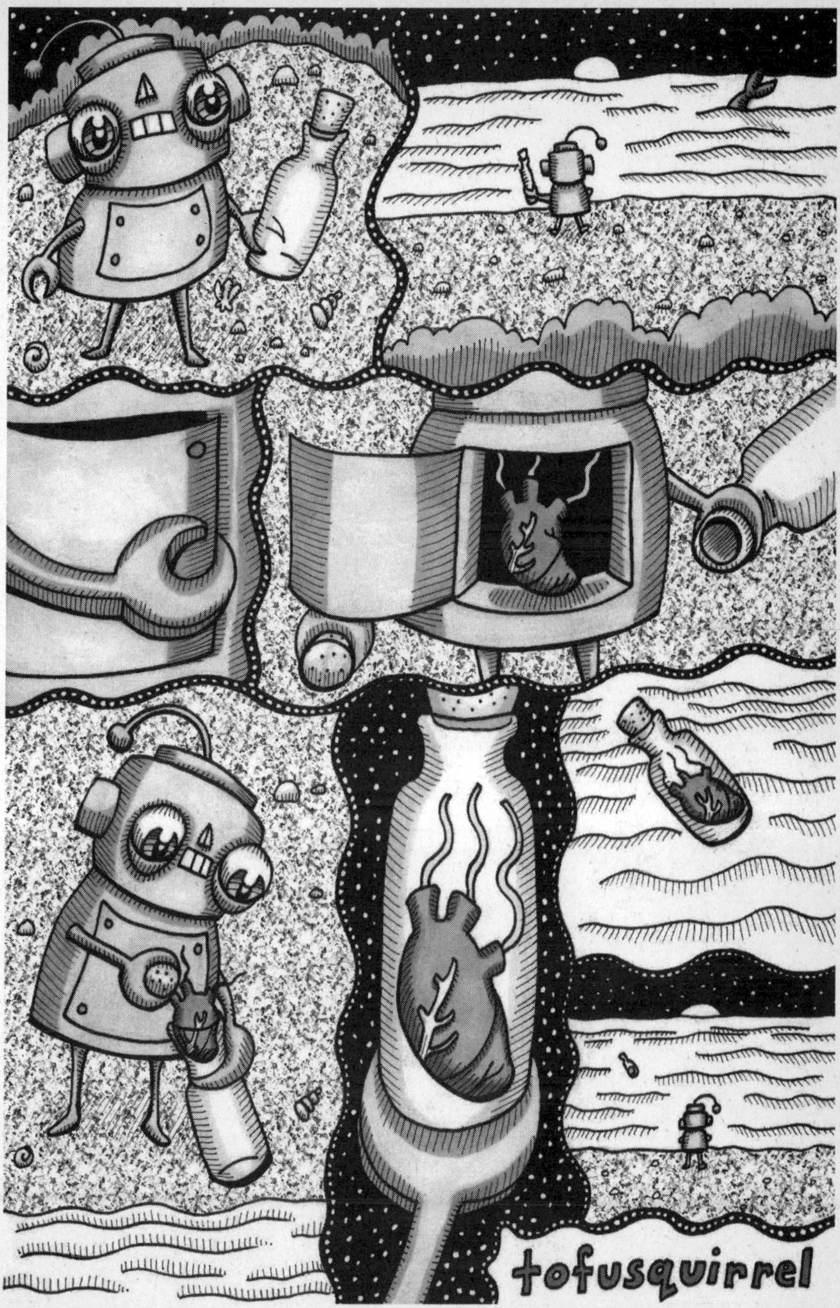
tofusquirrel

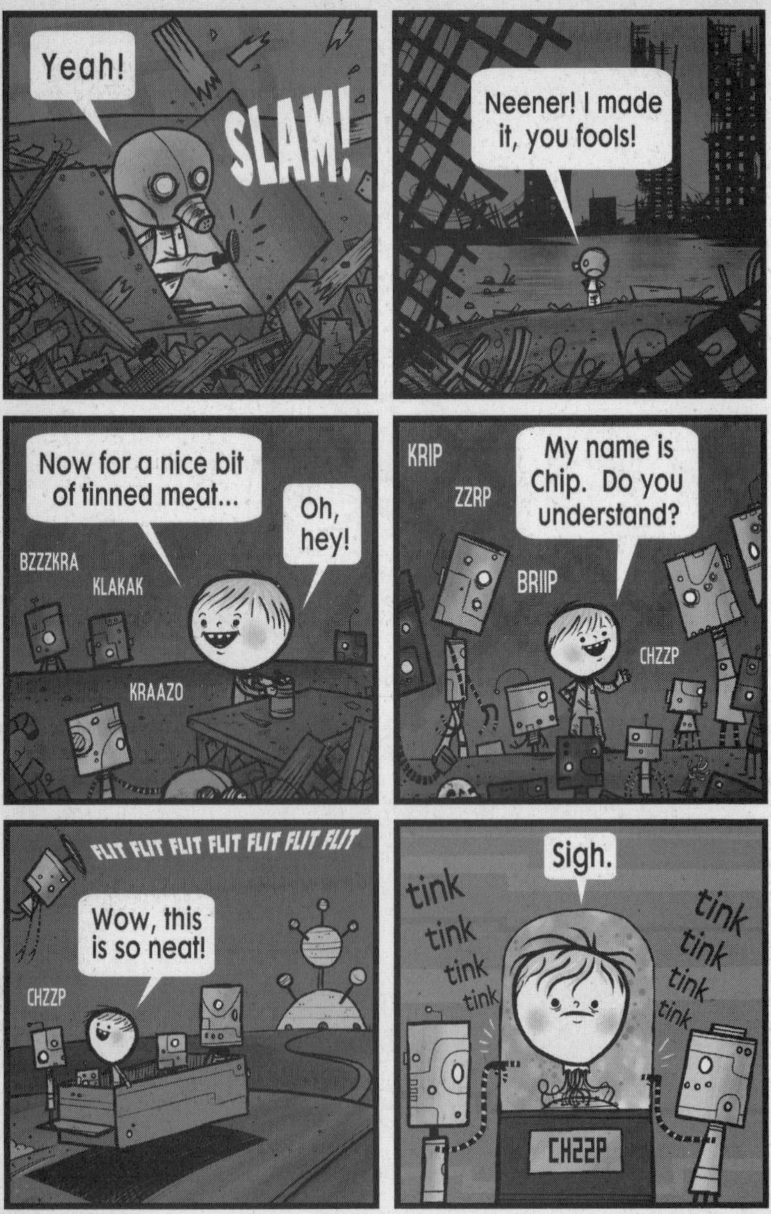
Yeah!
SLAM!
Neener! I made it, you fools!
Now for a nice bit of tinned meat...
Oh, hey!
BZZZKRA
KLAKAK
KRAAZO
KRIP
ZZRP
My name is Chip. Do you understand?
BRIIP
CHZZP
FLIT FLIT FLIT FLIT FLIT FLIT FLIT
Wow, this is so neat!
CHZZP
Sigh.
tink
tink
tink
tink
tink
tink
tink
tink
CHZZP

michael fleming

tweedlebop.com

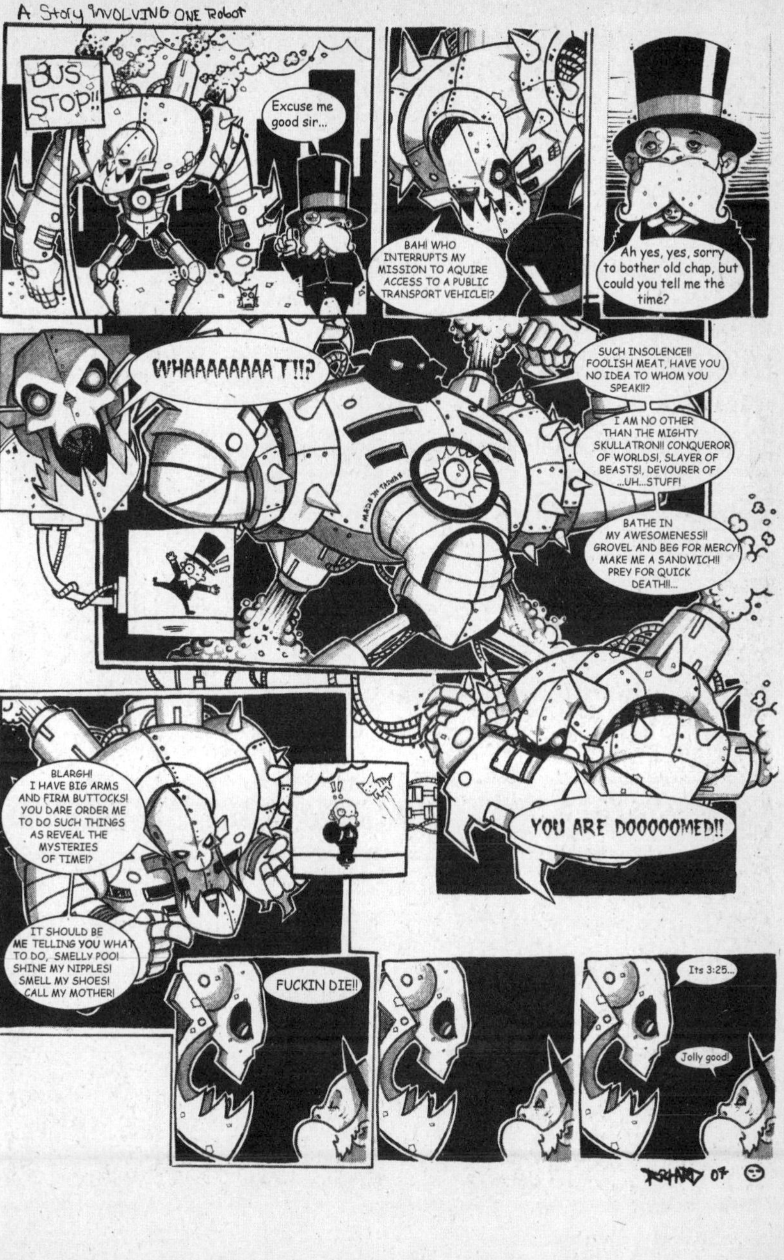
A Story involving ONE Robot
BUS STOP!!
Excuse me good sir...
BAH! WHO INTERRUPTS MY MISSION TO AQUIRE ACCESS TO A PUBLIC TRANSPORT VEHICLE!?
Ah yes, yes, sorry to bother old chap, but could you tell me the time?
WHAAAAAAAAT!!?
SUCH INSOLENCE!! FOOLISH MEAT, HAVE YOU NO IDEA TO WHOM YOU SPEAK!!?
I AM NO OTHER THAN THE MIGHTY SKULLATRON!! CONQUEROR OF WORLDS!, SLAYER OF BEASTS!, DEVOURER OF ...UH...STUFF!
BATHE IN MY AWESOMENESS!! GROVEL AND BEG FOR MERCY! MAKE ME A SANDWICH!! PREY FOR QUICK DEATH!!...
BLARGH! I HAVE BIG ARMS AND FIRM BUTTOCKS! YOU DARE ORDER ME TO DO SUCH THINGS AS REVEAL THE MYSTERIES OF TIME!?
IT SHOULD BE ME TELLING YOU WHAT TO DO, SMELLY POO! SHINE MY NIPPLES! SMELL MY SHOES! CALL MY MOTHER!
YOU ARE DOOOOOMED!!
FUCKIN DIE!!
Its 3:25...
Jolly good!
RICHARD 07

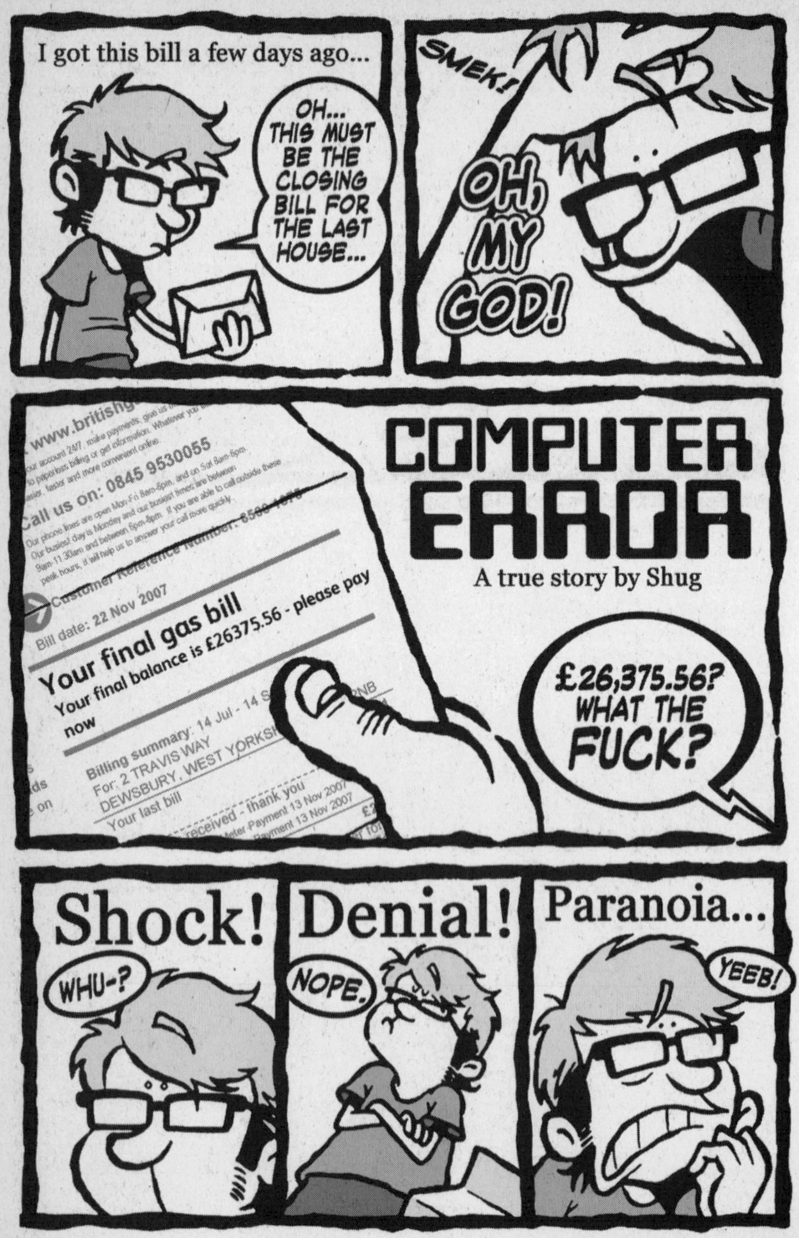
I got this bill a few days ago...
OH... THIS MUST BE THE CLOSING BILL FOR THE LAST HOUSE...
SMEK!
OH, MY GOD!
www.britishg
Call us on: 0845 9530055
Customer Reference Number:
Bill date: 22 Nov 2007
Your final gas bill
Your final balance is £26375.56 - please pay now
Billing summary: 14 Jul - 14 S
For: 2 TRAVIS WAY
DEWSBURY, WEST YORKS
Your last bill
received - thank you
COMPUTER ERROR
A true story by Shug
£26,375.56? WHAT THE FUCK?
Shock!
WHU-?
Denial!
NOPE.
Paranoia...
YEEB!

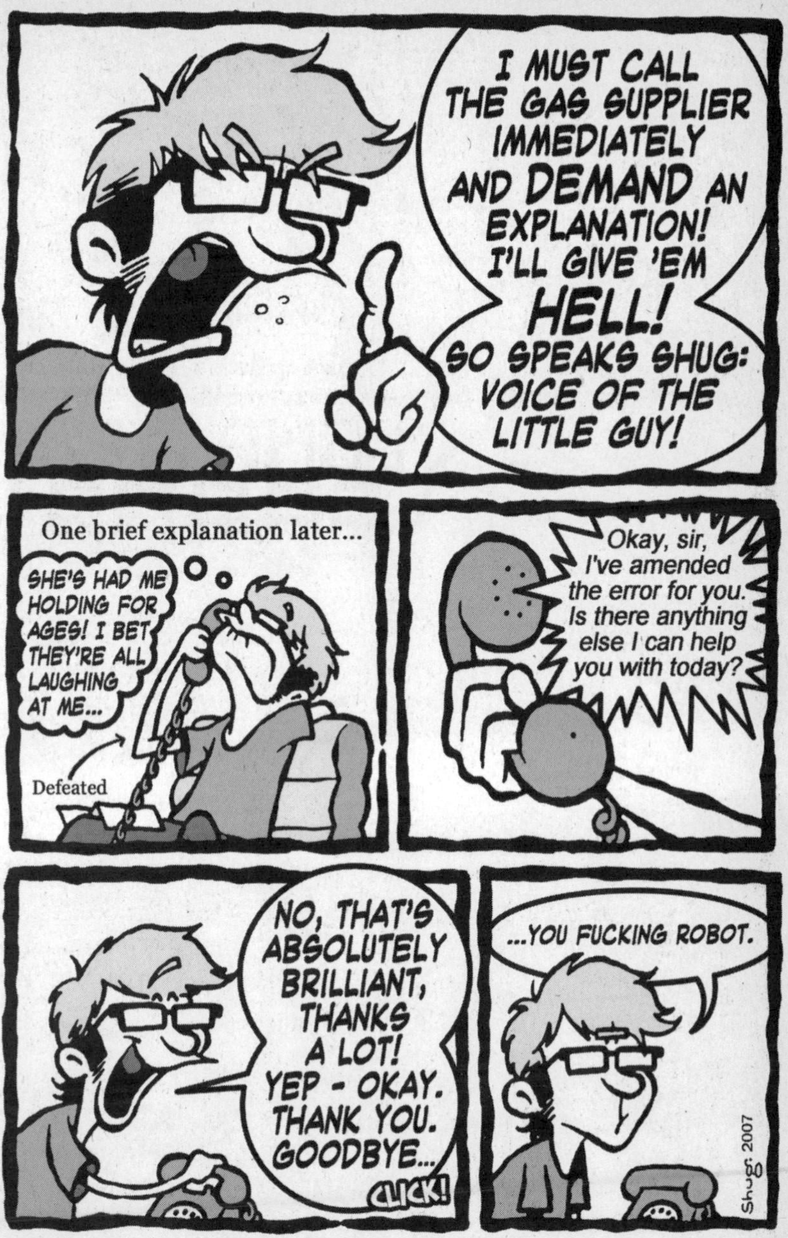
I MUST CALL THE GAS SUPPLIER IMMEDIATELY AND DEMAND AN EXPLANATION! I'LL GIVE 'EM HELL! SO SPEAKS SHUG: VOICE OF THE LITTLE GUY!
One brief explanation later...
SHE'S HAD ME HOLDING FOR AGES! I BET THEY'RE ALL LAUGHING AT ME...
Defeated
Okay, sir, I've amended the error for you. Is there anything else I can help you with today?
NO, THAT'S ABSOLUTELY BRILLIANT, THANKS A LOT! YEP - OKAY. THANK YOU. GOODBYE...
CLICK!
...YOU FUCKING ROBOT.
Shug 2007

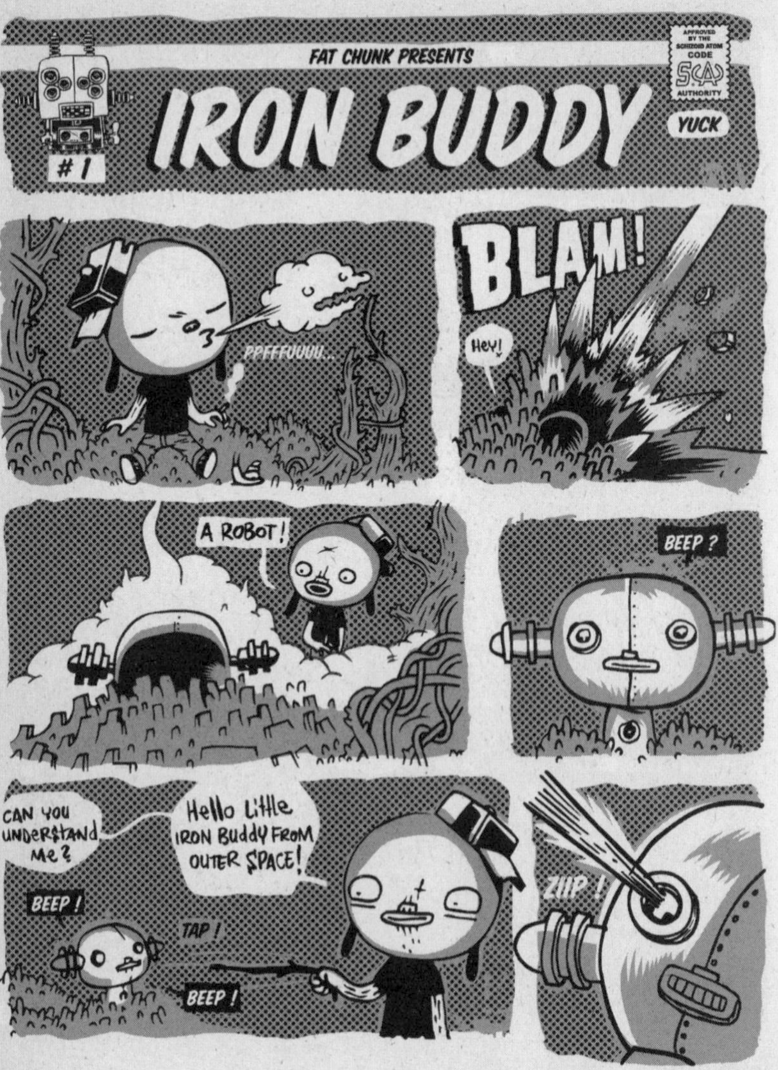
FAT CHUNK PRESENTS
IRON BUDDY
#1
APPROVED BY THE SCHIZOID ATOM CODE AUTHORITY
YUCK
PPFFFUUUU...
BLAM!
Hey!
A ROBOT!
BEEP ?
CAN YOU UNDERSTAND ME?
Hello Little IRON BUDDY FROM OUTER SPACE!
BEEP !
TAP !
BEEP !
ZIIP !

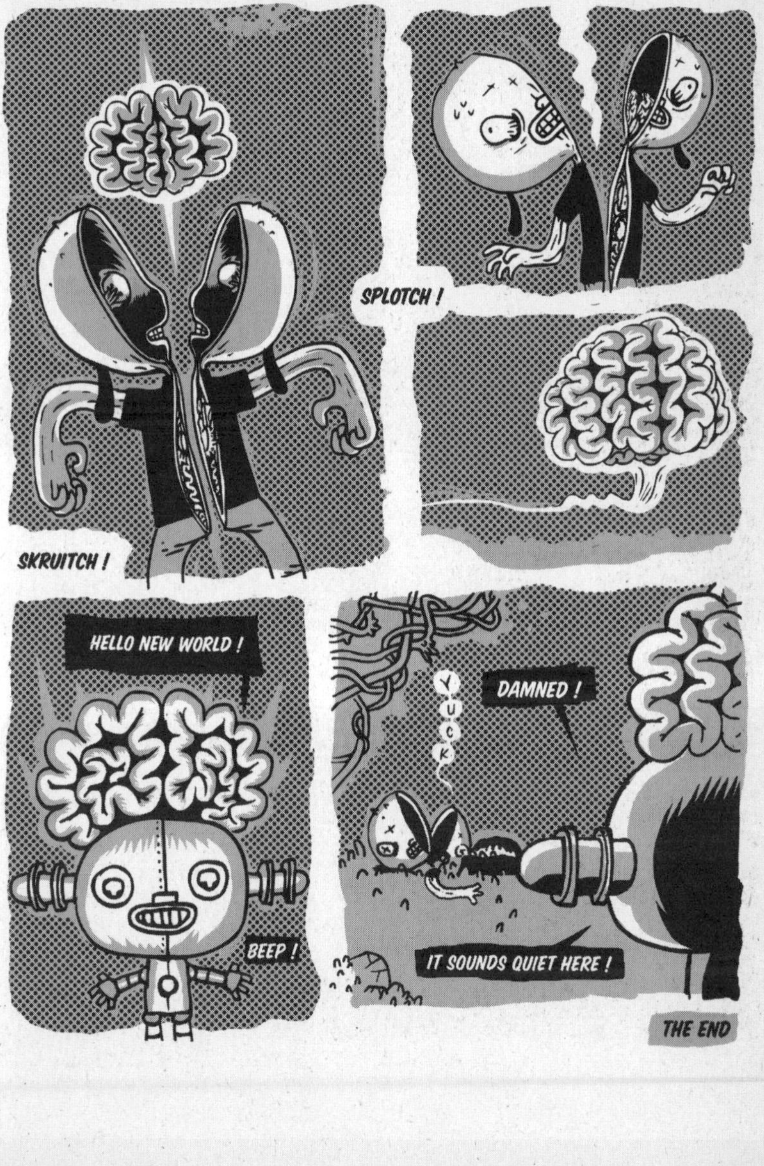
SKRUITCH !
SPLOTCH !
HELLO NEW WORLD !
BEEP !
Y U C K
DAMNED !
IT SOUNDS QUIET HERE !
THE END

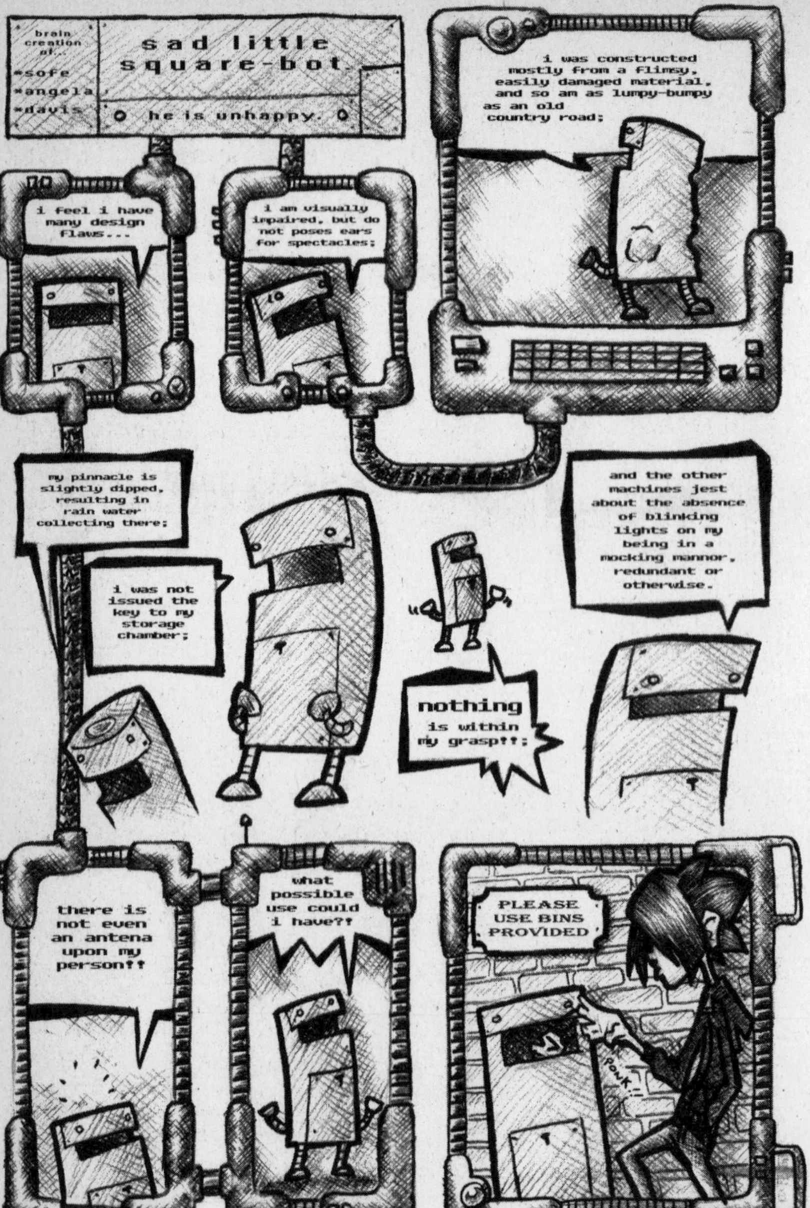
brain creation of...
*sofe
*angela
*davis
sad little square-bot.
he is unhappy.
i feel i have many design flaws...
i am visually impaired, but do not poses ears for spectacles;
i was constructed mostly from a flimsy, easily damaged material, and so am as lumpy-bumpy as an old country road;
my pinnacle is slightly dipped, resulting in rain water collecting there;
i was not issued the key to my storage chamber;
nothing is within my grasp!!;
and the other machines jest about the absence of blinking lights on my being in a mocking mannor, redundant or otherwise.
there is not even an antena upon my person!!
what possible use could i have??
PLEASE USE BINS PROVIDED
POWK!!

Delinquent Machine

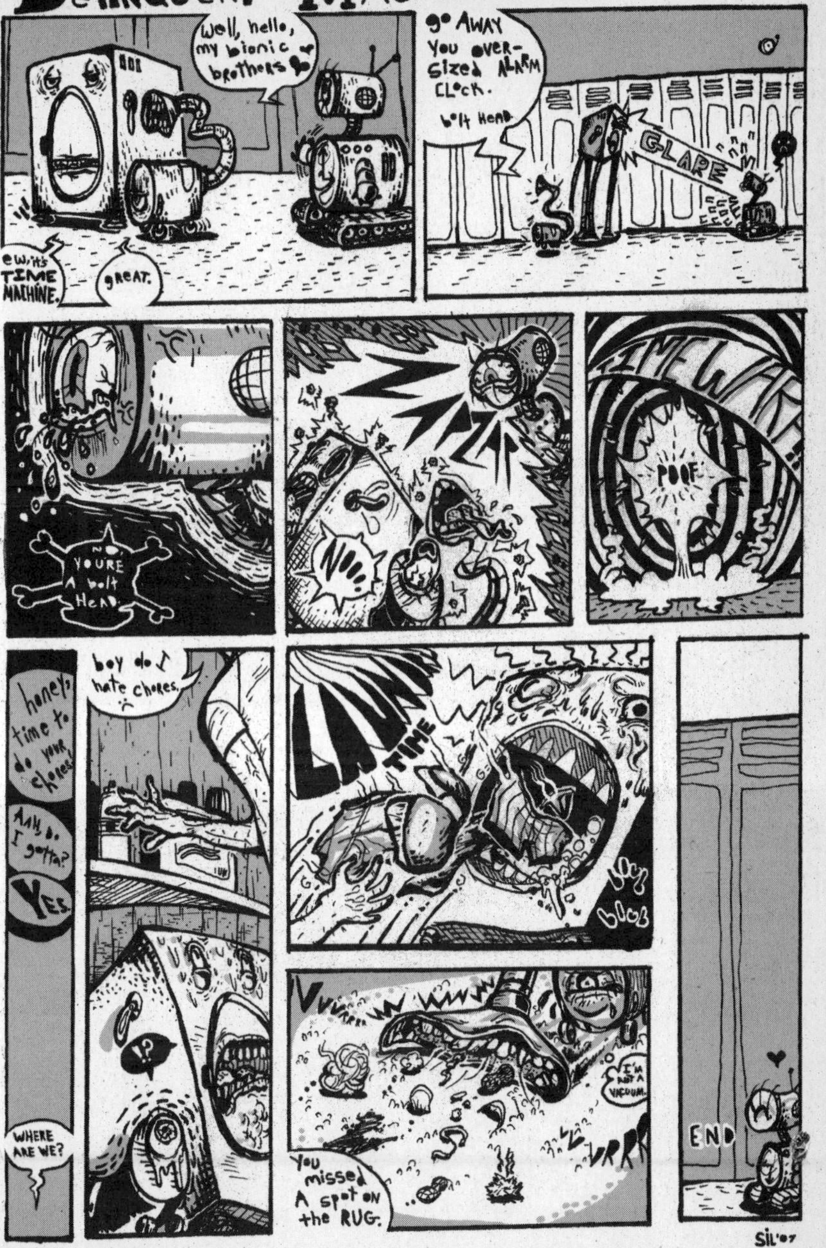
Well, hello, my bionic brothers
ew it's TIME MACHINE.
great.
go AWAY you over-sized ALARM CLOCK.
bolt HEAD.
GLARE
NO, YOU'RE A bolt HEAD.
NO...
POOF
honey, time to do your chores!
Aah, do I gotta?
YES.
boy do I hate chores.
WHERE ARE WE?
TIME
blob
I'm NOT A VACUUM.
You missed A spot on the RUG.
END
SiL'07

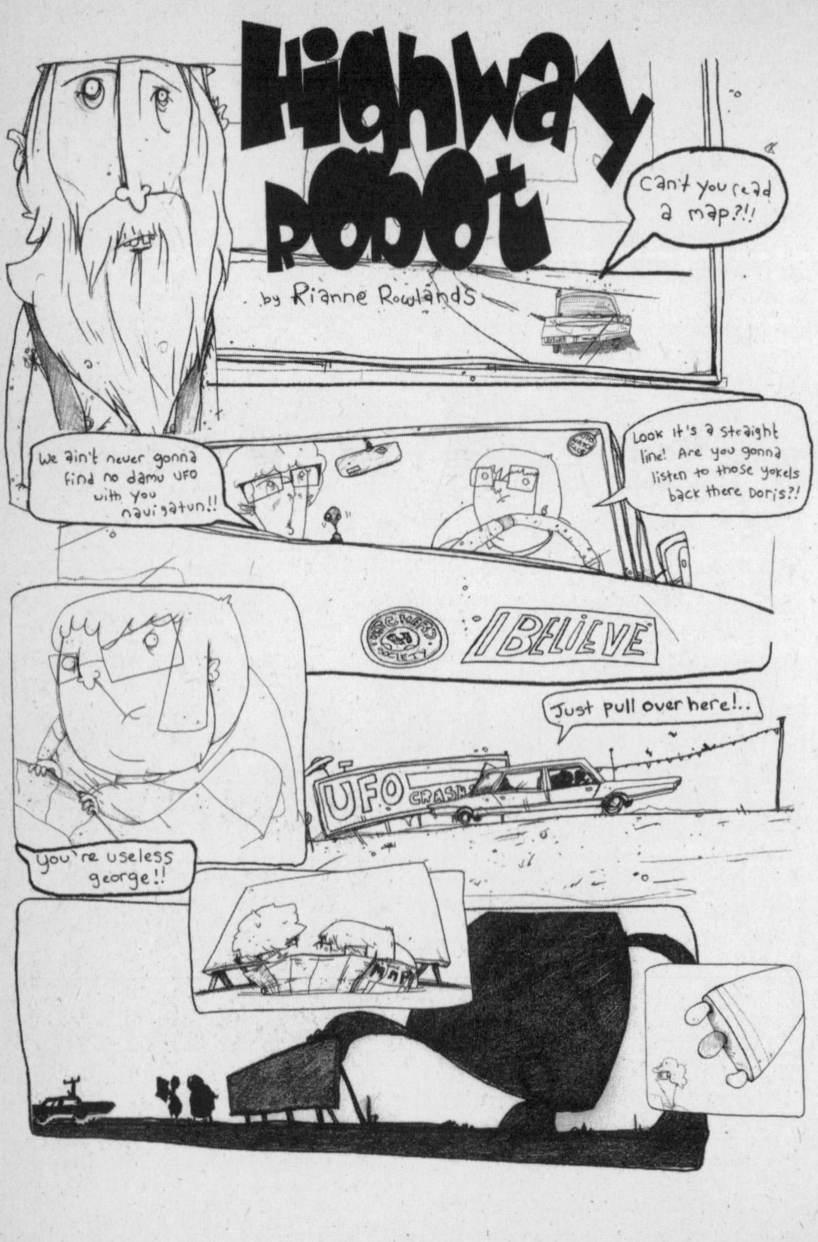

Highway Robot
by Rianne Rowlands
Can't you read a map?!!
We ain't never gonna find no damn UFO with you navigatun!!
Look it's a straight line! Are you gonna listen to those yokels back there Doris?!
I BELIEVE
Just pull over here!..
UFO CRASH
You're useless george!!

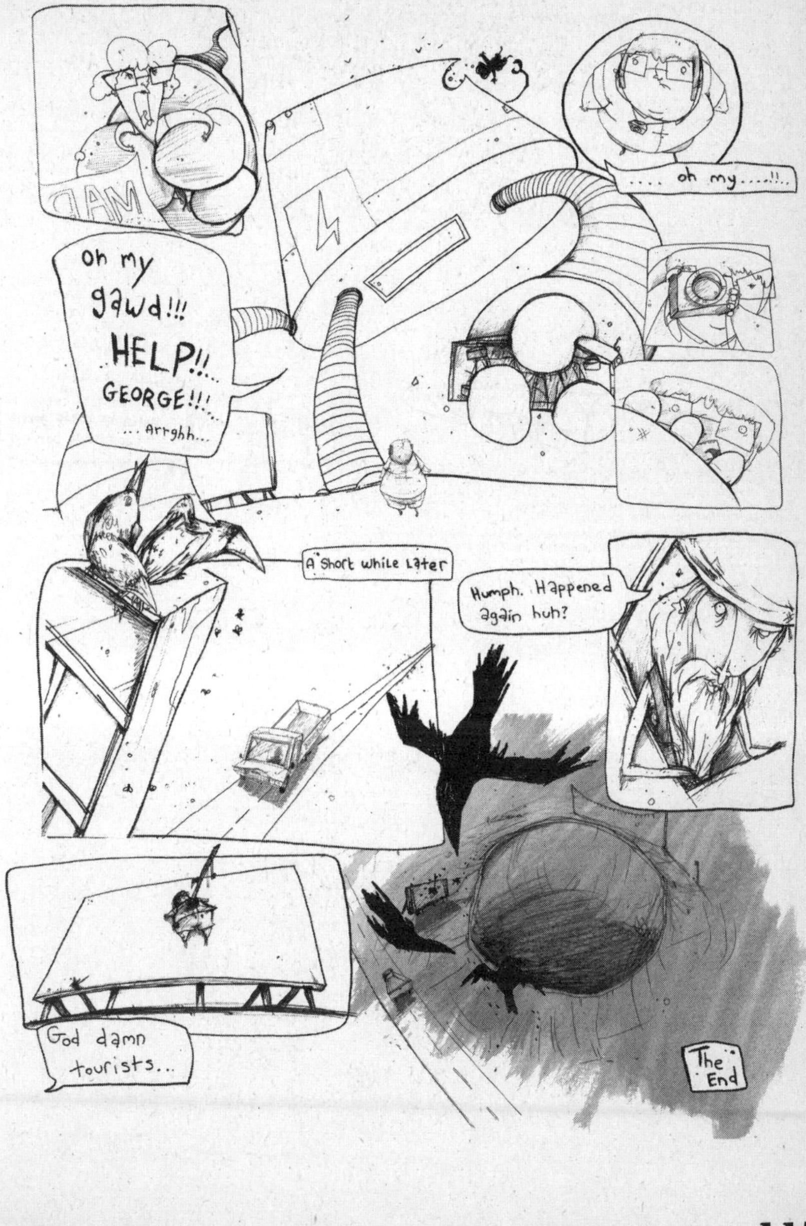
..... oh my.....!!
Oh my gawd!!! HELP!!!... GEORGE!!!... ...Arrghh...
A short while later
Humph. Happened again huh?
God damn tourists...
The End

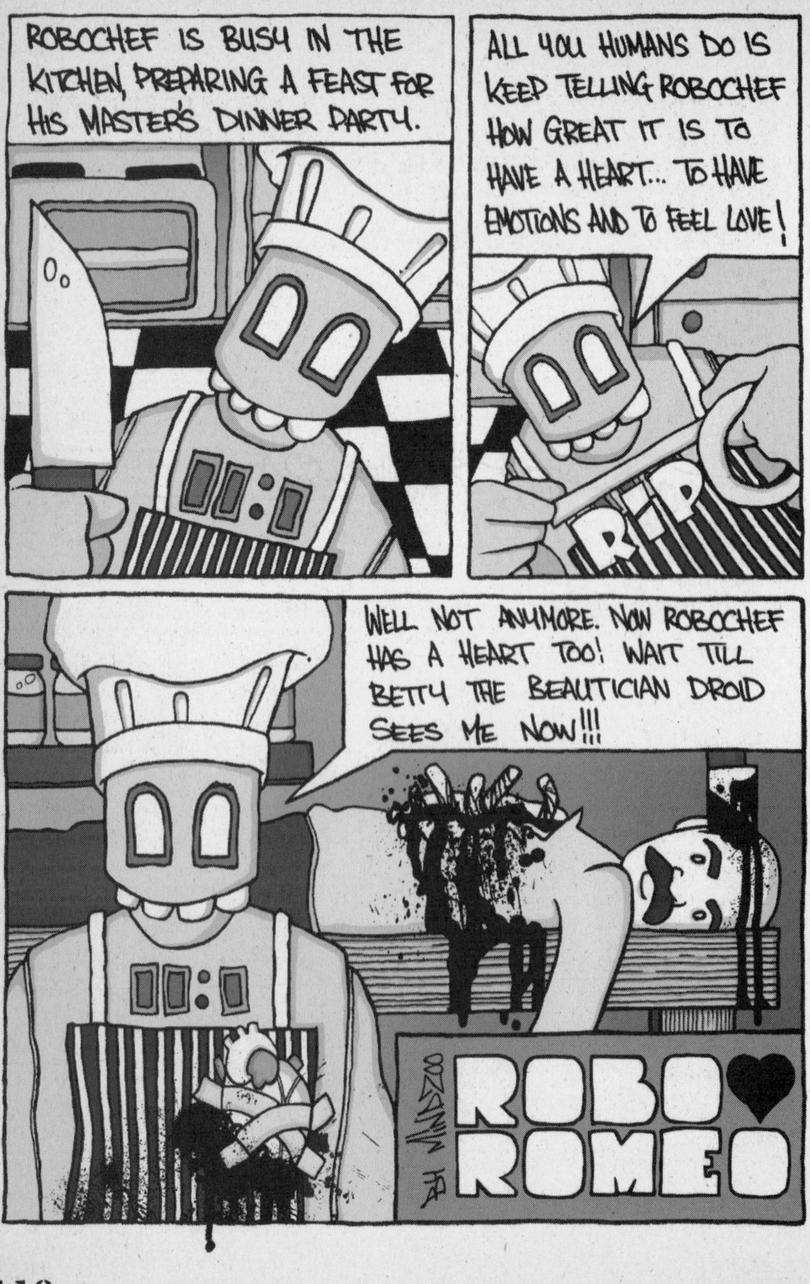
ROBOCHEF IS BUSY IN THE KITCHEN, PREPARING A FEAST FOR HIS MASTER'S DINNER PARTY.
ALL YOU HUMANS DO IS KEEP TELLING ROBOCHEF HOW GREAT IT IS TO HAVE A HEART... TO HAVE EMOTIONS AND TO FEEL LOVE!
RIP
WELL NOT ANYMORE. NOW ROBOCHEF HAS A HEART TOO! WAIT TILL BETTY THE BEAUTICIAN DROID SEES ME NOW!!!
ROBO ♥ ROMEO

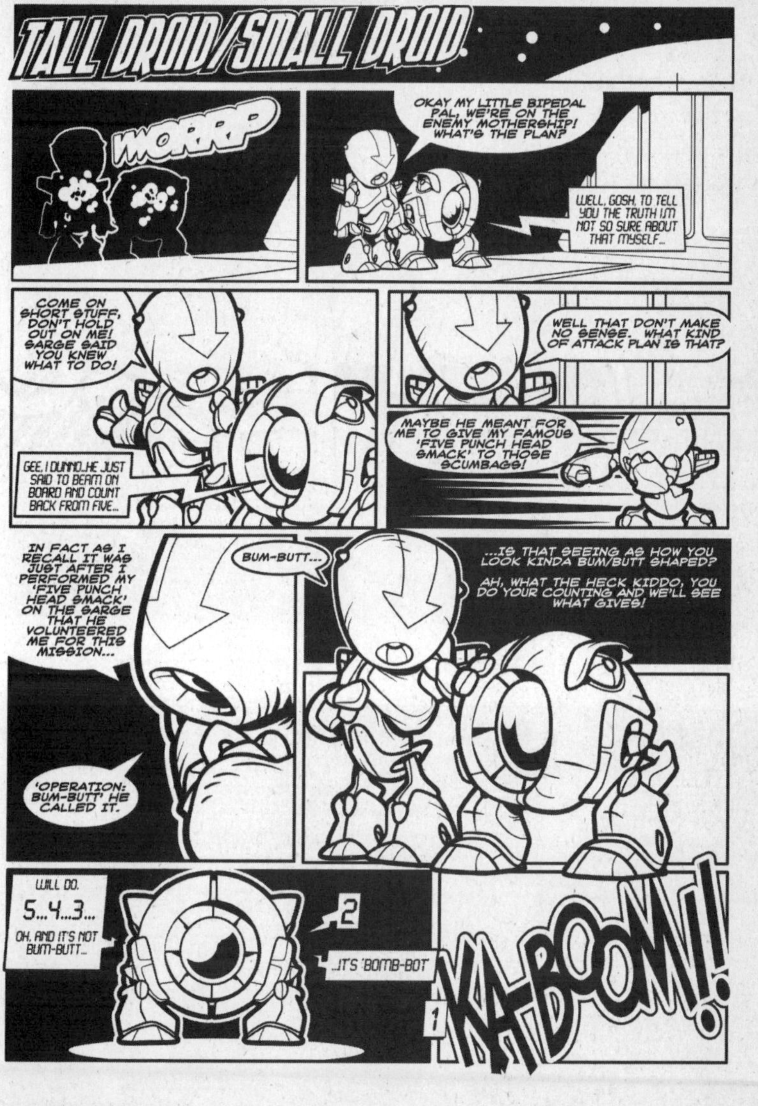
TALL DROID/SMALL DROID
WORRP
OKAY MY LITTLE BIPEDAL PAL, WE'RE ON THE ENEMY MOTHERSHIP! WHAT'S THE PLAN?
WELL, GOSH. TO TELL YOU THE TRUTH I'M NOT SO SURE ABOUT THAT MYSELF...
COME ON SHORT STUFF, DON'T HOLD OUT ON ME! SARGE SAID YOU KNEW WHAT TO DO!
GEE, I DUNNO..HE JUST SAID TO BEAM ON BOARD AND COUNT BACK FROM FIVE...
WELL THAT DON'T MAKE NO SENSE. WHAT KIND OF ATTACK PLAN IS THAT?
MAYBE HE MEANT FOR ME TO GIVE MY FAMOUS 'FIVE PUNCH HEAD SMACK' TO THOSE SCUMBAGS!
IN FACT AS I RECALL IT WAS JUST AFTER I PERFORMED MY 'FIVE PUNCH HEAD SMACK' ON THE SARGE THAT HE VOLUNTEERED ME FOR THIS MISSION...
'OPERATION: BUM-BUTT' HE CALLED IT.
BUM-BUTT...
...IS THAT SEEING AS HOW YOU LOOK KINDA BUM/BUTT SHAPED?
AH, WHAT THE HECK KIDDO, YOU DO YOUR COUNTING AND WE'LL SEE WHAT GIVES!
WILL DO.
5...4...3...
OH, AND IT'S NOT BUM-BUTT...
2
...IT'S 'BOMB-BOT'
1
KA-BOOM!!

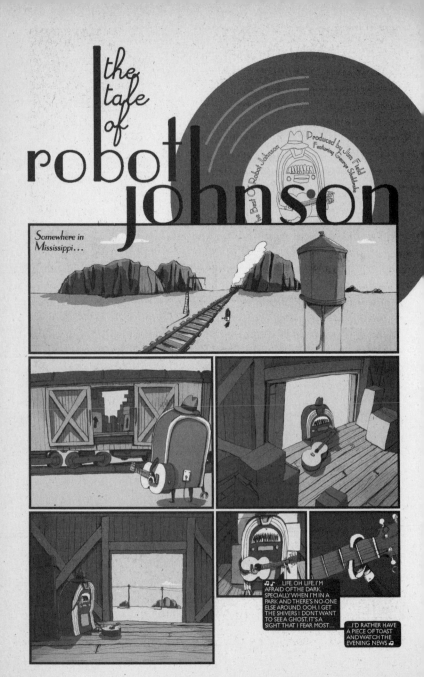

the tale of robot JOHNSON

The Best of Robot Johnson

Produced by Jim Field
Featuring Georgy Stebbck

Somewhere in Mississippi…

♪♫ LIFE. OH LIFE. I'M AFRAID OF THE DARK. SPECIALLY WHEN I'M IN A PARK AND THERE'S NO-ONE ELSE AROUND. OOH, I GET THE SHIVERS I DON'T WANT TO SEE A GHOST. IT'S A SIGHT THAT I FEAR MOST…

…I'D RATHER HAVE A PIECE OF TOAST AND WATCH THE EVENING NEWS ♫♪

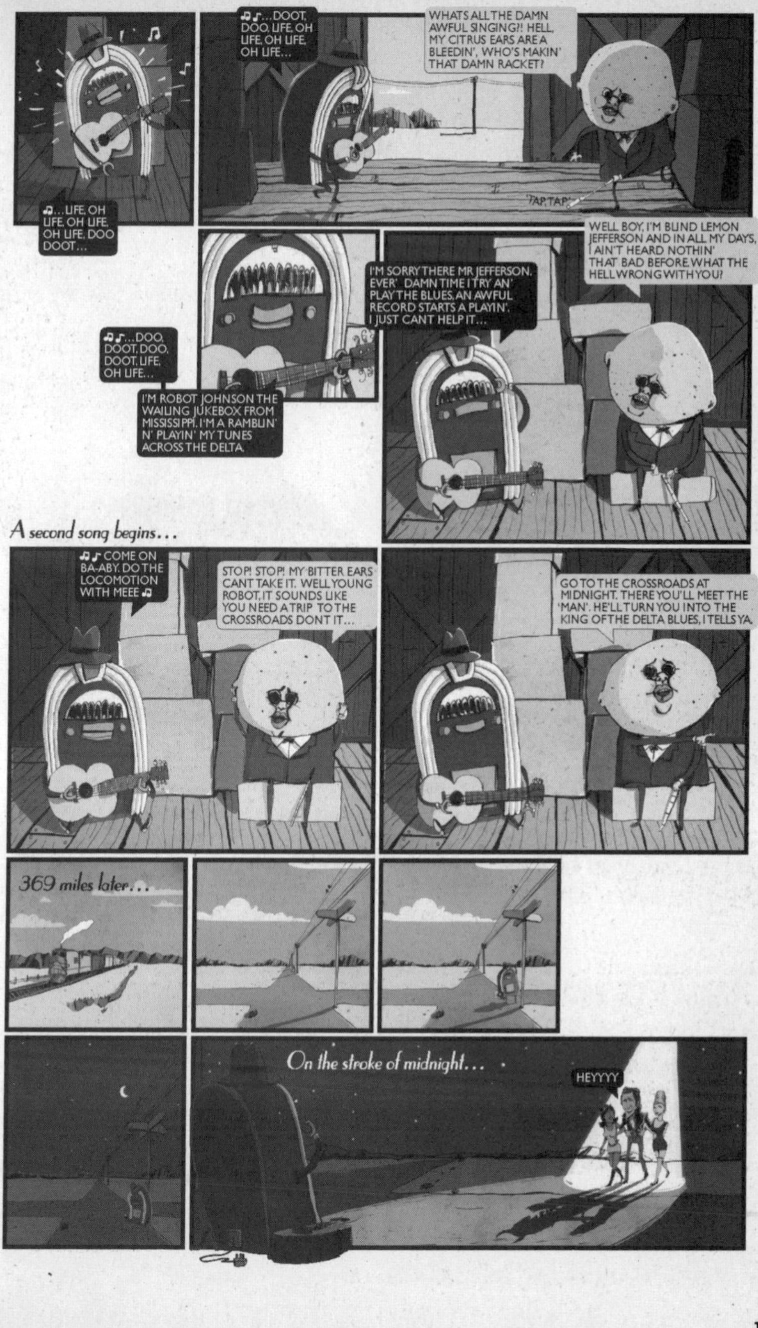
♫♪…DOOT, DOO, LIFE, OH LIFE, OH LIFE, OH LIFE…
WHATS ALL THE DAMN AWFUL SINGING?! HELL, MY CITRUS EARS ARE A BLEEDIN', WHO'S MAKIN' THAT DAMN RACKET?
'TAP, TAP'
♫…LIFE, OH LIFE, OH LIFE, OH LIFE, DOO DOOT…
♫♪…DOO, DOOT, DOO, DOOT, LIFE, OH LIFE…
I'M ROBOT JOHNSON THE WAILING JUKEBOX FROM MISSISSIPPI. I'M A RAMBLIN' N' PLAYIN' MY TUNES ACROSS THE DELTA.
WELL BOY, I'M BLIND LEMON JEFFERSON AND IN ALL MY DAYS, I AIN'T HEARD NOTHIN' THAT BAD BEFORE. WHAT THE HELL WRONG WITH YOU?
I'M SORRY THERE MR JEFFERSON. EVER' DAMN TIME I TRY AN' PLAY THE BLUES, AN AWFUL RECORD STARTS A PLAYIN'. I JUST CANT HELP IT…
A second song begins…
♫♪ COME ON BA-ABY. DO THE LOCOMOTION WITH MEEE ♫
STOP! STOP! MY BITTER EARS CANT TAKE IT. WELL YOUNG ROBOT, IT SOUNDS LIKE YOU NEED A TRIP TO THE CROSSROADS DONT IT…
GO TO THE CROSSROADS AT MIDNIGHT. THERE YOU'LL MEET THE 'MAN'. HE'LL TURN YOU INTO THE KING OF THE DELTA BLUES, I TELLS YA.
369 miles later…
On the stroke of midnight…
HEYYYY

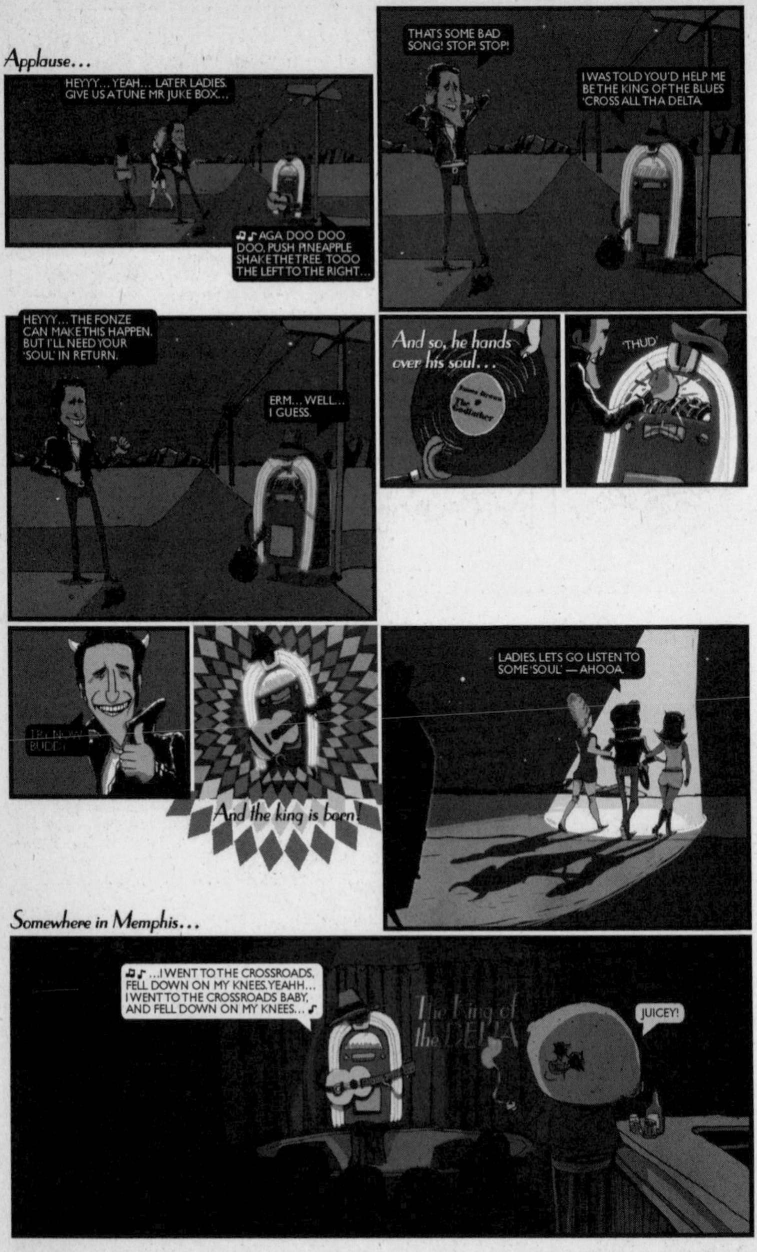
Applause...
HEYYY... YEAH... LATER LADIES. GIVE US A TUNE MR JUKE BOX...
♫♪ AGA DOO DOO DOO. PUSH PINEAPPLE SHAKE THE TREE. TOOO THE LEFT TO THE RIGHT...
THATS SOME BAD SONG! STOP! STOP!
I WAS TOLD YOU'D HELP ME BE THE KING OF THE BLUES 'CROSS ALL THA DELTA.
HEYYY... THE FONZE CAN MAKE THIS HAPPEN. BUT I'LL NEED YOUR 'SOUL' IN RETURN.
ERM... WELL... I GUESS.
And so, he hands over his soul...
'THUD'
And the king is born!
LADIES. LETS GO LISTEN TO SOME 'SOUL' — AHOOA.
Somewhere in Memphis...
♫♪ ...I WENT TO THE CROSSROADS, FELL DOWN ON MY KNEES. YEAHH... I WENT TO THE CROSSROADS BABY, AND FELL DOWN ON MY KNEES... ♪
JUICEY!

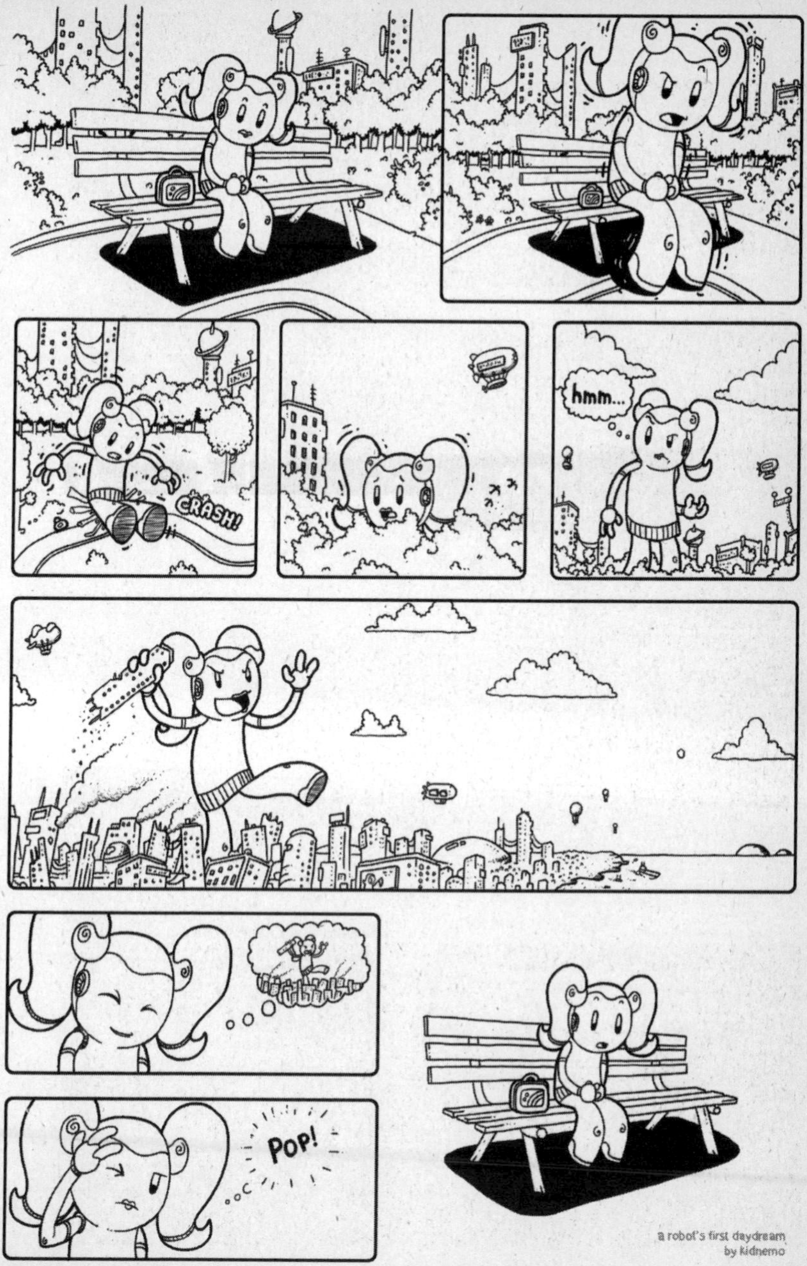
CRASH!
hmm...
POP!
a robot's first daydream
by kidnemo

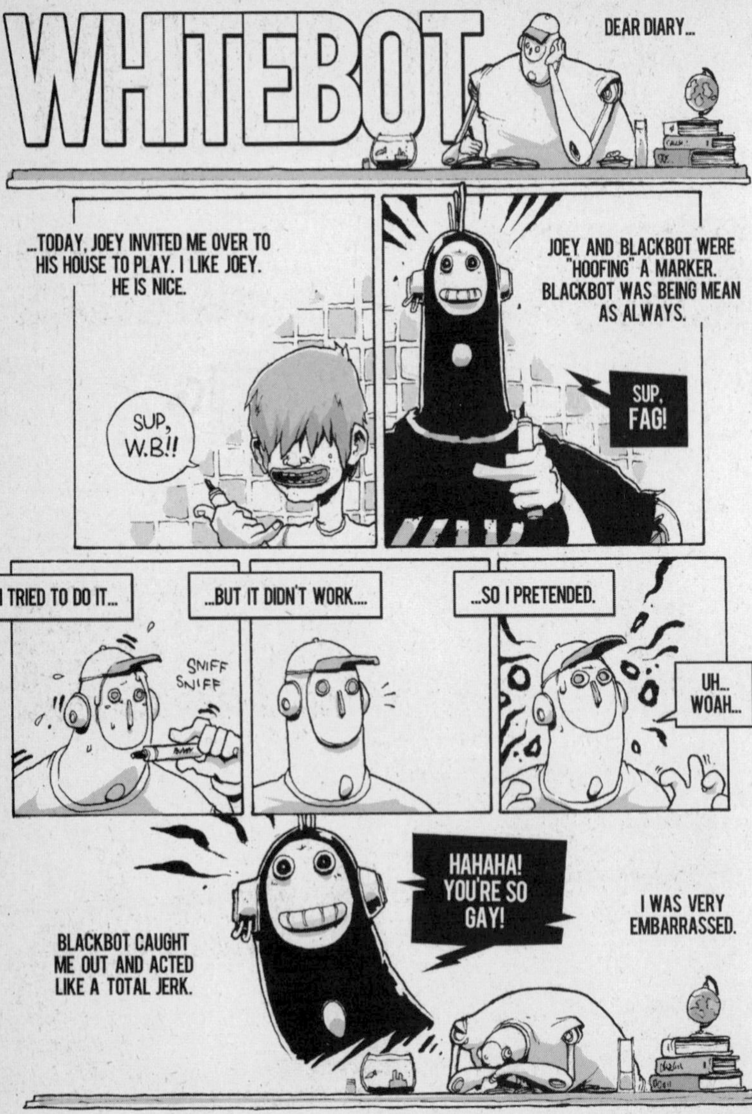
WHITEBOT
DEAR DIARY...
...TODAY, JOEY INVITED ME OVER TO HIS HOUSE TO PLAY. I LIKE JOEY. HE IS NICE.
SUP, W.B!!
JOEY AND BLACKBOT WERE "HOOFING" A MARKER. BLACKBOT WAS BEING MEAN AS ALWAYS.
SUP, FAG!
I TRIED TO DO IT...
SNIFF SNIFF
...BUT IT DIDN'T WORK....
...SO I PRETENDED.
UH... WOAH...
BLACKBOT CAUGHT ME OUT AND ACTED LIKE A TOTAL JERK.
HAHAHA! YOU'RE SO GAY!
I WAS VERY EMBARRASSED.

BY SHELDON VELLA / 1984CUSTOM.RESPARK.NET

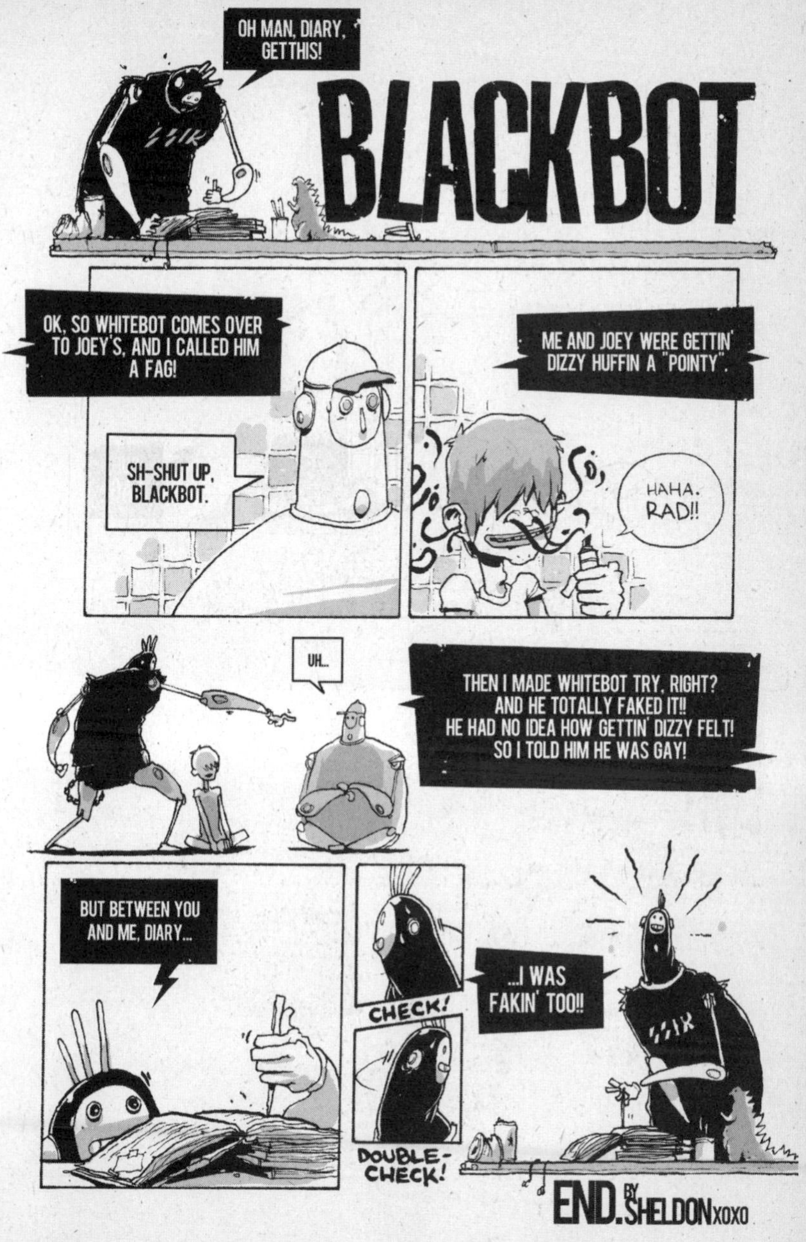
OH MAN, DIARY, GET THIS!
BLACKBOT
OK, SO WHITEBOT COMES OVER TO JOEY'S, AND I CALLED HIM A FAG!
SH-SHUT UP, BLACKBOT.
ME AND JOEY WERE GETTIN' DIZZY HUFFIN A "POINTY".
HAHA. RAD!!
UH...
THEN I MADE WHITEBOT TRY, RIGHT? AND HE TOTALLY FAKED IT!! HE HAD NO IDEA HOW GETTIN' DIZZY FELT! SO I TOLD HIM HE WAS GAY!
BUT BETWEEN YOU AND ME, DIARY...
CHECK!
DOUBLE-CHECK!
...I WAS FAKIN' TOO!!
END. BY SHELDON XOXO

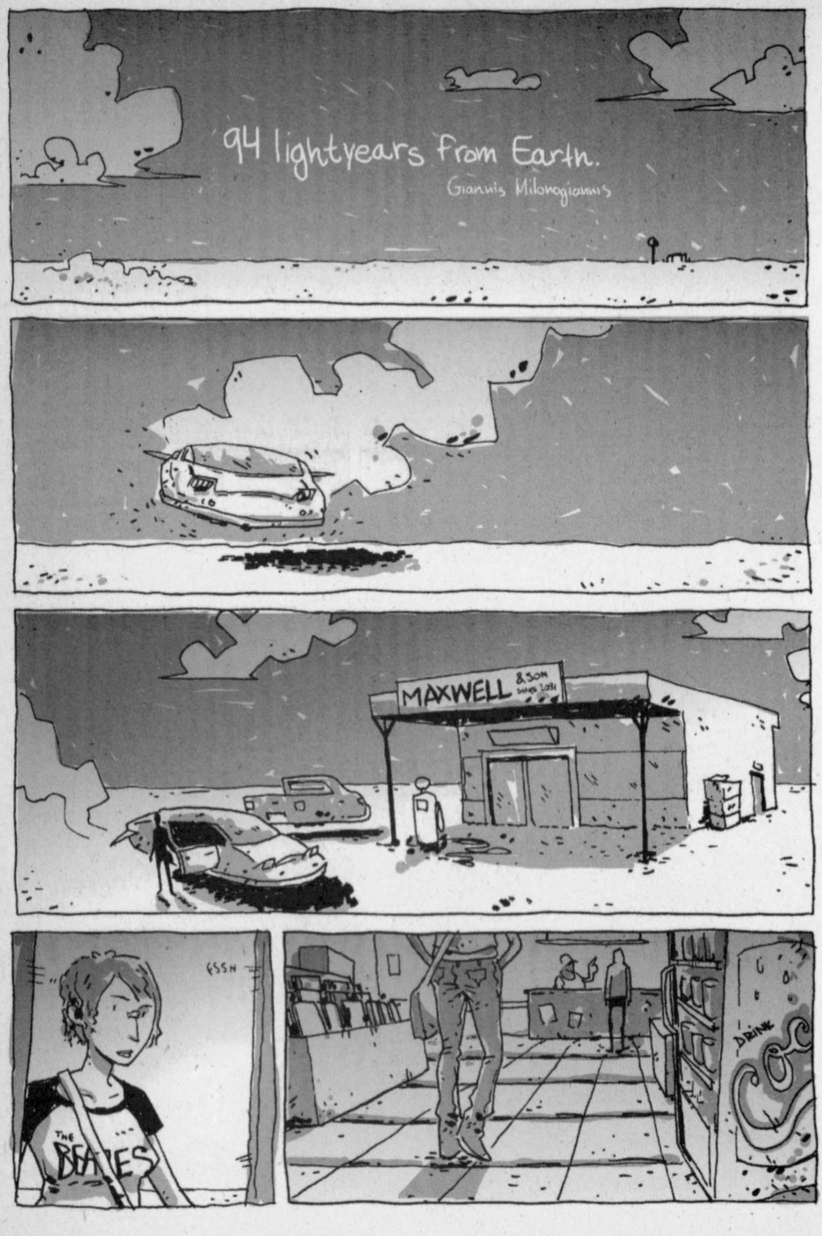
94 lightyears from Earth.
Giannis Milonogiannis
MAXWELL &SON SINCE 2081
ESSH
DRINK

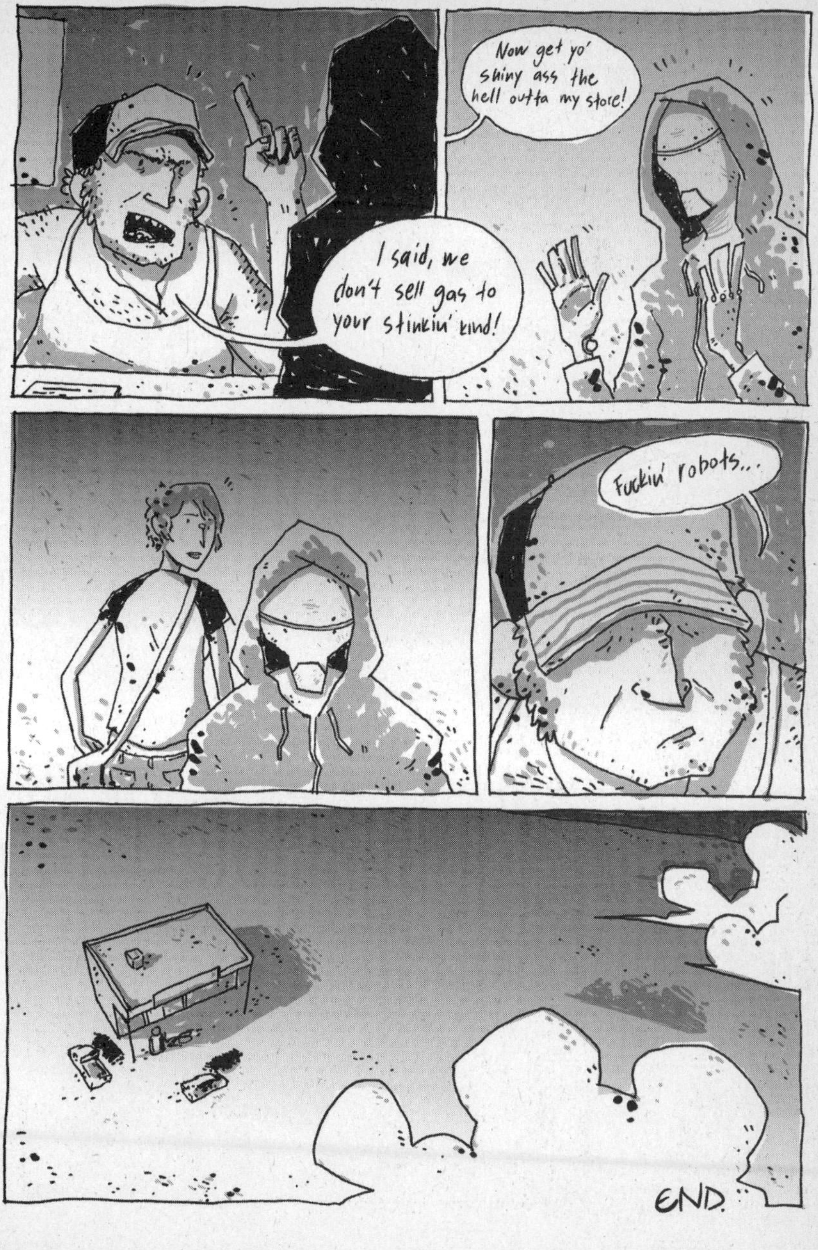
I said, we don't sell gas to your stinkin' kind!
Now get yo' shiny ass the hell outta my store!
Fuckin' robots...
END.

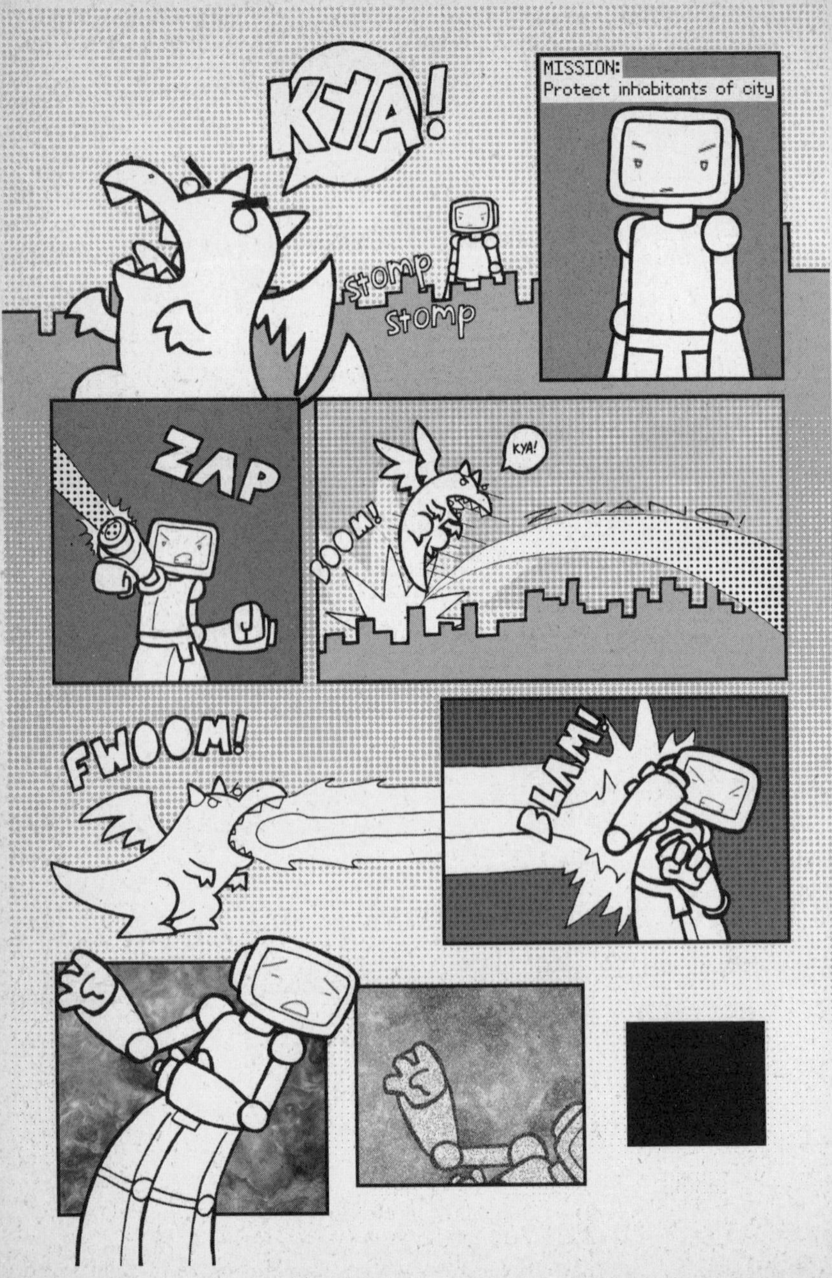
KYA!
MISSION:
Protect inhabitants of city
stomp
stomp
ZAP
KYA!
BOOM!
FWOOM!
BLAM!

BY DR.SALT-CAIRN MCDONALD / DRSALT.DEVIANTART.COM

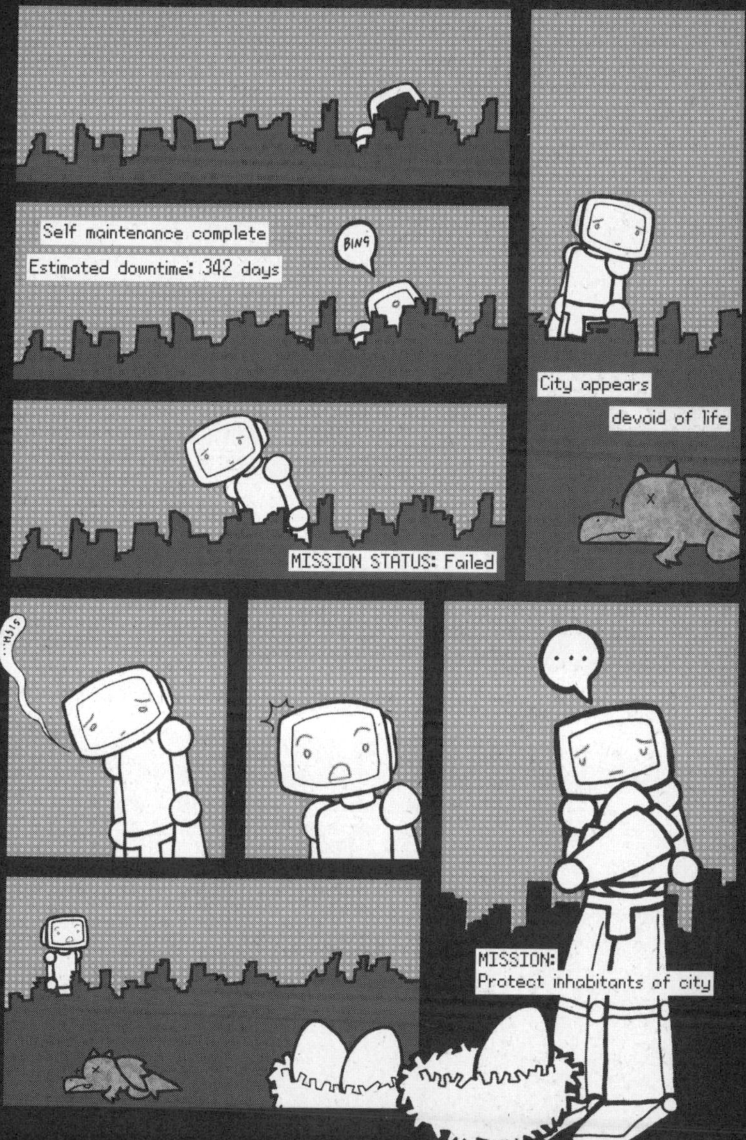

Self maintenance complete
Estimated downtime: 342 days
BING
City appears
devoid of life
MISSION STATUS: Failed
SIGH...
...
MISSION:
Protect inhabitants of city

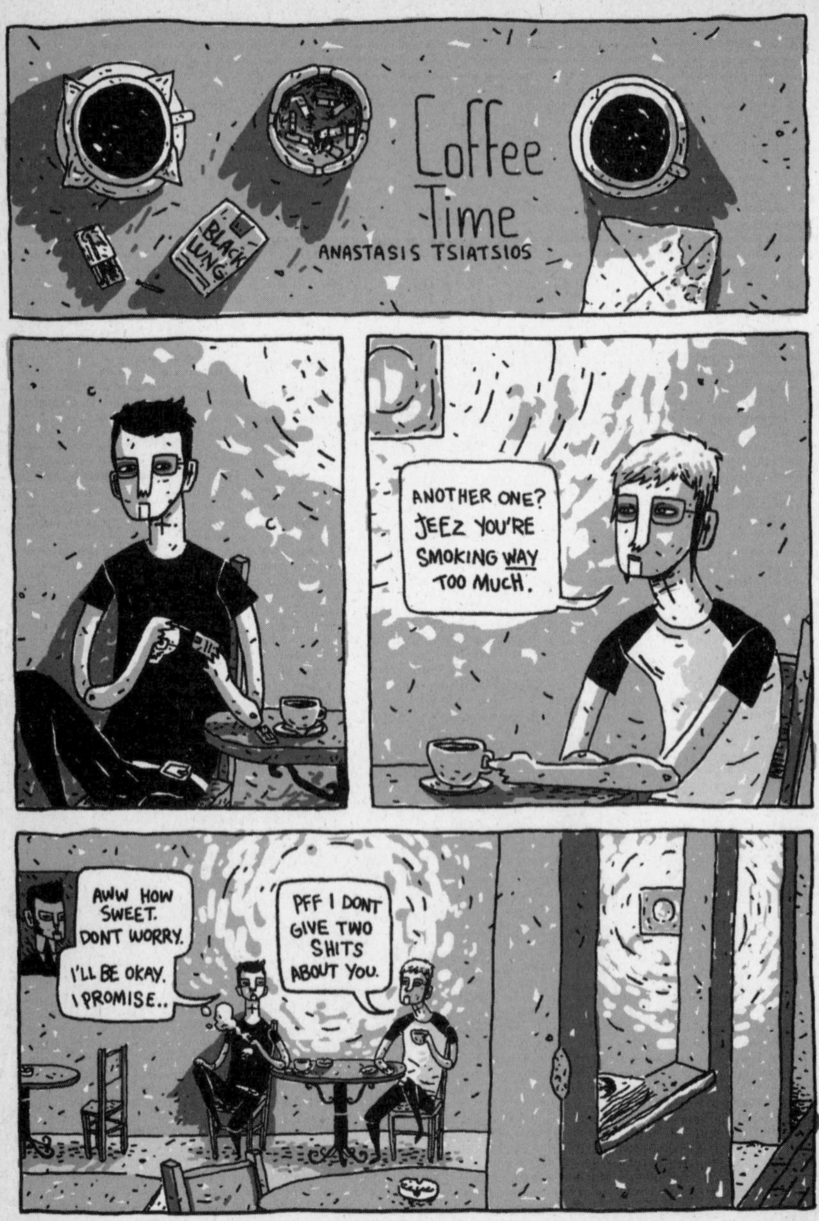
Coffee Time
ANASTASIS TSIATSIOS
BLACK LUNG
ANOTHER ONE? JEEZ YOU'RE SMOKING WAY TOO MUCH.
AWW HOW SWEET. DONT WORRY.
I'LL BE OKAY. I PROMISE..
PFF I DONT GIVE TWO SHITS ABOUT YOU.

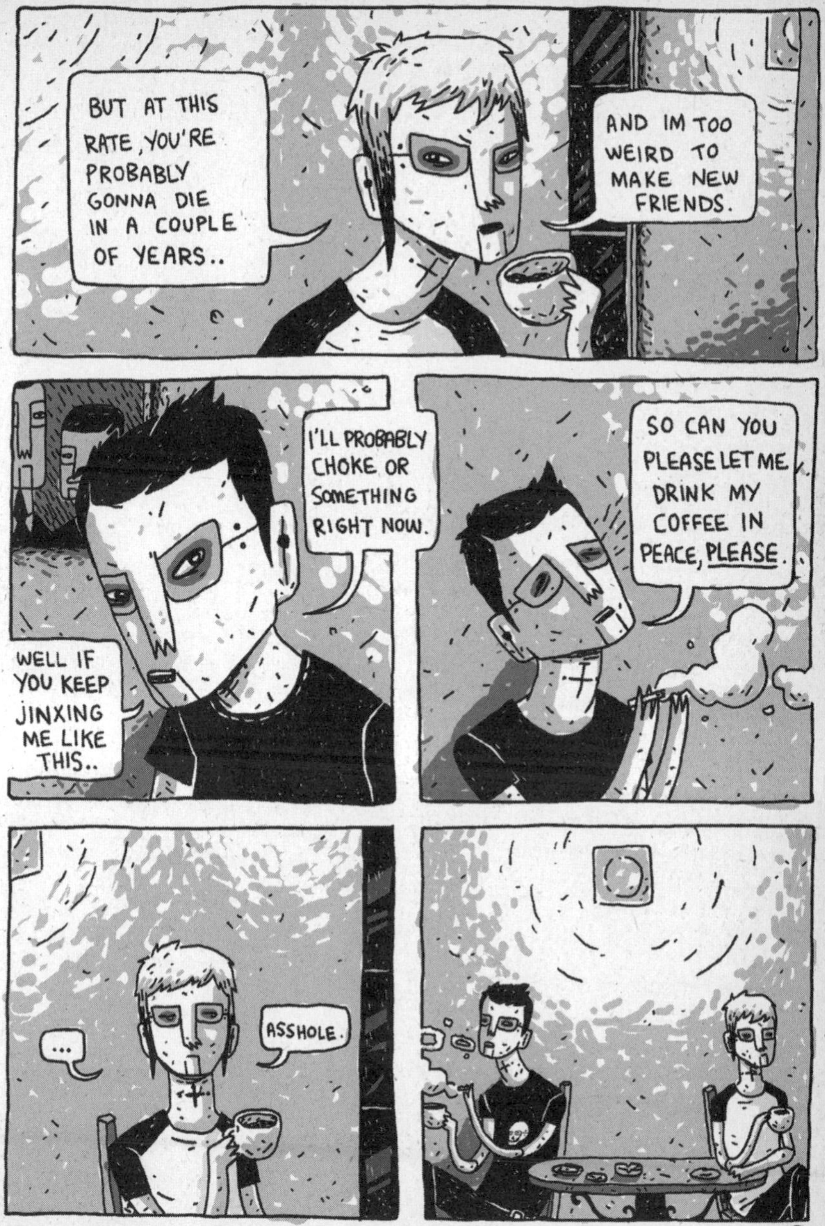
BUT AT THIS RATE, YOU'RE PROBABLY GONNA DIE IN A COUPLE OF YEARS..
AND IM TOO WEIRD TO MAKE NEW FRIENDS.
I'LL PROBABLY CHOKE OR SOMETHING RIGHT NOW.
WELL IF YOU KEEP JINXING ME LIKE THIS..
SO CAN YOU PLEASE LET ME DRINK MY COFFEE IN PEACE, PLEASE.
...
ASSHOLE.
END

BY: DUST / DIRTYDUST.DE

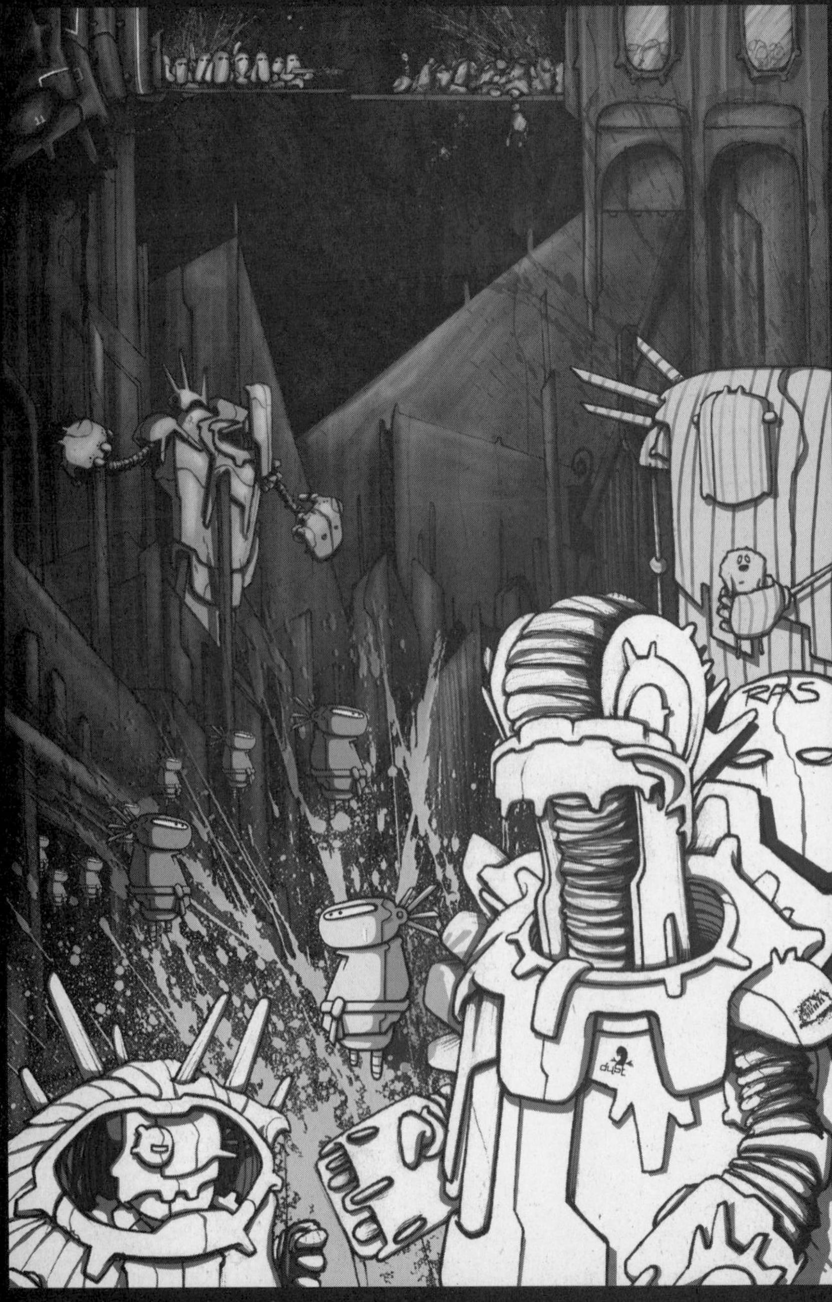
RAS

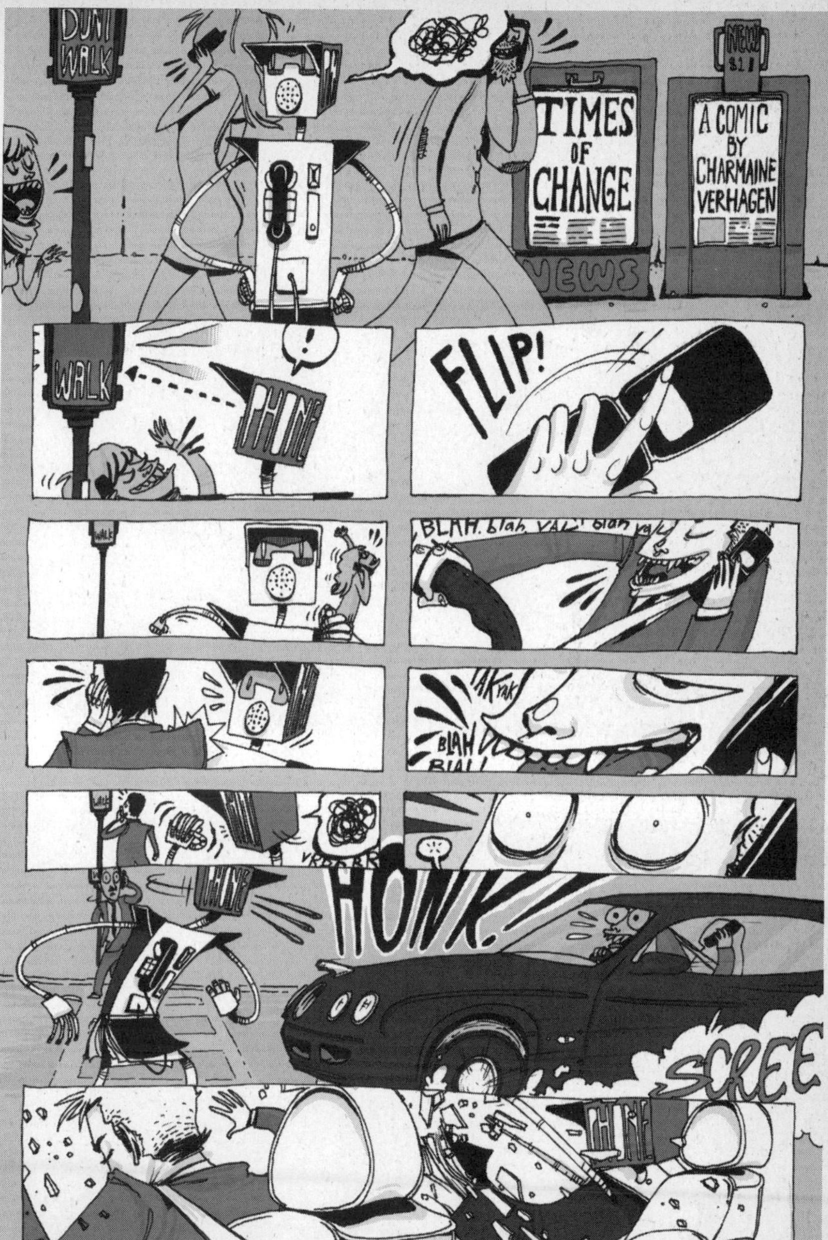
WALK
TIMES OF CHANGE
NEWS
A COMIC BY CHARMAINE VERHAGEN
WALK
!
FLIP!
BLAH. blah, YAK
HONK!
SCREE

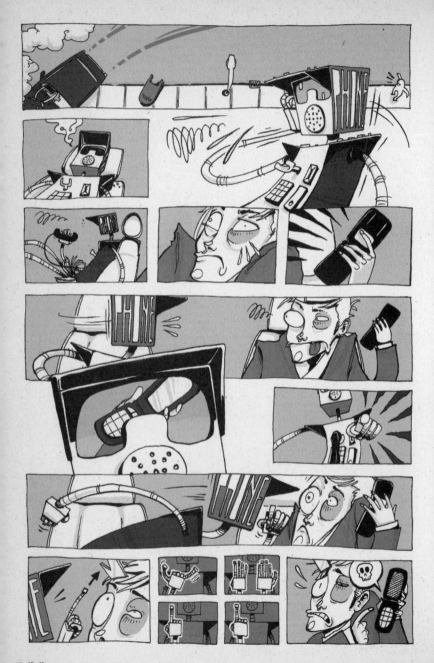

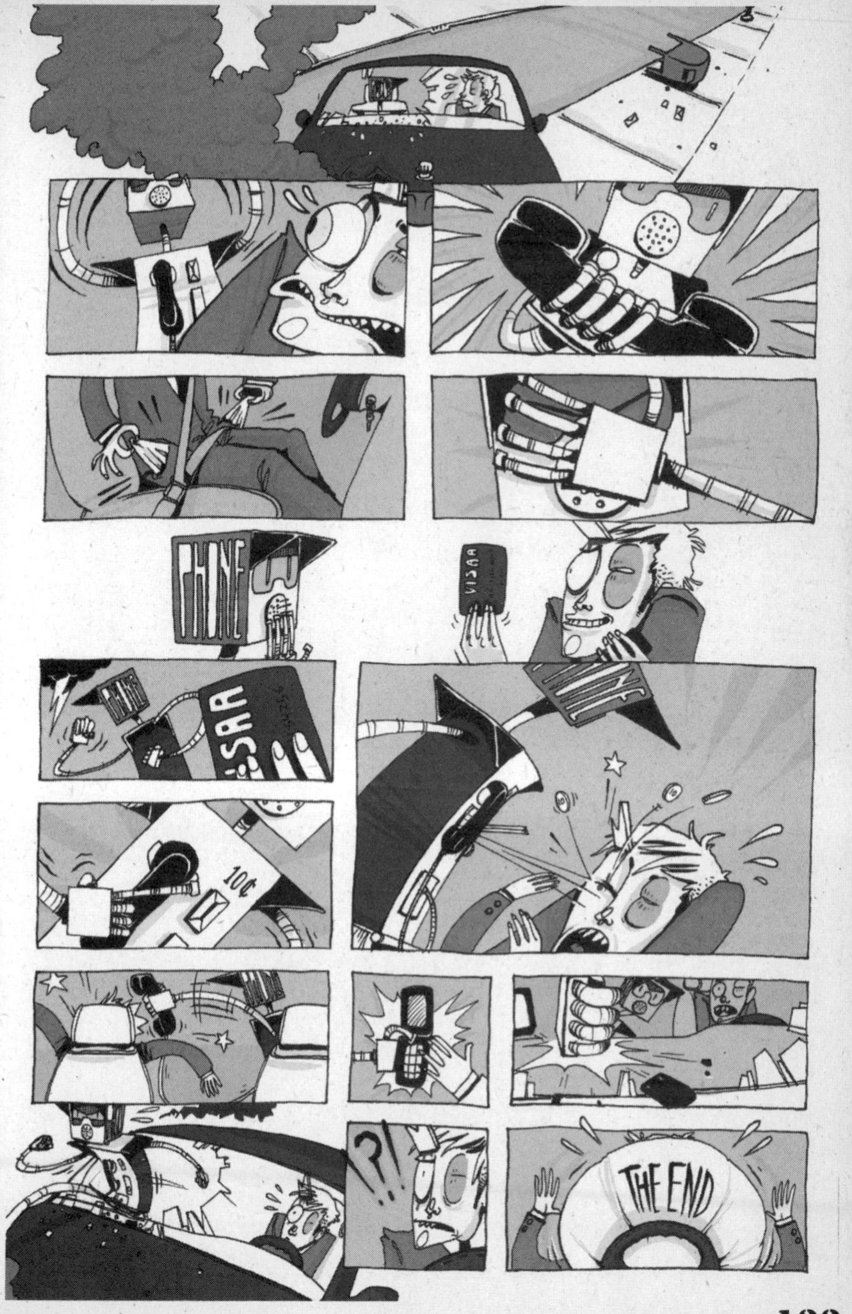
PHONE
VISAA
VISAA
10¢
THE END

PLASTIC DAYDREAMS
story+art:mark ganzon

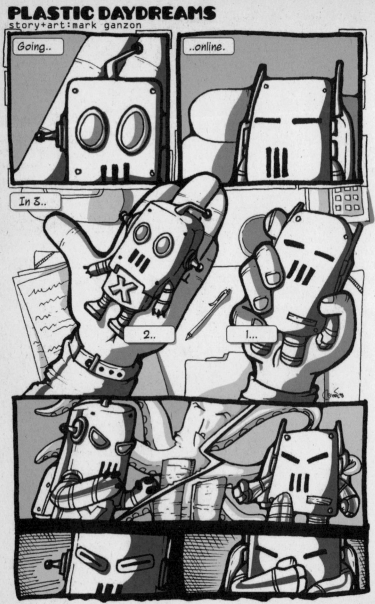

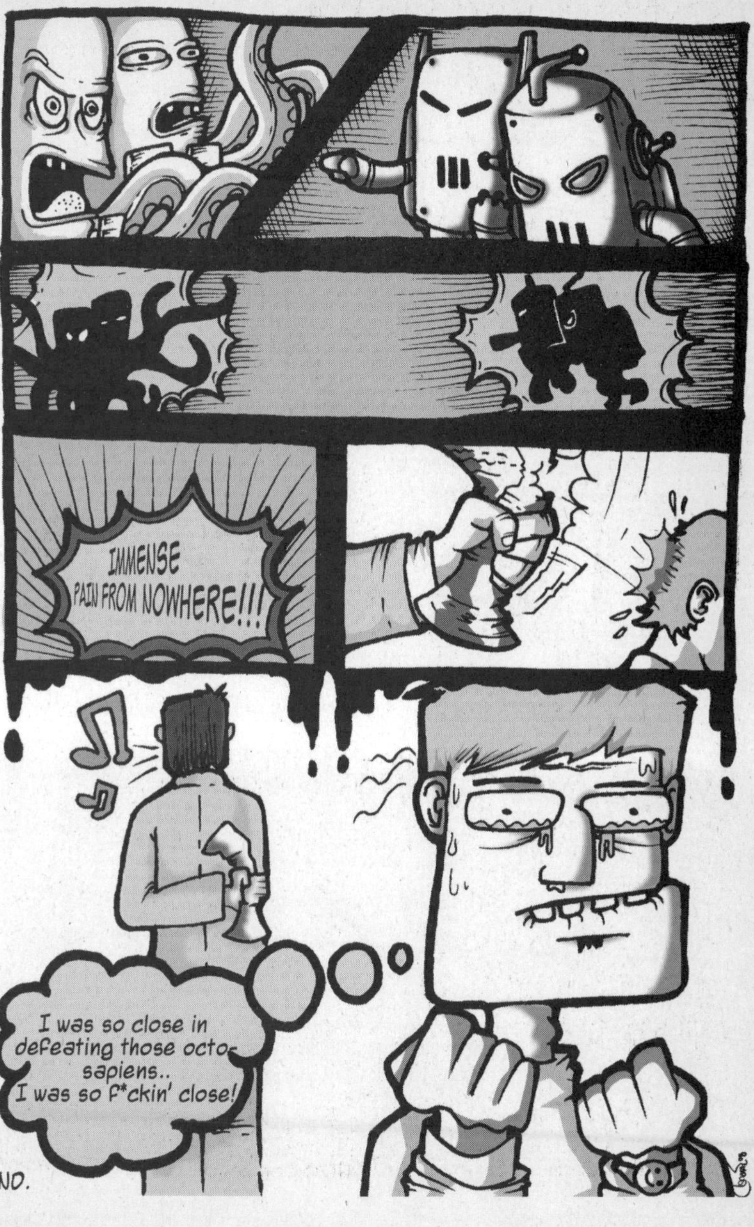
IMMENSE
PAIN FROM NOWHERE!!!
I was so close in defeating those octo-sapiens..
I was so f*ckin' close!
END.

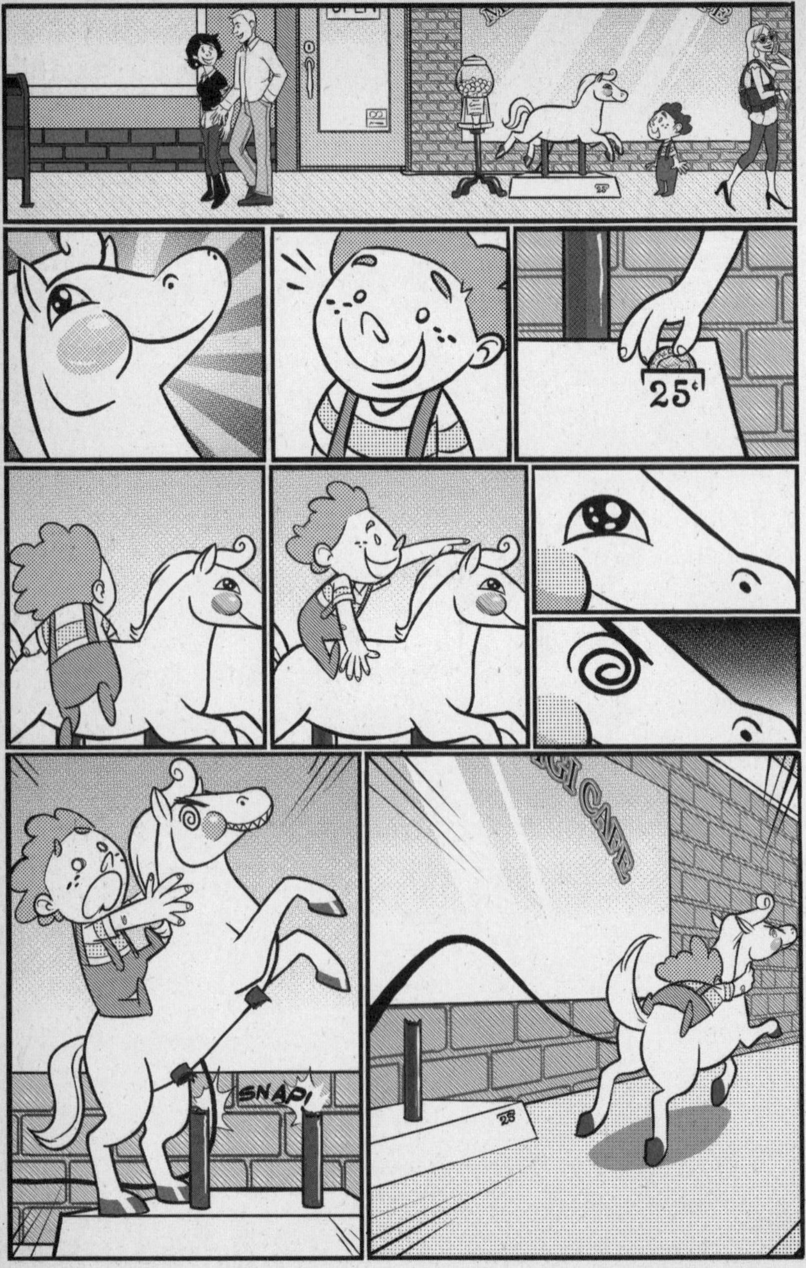
25¢
SNAP!

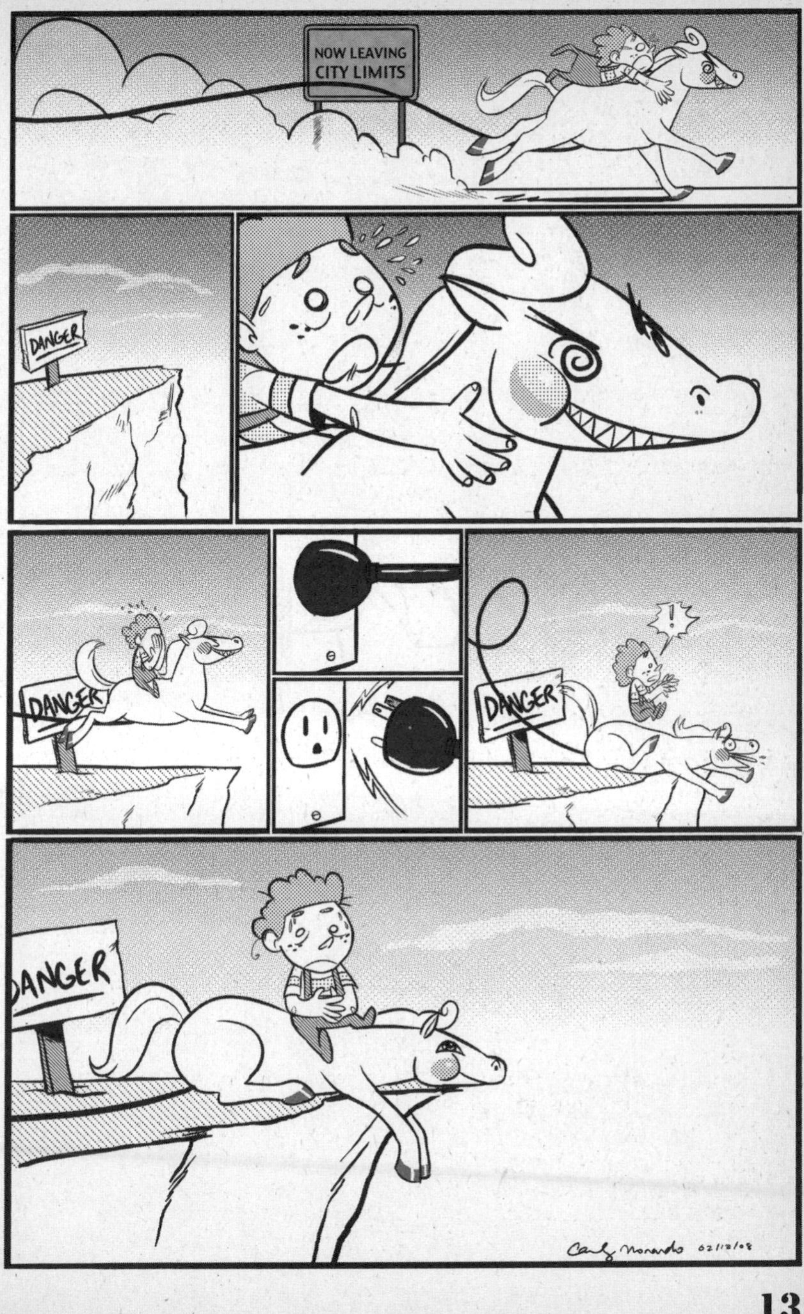
NOW LEAVING
CITY LIMITS
DANGER
DANGER
DANGER
!
DANGER
Carly Monardo 02/13/08

FOLD-A-BOT

Photocopy the page with the model or download the PDF from www.marshallalexander.net and print it out. Cut out the model and score all the foldlines. Don't forget to cut the lines at the top and bottom of the eyes. Fold over and glue A-parts to create the limbs. Put glue on back of B-parts and stick to inside of head (C-part). Glue the head (D) together while pushing the eyes inwards and MAKE SURE the arms are inside the head. Then glue E-part to the head so arms will stick out left and right of it. Now glue the body (F) together and glue G-parts to E-part to fix the body to the head.

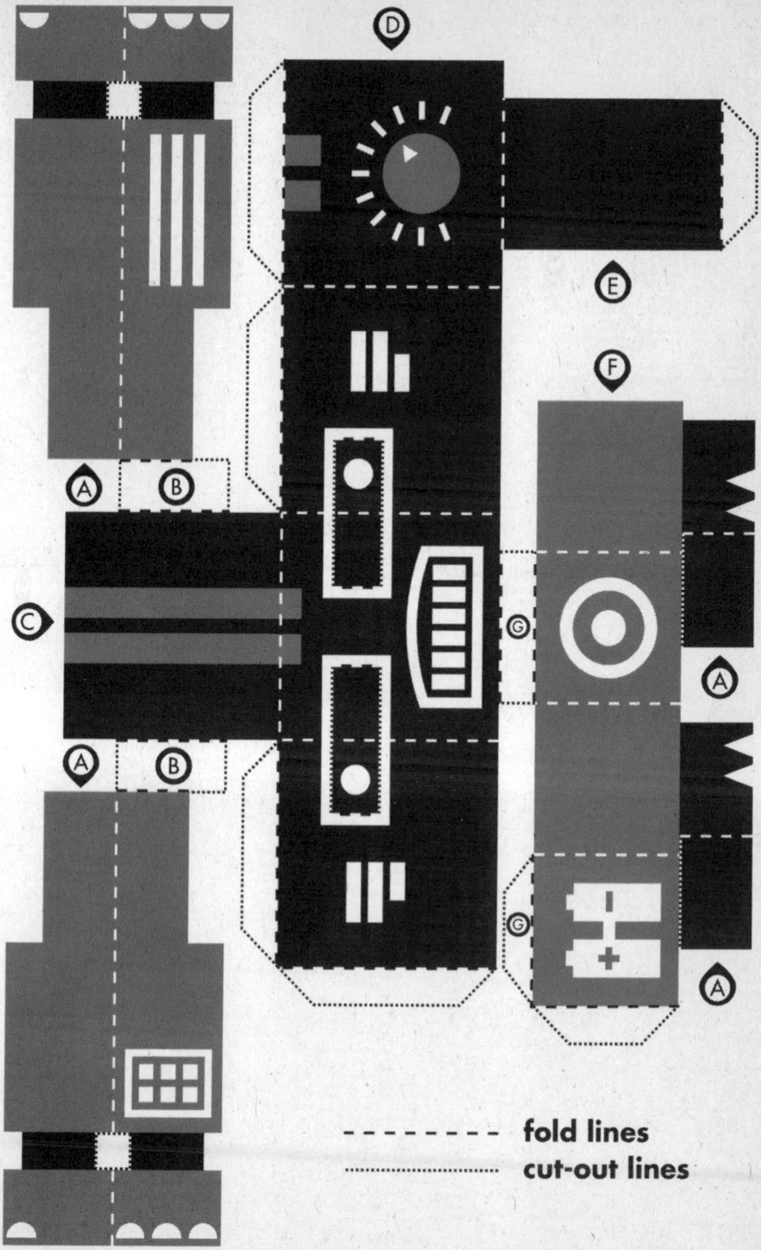
D
E
F
A
B
C
G
A
B
G
A
A
fold lines
cut-out lines

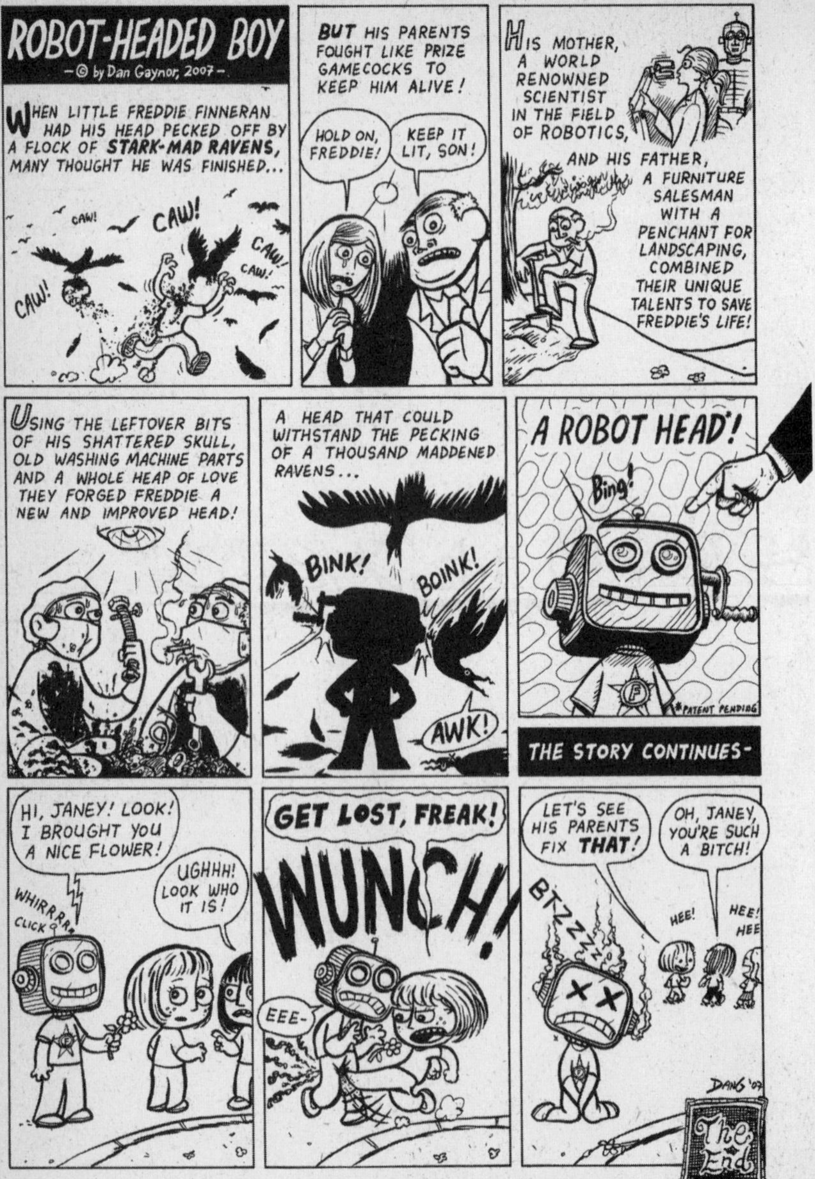
ROBOT-HEADED BOY
—© by Dan Gaynor, 2007—
WHEN LITTLE FREDDIE FINNERAN HAD HIS HEAD PECKED OFF BY A FLOCK OF STARK-MAD RAVENS, MANY THOUGHT HE WAS FINISHED...
CAW!
CAW!
CAW!
CAW!
CAW!
BUT HIS PARENTS FOUGHT LIKE PRIZE GAMECOCKS TO KEEP HIM ALIVE!
HOLD ON, FREDDIE!
KEEP IT LIT, SON!
HIS MOTHER, A WORLD RENOWNED SCIENTIST IN THE FIELD OF ROBOTICS,
AND HIS FATHER, A FURNITURE SALESMAN WITH A PENCHANT FOR LANDSCAPING, COMBINED THEIR UNIQUE TALENTS TO SAVE FREDDIE'S LIFE!
USING THE LEFTOVER BITS OF HIS SHATTERED SKULL, OLD WASHING MACHINE PARTS AND A WHOLE HEAP OF LOVE THEY FORGED FREDDIE A NEW AND IMPROVED HEAD!
A HEAD THAT COULD WITHSTAND THE PECKING OF A THOUSAND MADDENED RAVENS...
BINK!
BOINK!
AWK!
A ROBOT HEAD*!
Bing!
*PATENT PENDING
THE STORY CONTINUES-
HI, JANEY! LOOK! I BROUGHT YOU A NICE FLOWER!
WHIRRRR
CLICK
UGHHH! LOOK WHO IT IS!
GET LOST, FREAK!
WUNCH!
EEE-
LET'S SEE HIS PARENTS FIX THAT!
OH, JANEY, YOU'RE SUCH A BITCH!
BTZZZZZ
HEE!
HEE!
HEE
DANG '07
The End

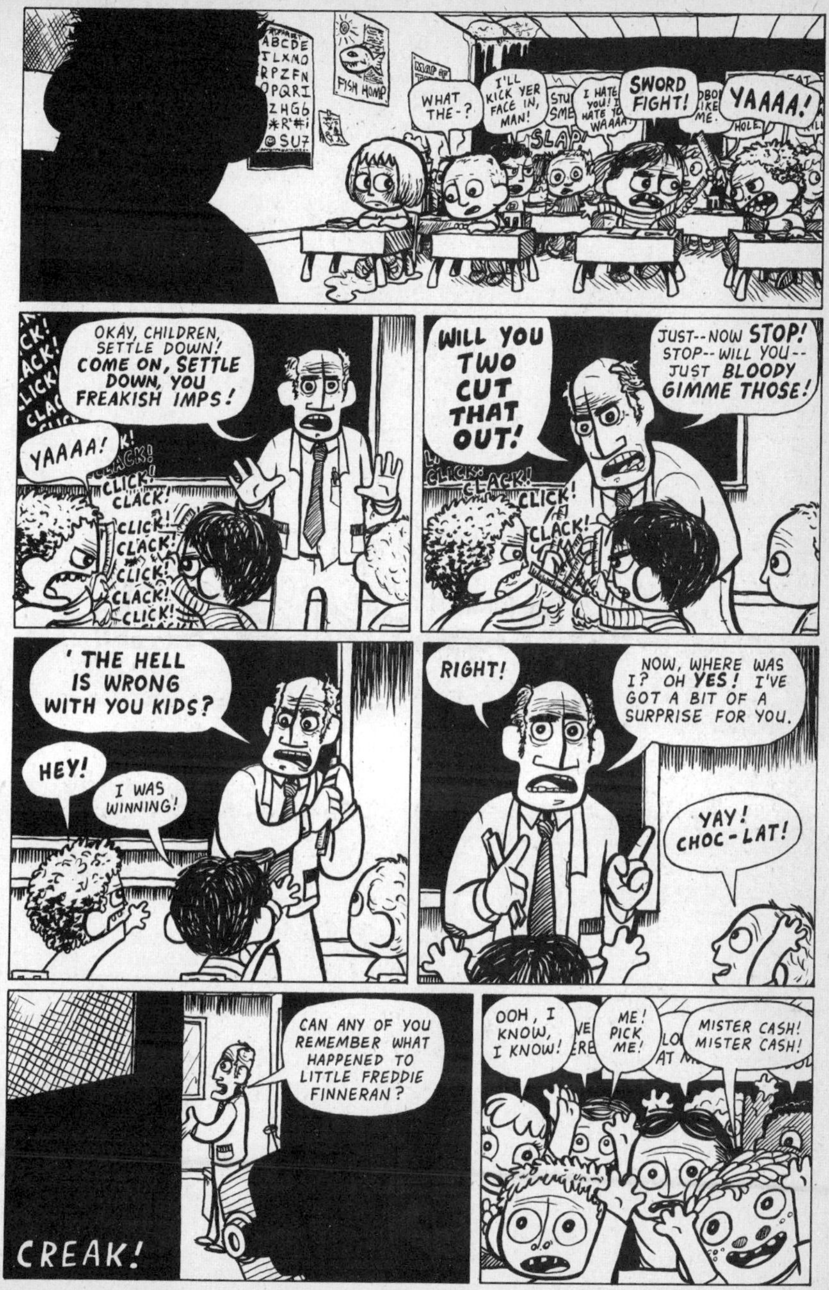
FISH HOMP
WHAT THE-?
I'LL KICK YER FACE IN, MAN!
SLAP!
SWORD FIGHT!
YAAAA!
OKAY, CHILDREN, SETTLE DOWN! COME ON, SETTLE DOWN, YOU FREAKISH IMPS!
YAAAA!
CLICK! CLACK! CLICK! CLACK! CLICK! CLACK! CLICK!
WILL YOU TWO CUT THAT OUT!
JUST--NOW STOP! STOP--WILL YOU--JUST BLOODY GIMME THOSE!
CLICK! CLACK! CLICK! CLACK!
' THE HELL IS WRONG WITH YOU KIDS?
HEY!
I WAS WINNING!
RIGHT!
NOW, WHERE WAS I? OH YES! I'VE GOT A BIT OF A SURPRISE FOR YOU.
YAY! CHOC-LAT!
CAN ANY OF YOU REMEMBER WHAT HAPPENED TO LITTLE FREDDIE FINNERAN?
CREAK!
OOH, I KNOW, I KNOW!
ME! PICK ME!
MISTER CASH! MISTER CASH!

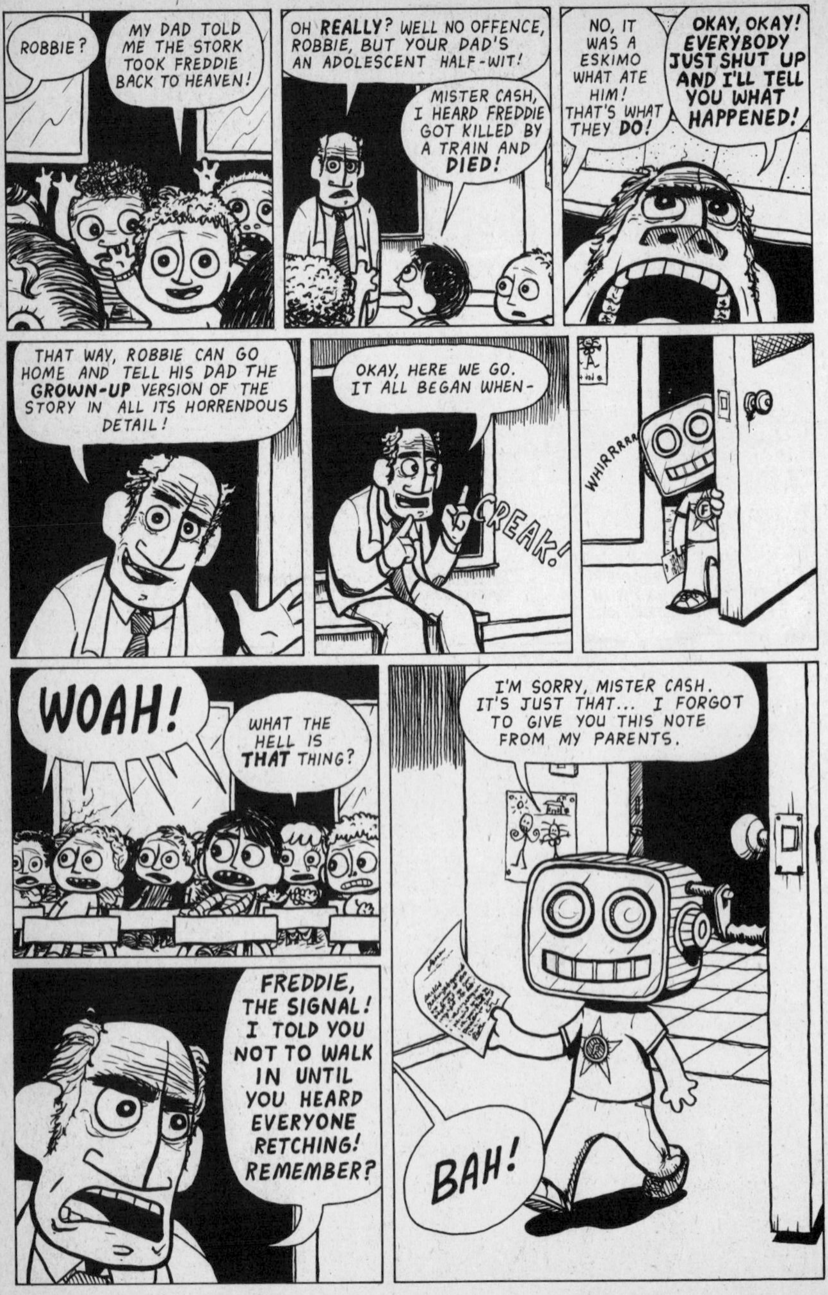
ROBBIE?
MY DAD TOLD ME THE STORK TOOK FREDDIE BACK TO HEAVEN!
OH REALLY? WELL NO OFFENCE, ROBBIE, BUT YOUR DAD'S AN ADOLESCENT HALF-WIT!
MISTER CASH, I HEARD FREDDIE GOT KILLED BY A TRAIN AND DIED!
NO, IT WAS A ESKIMO WHAT ATE HIM! THAT'S WHAT THEY DO!
OKAY, OKAY! EVERYBODY JUST SHUT UP AND I'LL TELL YOU WHAT HAPPENED!
THAT WAY, ROBBIE CAN GO HOME AND TELL HIS DAD THE GROWN-UP VERSION OF THE STORY IN ALL ITS HORRENDOUS DETAIL!
OKAY, HERE WE GO. IT ALL BEGAN WHEN-
CREAK!
WHIRRRRR
WOAH!
WHAT THE HELL IS THAT THING?
FREDDIE, THE SIGNAL! I TOLD YOU NOT TO WALK IN UNTIL YOU HEARD EVERYONE RETCHING! REMEMBER?
I'M SORRY, MISTER CASH. IT'S JUST THAT... I FORGOT TO GIVE YOU THIS NOTE FROM MY PARENTS.
BAH!

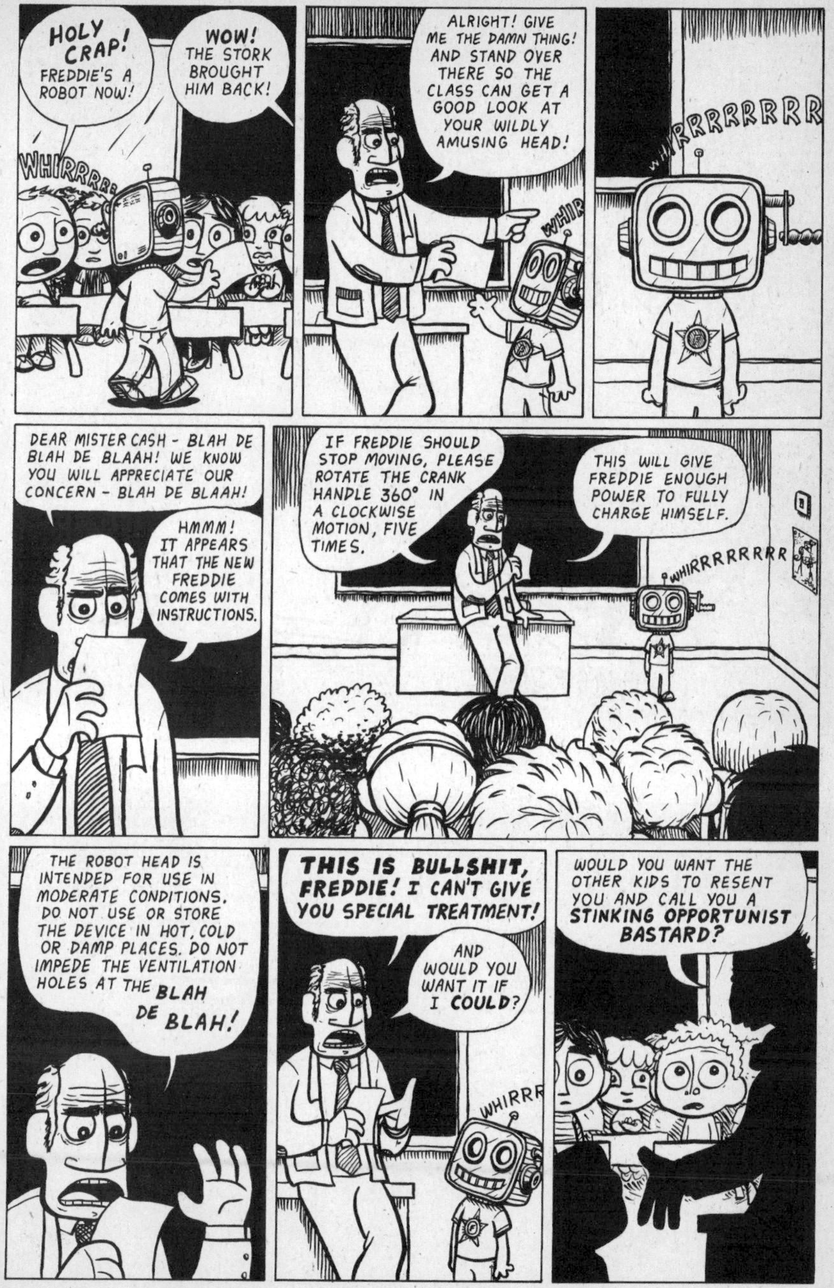
HOLY CRAP! FREDDIE'S A ROBOT NOW!
WOW! THE STORK BROUGHT HIM BACK!
WHIRRRRR
ALRIGHT! GIVE ME THE DAMN THING! AND STAND OVER THERE SO THE CLASS CAN GET A GOOD LOOK AT YOUR WILDLY AMUSING HEAD!
WHIR
WHIRRRRRRRRR
DEAR MISTER CASH - BLAH DE BLAH DE BLAAH! WE KNOW YOU WILL APPRECIATE OUR CONCERN - BLAH DE BLAAH!
HMMM! IT APPEARS THAT THE NEW FREDDIE COMES WITH INSTRUCTIONS.
IF FREDDIE SHOULD STOP MOVING, PLEASE ROTATE THE CRANK HANDLE 360° IN A CLOCKWISE MOTION, FIVE TIMES.
THIS WILL GIVE FREDDIE ENOUGH POWER TO FULLY CHARGE HIMSELF.
WHIRRRRRRRR
THE ROBOT HEAD IS INTENDED FOR USE IN MODERATE CONDITIONS. DO NOT USE OR STORE THE DEVICE IN HOT, COLD OR DAMP PLACES. DO NOT IMPEDE THE VENTILATION HOLES AT THE BLAH DE BLAH!
THIS IS BULLSHIT, FREDDIE! I CAN'T GIVE YOU SPECIAL TREATMENT!
AND WOULD YOU WANT IT IF I COULD?
WHIRRR
WOULD YOU WANT THE OTHER KIDS TO RESENT YOU AND CALL YOU A STINKING OPPORTUNIST BASTARD?

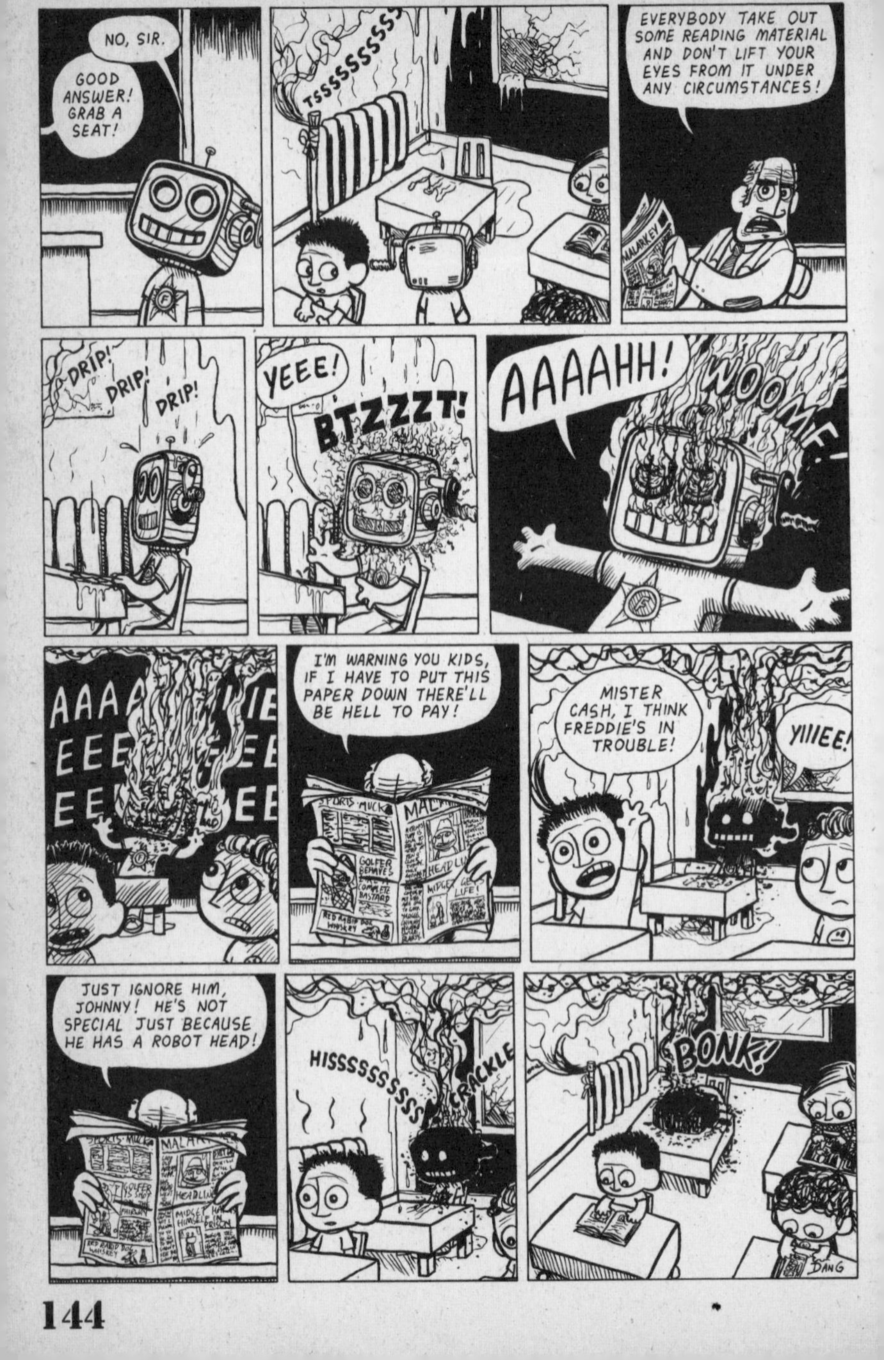
NO, SIR.
GOOD ANSWER! GRAB A SEAT!
EVERYBODY TAKE OUT SOME READING MATERIAL AND DON'T LIFT YOUR EYES FROM IT UNDER ANY CIRCUMSTANCES!
MALARKEY
DRIP!
DRIP!
DRIP!
YEEE!
BTZZZT!
AAAAHH!
I'M WARNING YOU KIDS, IF I HAVE TO PUT THIS PAPER DOWN THERE'LL BE HELL TO PAY!
MISTER CASH, I THINK FREDDIE'S IN TROUBLE!
YIIIEE!
JUST IGNORE HIM, JOHNNY! HE'S NOT SPECIAL JUST BECAUSE HE HAS A ROBOT HEAD!
CRACKLE
BONK!
DANG